The Battle of Savo Island

The Battle of Savo Island

Richard F. Newcomb

An Owl Book

Henry Holt and Company   New York

For Alice, Carol, and Susan, a loyal crew

Henry Holt and Company, LLC
Publishers since 1866
115 West 18th Street
New York, New York 10011

Henry Holt® is a registered trademark
of Henry Holt and Company, LLC.

Library of Congress Cataloging-in-Publication Data
Newcomb, Richard F.
  [Savo]
  The battle of Savo Island / Richard F. Newcomb.
  —1st Owl books ed.
    p. cm.
  "An Owl book."
  Originally published: Savo. New York :
  Holt, Rinehart and Winston, 1961.
  Includes bibliographical references and index.
  ISBN 0-8050-7072-9 (pbk.)
  1. Savo Island, Battle of, 1942. I. Title.

D774.S318 N4 2002
940.54'26—dc21   2002017204

Henry Holt books are available for special
promotions and premiums.
For details contact: Director, Special Markets.

First published in hardcover in 1961
by Holt, Rinehart and Winston

First Owl Books Edition 2002

Designed by Ernst Reichl

Printed in the United States of America

1 3 5 7 9 10 8 6 4 2

If I were a king, the worst punishment I could inflict on my enemies would be to banish them to the Solomons. On second thought, king or no king, I don't think I'd have the heart to do it.

Jack London—1908
(*The Cruise of the Snark*)

introduction

The Solomon Islands campaign is a unique and fascinating chapter in naval history. Covering a period of seventeen months in 1942–43, it was marked by unremitting warfare, by sudden and vicious surface engagements, most of them at night, most at very close range, and all of them deadly. It will never be repeated, and those who took part will never forget it.

This is the story of the opening engagement, what is now called the Battle of Savo Island. It was the first surface engagement for a co-ordinated American force in nearly half a century, and it was a bad start. Courage and will were never lacking, but a new tactic had been perfected by the Imperial Japanese Navy and was introduced here with devastating effect. Admiral Alfred Thayer Mahan once said that history shows military men reluctant to change tactics but "the one who does will go into battle with a great advantage—a lesson in itself of no mean value." Savo was proof of this.

The bright harvest of this battle, for Americans, was the speed and ingenuity with which the U. S. Navy adapted to the enemy's tactic, mastered it, and turned it against him. In a way, the Pacific sea war was fought and won in these dark waters, for the enemy could never recover from the punishment sustained here. It was a heroic period in the history of the United States Navy, of which this is only the first chapter.

In addition to the works listed at the end of this book, I have consulted the magazines, newspapers, and periodicals mentioned in the text, and others not mentioned. I have talked or corresponded with many officers and enlisted men who took part in the battle and I wish to thank them for their contributions or suggestions. Among a great many individuals who were most helpful I must list Rear Admiral Ernest M. Eller, Director of Naval History; Captain F. Kent Loomis, Assistant Director of Naval History; Dean Allard, Naval Records Management Center; Elbert L. Huber, National Archives; H. O. Werner, U.S. Naval Institute; Commander G. Hermon Gill, official historian, Royal Australian Navy; Commander Eric A. Feldt, RAN; Rear Admiral G. C. O. Gatacre, RAN; Susumu Nishiura, War History Office, Tokyo; Rear Admiral Walter H. Price; Rear Admiral Donald J. Ramsey; Commander Herbert J. Gimpel; Commander Russell L. Bufkins, and Lieutenant J. M. Hession of the Office of Information, U.S. Navy, and Albro F. Downe, who did the charts and end papers.

The views expressed here are my own.

—R.F.N.

The Battle of Savo Island

chapter
1

The Solomon Islands have always been a swindle. A double-strand choker of emeralds, set in a blue-green sea, they delight the senses from afar and seem to promise all the mysteries and enchantments of the South Seas. They speak of soft winds and swaying palms, of tropic nights and languor in a land without cares. But alas, it is not so; in the end there is nothing here but disappointment and death, and it has always been thus.

Ever since the Spaniards, to their sorrow, listened to the Inca seer, the false dream persisted until, nearly four centuries later, it was finally exorcised in an orgy of suffering and death.

Then the exotic names—Guadalcanal, Tulagi, Savo, Rendova, Vella Lavella, Kula Gulf, Kolombangara, and Bougainville—burst on the world, and centuries of obscurity were blasted away in seventeen months of the most vicious land and sea fighting ever known. When it had passed, the Solomons were known throughout the world for what they truly are—a land of jungle and stinking swamp, of disease and death, heartbreak, and horror.

Pedro Sarmiento de Gamboa, one of the most celebrated navigators of the sixteenth century, first fell prey to the dream when he listened to Tupac Inca Yupanqui sing of the islands rich as Solomon's mines lying only 600 leagues to the west of Peru. He bought the dream and he sold it to the Viceroy of Peru, Governor-General Lope Garcia de Castro, who in turn sold it to King Philip II of Spain, and the king authorized an expedition, not, of course, for gold, but "to convert all infidels to Christianity."

The Governor-General chose his nephew, Álvaro de Mendaña de Neira, to command the voyage and two vessels were quickly fitted out, the *Capitana,* of 250 tons, and the *Almiranta,* 107 tons. The haste was not for fear that the natives might escape God but that the gold might escape the Spaniards.

Mendaña, only twenty-six years of age, was wise beyond his years, a fortunate circumstance, for his expedition was riven with hatred before it sailed. He had chosen Hernan Gallego as his chief pilot, a post coveted by Sarmiento, and the later was sullen, disloyal, and disobedient throughout the entire voyage. Mendaña took aboard a total complement of 150 men, including some 70 soldiers, 4 Franciscan friars, and a number of black slaves, and the expedition cleared the harbor of Callao, port of Lima, on Wednesday, November 19, 1567.

At the end of twenty-six days of westward sailing there was no land, and doubts began to arise that the Inca knew anything of these waters. On the advice of Gallego the ships wore off on a more northerly course, but by year's end there was still no land. Gallego, to ease the rising discontent, promised that there would be land by the end of January. As that time approached, a low island, hardly more than a sand spit, was sighted, but Gallego refused to stop. He maneuvered the vessels so they passed and could not beat back against the wind and current. It was a daring thing to do, but Gallego was a man of strong intuitions and shortly he was able to record in his log:

> And it was Saturday, the 7th of the said month of February, at the end of eighty days counted from the day we set out from Callao, the Port of the City of the Kings; and that day, in the morning, I ordered a sailor to climb to the maintop and look toward the south for land, because there appeared to me something very high in that quarter. And the sailor reported land, and presently it was visible to us. And we hoisted a flag, so that the *Almiranta,* which was half a league from the *Capitana,* should know it, and everybody received the news with great joy and gratitude for the grace that God had vouchsafed to us through the intercession of the Virgin of Good Fortune, the Glorious Mother of God, whom we all worshiped, to whom we all prayed, singing the *Te Deum Laudamus.*

It was an immense island, and they named it Santa Ysabel because they had sailed on that saint's day from Callao. As they sought a passage over the reef, a star appeared, a wonderful daytime manifestation, and guided them into a bay, which they named the Bay of the Star, thinking this a good augury. The boats were put over and the friars led a party ashore, where a cross was immediately erected and thanks given to God for leading them to the Isles of Solomon.

It was one of the great ironies of the Age of Exploration, for here was no gold, no treasure, no riches of any kind. The first gift from the natives was the quarter of a boy, laid at the feet of Mendaña, the arm and hand still attached. The men recoiled in disgust, and buried the bloody torso. From this day on, though hope died hard, these islands gave the lie to the Inca seer.

The natives promised food, but brought none, and their smiles of friendship were really leers of anticipation, for they were not only cannibals but head-hunters. Sarmiento led a party inland and had to fight his way back to the beach. The natives followed and threw stones from the jungle and finally it was necessary to drive them off by firing arquebuses, the sound of which terrified them.

Mendaña, wishing to explore further and not willing to risk his vessels among the coral reefs, ordered a brigantine built of green wood. This vessel, of 4 or 5 tons, sailed southeastward down the coast on April 7, Gallego in command, and Pedro de Ortega, the Master of the Camp, on board with a party of some forty men. Passing the end of Santa Ysabel, they sighted the huge island of Malaita and doubled back on Easter morning around an island they named Florida. To the south was another great island with high mountains and they decided to go ashore.

The brigantine tossed all night in a cross sea in the lee of a tiny volcanic island they named Sesarga, because it looked like an island of that name near La Coruña.

The volcano was partly in eruption, and smoke and ash fumed up from its flat round top, casting a pall over the Sound. This island, scarcely three miles in diameter, was called Sabu by the natives, and centuries later became known to the world as Savo, a symbol of horror alike to Japanese and Americans. The bay over which it brooded, first known as Savo Sound, was later, perforce, renamed Ironbottom Sound, and is so known today. As a graveyard for fighting men and ships it has no equal in the world.

After the night off Savo, the Spaniards went next morning to the great island to the south. Pedro de Ortega named it Guadalcanal, after his native place in Spain.

Gallego recorded the landing:

Another day, which was the 19th of April, we came to the large island which we had seen, and there was a village of the Indians, and a large river. There came out canoes to the brigantine, and some Indians swimming, and some women and boys. We gave them a rope and, drawing it, they brought us to land; and when we were near the land they began throwing stones at us, saying 'Mate! Mate,' meaning that they would kill us. Firing some arquebuses at them, we killed two of them, and immediately they left us and fled away. The Master of the Camp landed with twenty men and took possession; as in the other villages there was found a great quantity of food of roots and ginger collected in small baskets, of which there was a great quantity in the island. We put into the brigantine what we could, including a pig, and the same evening we went on board.

To this island we gave the name of Guadalcanal, and we called the river Ortega.

The brigantine came back to Guadalcanal in June, and this time there was an ambush and 9 men from the party were killed. The Spaniards left and did not return.

Everywhere in the islands it was the same. The natives were hostile and the land was hostile, refusing to yield gold, or silver, or gems, or even food. This land, that looked so rich, was not only poor but belligerently poor, teeming with decay and putrefaction. In the rain forests the rotting vegetable matter gave off revolting vapors and the jungles abounded with strange and deadly reptiles, huge rats, and a species of giant frog weighing three pounds. The waters, so blue and benign by day, turned black at night, and swift and treacherous currents ran among the islands. There was nothing in this whole place but frustration and foreboding, and the men cheered when they learned they were going home.

Mendaña, reluctant to return without the treasure he had been sent for, nevertheless realized that he must. His ships were wearing, and the rigging and sails could not be replaced, nor could his food, except for a few roots and some pigs traded from the natives for hostages caught in the bush.

The vessels sailed August 11, 1568, steering north to catch the westerly winds. On board, as captives, were 6 natives—a man and wife with child at breast, a young girl, and 2 boys. In December, after great travail, with food and water nearly exhausted, and both vessels having been dismasted in October hurricanes, they raised the coast of Lower California, one-third of the party of 150 having died. Stopping often en route down the coast, the expedition reached Callao on September 11, 1569, after a voyage of nearly two years.

There was some attempt to hide the failure and disappointment of the quest, but it was obvious that it had been unsuccessful. Mendaña wanted to go back to colonize the islands, but it was 1595 before he could raise another expedition and then he reached only as far as the Santa Cruz Islands, where he died. The islands were forgotten (a capital idea!) for two centuries, until the French returned under De Bougainville, who called them Terre des Arsacides (Land of the Assassins). The British stopped by a few years later, to name one island New Georgia, after the King. But no one wanted them and finally, late in the nineteenth century, they went almost by default to the Germans, who took Bougainville, and to the British, who took the rest. Missionaries went out and a few palm plantations were started. A famous tourist, Jack London, stopped there in 1908 in the *Snark* and was glad to get away, writing later:

"If I were a king, the worst punishment I could inflict on my enemies would be to banish them to the Solomons. On second thought, king or no king, I don't think I'd have the heart to do it."

It seemed a fitting requiem for a place of pestilence, and thereafter America, and the world, once more forgot the Solomon Islands. How wonderful, indeed, if they had never been heard of again!

chapter
2

After the Battle of Midway in 1942, Rear Admiral Gunichi Mikawa returned to his home in Setagaya, a suburb of Tokyo, to await his next assignment. There was not much time, but he was thankful for the several weeks allowed him, time in which to assess the awesome results of Midway, to restore his spirit, and to begin to think of what now must be done. There were lessons to be learned from Midway, and they must be learned well, for Japan could not again accept such losses and still expect ultimate victory in the war.

The admiral, at fifty-three, was a soft-spoken, gentle man of a somewhat intellectual cast, but it would have been a mistake to think him not a man of action. The Navy Section of Imperial General Headquarters knew him as one competent in tactics, inspiring in leadership, and above all courageous and aggressive. At the start of the war, as a rear admiral he had been given command of the Support Force, second in command to Vice Admiral Chuichi Nagumo of the Pearl Harbor Striking Force. Thereafter, in days filled with action, his force of battleships and cruisers had prowled the oceans over one-third of the world in support of Nagumo's carriers. Without mercy they had rained blows on the Allies from Pearl Harbor all the way to Ceylon. In this campaign, little known even today, the Japanese exhibited the brilliant planning and tactics which had occupied them for years before the outbreak of hostilities. Using battleships to cover fast carriers (a tactic both the Americans and British were to copy), the powerful force roamed the seas at will, attacking where it chose and returning to Japan in April, 1942, without damage to a single ship.

In its rampage, having no parallel in naval history, the force had sunk 5 battleships, 1 aircraft tender, 1 cruiser, and 7 destroyers; damaged 3 battleships, 3 cruisers, and 1 destroyer. In addition, thousands of tons of merchant shipping had been sunk, hundreds of aircraft destroyed, and docks, hangars, and bases smashed through 120 degrees of longitude. Scant wonder the proud force scarcely noticed the Doolittle raid on the very day it re-entered home waters, April 18, 1942.

But the raid was the shadow of things to come. Less than a month later, the Battle of the Coral Sea brought the Japanese up short, five months after Pearl Harbor. Admiral Mikawa missed this engagement; he was in Tokyo, planning for Midway. News of the Coral Sea loss and the failure to take Port Moresby was sobering, but it was by no means a disaster. Midway was. The admiral had little time to dwell on it during those weeks in late June and early July, but the defeat had been staggering.

The Midway campaign was intended to complete the work of Pearl Harbor—draw out the remainder of the American fleet and smash it, particularly the carriers. It was planned with great care, and all of the nation's resources were thrown into it. Admiral Isoroku Yamamoto assembled for it 350 ships and 100,000 men, the largest force ever seen in the Pacific up to that time. The force put to sea on schedule, in deep secrecy and with high hope, and was brought to battle on the morning of June 4, 1942.

The United States Navy, inferior in every category of weapon except courage, met the armada and turned it back in the most crucial battle of the Pacific war. By nightfall of June 4 the Japanese had lost 4 first-line aircraft carriers, over 300 planes, and more than 100 pilots. Admiral Yamamoto was forced to order the vast operation canceled, and the fleet skulked back to Japan in such secrecy that the wounded were trundled ashore at night in well-guarded ports.

It was the first Japanese defeat in modern times, and the ignominy and magnitude of it were a carefully kept secret from the Japanese nation until long after the war was over. Within the Navy the truth could not be disguised: the carriers and the planes might be replaced in time, but the pilots could never be. They were the flower of the peacetime training program, a regimen of utmost rigor which only the most gifted fliers survived. Never again would Japan have time to train such men.

Nevertheless, the war was not over. Admiral Mikawa's new orders arrived on July 12, and that very day his operational staff officer, Commander Toshikazu Ohmae, came to his home. The orders were a great satisfaction to Mikawa, and at the same time reflected the new state of things since Midway. The High Command had not been idle; changes had already been made.

Admiral Mikawa was given command of a new force, the Eighth Fleet, to be known operationally as the Outer South Seas Force, with headquarters at Rabaul, New Britain. For his flagship, he was assigned the *Chokai,* a heavy cruiser of strange (to American eyes) but powerful appearance, and his force at first included four heavy cruisers of Cruiser Division 6, the *Aoba, Kinugasa, Furutaka,* and *Kako,* the two light cruisers of Cruiser Division 18, *Tenryu* and *Yubari,* and such destroyers as might be assigned.

It was a respectable force, of good speed and firepower, and most important the officers and men were soundly trained and had seen much action. Rear Admiral Aritomo Goto had led Cruiser Division 6 in the capture of Guam and Wake, and at Coral Sea he was in command of the Invasion Forces and Supporting Forces, with the same ships plus the aircraft carrier *Shoho.* The two light cruisers, which had operated with Admiral Goto's force at Guam and Wake, were now commanded by Rear Admiral Mitsuharu Matsuyama. For his staff, Admiral Mikawa had Rear Admiral Shinzo Ohnishi as Chief of Staff,

Captain Shigenori Kami as Flag Captain, and Commander Ohmae as operational officer.

As Mikawa and Ohmae talked over tea, the bright leaves shimmering in the summer sun, the admiral mused on the task awaiting him.

He knew little of his mission as yet, but it was plain that the battle area was solidifying. The Japanese had no clear plan after Pearl Harbor, except to extend the arc of control as far east as was feasible, to keep the Americans as far as possible from the home islands and protect the vast empire seized in China, the Philippines, and Southeast Asia. It had once been planned to seize Port Moresby, New Caledonia, and the Fiji Islands, thus dominating Australia and its life line to the United States. The battles in the Coral Sea and at Midway had now delineated the arc of defense. The Japanese line would run southward from the Kuriles through the Marshalls, and Gilberts and turn westward through Rabaul and New Guinea. The Japanese still meant to capture New Guinea, operating from the Rabaul bastion, which was to be protected by the Solomon Islands. It was a vast theater of war and Admiral Mikawa's segment of it was a challenging assignment. Rabaul was the hot corner, nearest to the vital United States-Australia line. Here the Americans would have to fight, but Mikawa intended to get there first.

Mikawa proposed that Commander Ohmae fly down to Truk and talk with Vice Admiral Shigeyoshi Inoue, Commander of the Fourth Fleet. Part of Admiral Inoue's fleet, and part of his domain, were being carved off for the new Eighth Fleet. Now that Coral Sea and Midway had shrunk the area of battle, the Imperial Navy could bring more weight to bear within the circle. This time Port Moresby *would* be taken, not by sea but by troops overland from Buna. Rabaul would be the new fortress, and with New Guinea and the Solomons on the flanks, the Bismarck Barrier would be impregnable.

Commander Ohmae left Tokyo two days later, stopped at Truk for a briefing by staff officers of the Fourth Fleet, and arrived in Rabaul early on the morning of July 20. He was not impressed. Behind the harbor an active volcano belched sulphurous clouds and at a dock in the foreground a rusting, half-sunken freighter contrasted sharply with the clear blue waters of the lagoon. Small vessels were grouped together with no thought of protection against enemy raids, and he soon learned that this was the spirit which pervaded the shore forces. Two small airfields were under construction by the Eighth Base Force. The 25th Air Flotilla was already operating, but its headquarters was far off on Tinian, in the Mariana Islands. There was friction between the base force and the airmen, and the whole operation needed direction and command. Admiral Mikawa would provide it—if he had time.

There was no feeling that he would not, but here he reckoned without Admiral King. In his sixty-fourth year and just short of retirement, Admiral Ernest J. King was summoned to Washington the day after Pearl Harbor. Twelve days later he became Commander in Chief, United States Fleet, or COMINCH. (The old abbreviation, CINCUS, pronounced Sink Us, had been dropped for painfully obvious reasons.) Despite his vast responsibilities across the world, almost his first thought was for the Pacific and there, throughout the war, his heart lay. From the first he fought the battle for the Pacific Fleet in the highest councils, and it is well that he did.

He saw at once the absolute necessity of seizing bases on the route to Australia and he was not a man to brook interference. He enunciated his plans in February, 1942, and thereby set the course of the war in the South Pacific for the next two years.

"The general scheme or concept of operations," he wrote, "is not only to protect the line of communications with Australia but, in so doing, set up 'strong points' from which a step-by-step general advance can be made through the New Hebrides, Solomons and the Bismarck Archipelago. It is to be expected that such a step-by-step general advance will draw Japanese forces to oppose it, thus relieving pressure in other parts of the Pacific—and that the operation will of itself be good cover for the communications with Australia."

No prophet could have written more clearly, and it should be noted that his plan was no static defense, but actually the beginning of the offensive.

Ragtag forces of the Army, Navy, and Marines were seized wherever they could be found and thrown into the breach. Army and Navy forces arrived in New Caledonia on March 12, occupied Efate in the New Hebrides on March 29, and on May 28 moved up to Espiritu Santo. Other forces occupied the Fiji Islands, the Tongas, and the Society Islands and began building runways, fueling bases, and fleet anchorages. The Japanese gambled everything on Midway, and in losing it lost more than they knew. King's men had been busy in the southeast.

From Rabaul, small Japanese forces had been drifting down the Solomons chain and early in May had occupied Tulagi. In June they crossed Savo Sound and moved into Guadalcanal. The terrain was better there and they began burning off the kunai grass to build an airfield. It would be ready in a few weeks.

Commander Ohmae was unsettled by the complacency he found at Rabaul. He was no stranger to interservice bickering, but he was upset by it here. He had the feeling that forces then present resented a new command coming in. It quickly became more than a feeling.

When he sought to discuss staff quarters for the admiral, he was told there were none. It was suggested that any naval commander would prefer to have his command afloat. Commander Ohmae was able to answer that. Admiral Mikawa had told him that he planned to keep his forces in safer areas to the rear—behind New Ireland, which arcs like a cutlass to the north—but would require space ashore to direct operations from Rabaul. In the end it was agreed that the admiral would have accommodations ashore—if he could find them.

Commander Ohmae returned to Truk in time for a dinner in honor of Lieutenant General H. Hyakutake, commander of the 17th Army. During an evening made convivial with sake and beer, Ohmae learned that the 17th was destined for the Port Moresby operation. He heard little talk of the Solomons. No concern was felt in that area.

Two days later, on July 25, Admiral Mikawa arrived at Truk. When Commander Ohmae saw the *Chokai* in the anchorage, her fat forward stack sharply canted back and the slim second stack pointing straight up, he hurried out to report. Admiral Mikawa listened closely as Ohmae recounted what he had learned in the past ten days.

His anxiety rising as the account progressed, Admiral Mikawa requested an immediate conference with Vice Admiral Inoue, and they met that afternoon with their staffs. Admiral Mikawa could not feel easy until he had taken steps to overcome the vacuum of authority in the immense area now under his command. Some of his anxiety leaked out during the conference, but when his staff officers raised questions of possible enemy invasion of the Solomons or eastern New Guinea, Fourth Fleet officers dismissed them. There was nothing to fear, they said. The enemy was still reeling from the shock of defeats from Pearl Harbor to India.

Secretly it seemed that Admiral Inoue was as anxious to be rid of that huge southern part of his command as Admiral Mikawa was to assume it. The transfer was effected as of midnight July 26. The *Chokai* left the harbor that afternoon, en route for Rabaul. At precisely the same hour, though Mikawa could not have conceived it, the first Allied offensive was gathering far off to the southeast, behind the Fiji Islands. Operation Watchtower was already under way. If either side could have known what awaited exactly two weeks from this day . . .

But for the moment Mikawa was happy to be at sea again, the *Chokai's* turbines throbbing under him. He was heading away from the complacency of Truk and toward Rabaul, where command would be truly his. The *Chokai* entered Simpson Harbor, Rabaul, on the morning of July 30, and Admiral Mikawa went ashore the same day. It was as bad as Commander Ohmae had said, but finally they found a dilapidated building near the airfield and the admiral ran up his flag over it. Even toilet facilities were lacking, but Mikawa was not dismayed. He commandeered planning rooms from the Eighth Base Force, called a meeting with the 17th Army, and set about the work of the Port Moresby operation. Some of the troops, landing at Buna, New Guinea, had started up the Owen Stanley Mountains and advanced as far as Kokoda. The Eighth Fleet must carry more troops and supplies to Buna, and at the same time capture other bases on the tip of the island, near Milne Bay. By mid-August, the assault on Port Moresby, by sea and over the mountains from the north, must be ready. Once Port Moresby fell, Australia would lie unobstructed before the Japanese.

Through the next days, all eyes to the southwest, the Japanese were nevertheless aware of increasing activity to the southeast. The airfield on Gaudalcanal was nearly ready, and Lieutenant T. Okamura, commanding officer of the construction forces there, several times requested planes for the base. There was no reply from Eleventh Air Base headquarters. The seaplane base at Tulagi reported that enemy planes were coming over daily now. On August 1, 10 B-17's appeared, 11 the next day, and 3 or more daily thereafter. Japanese intelligence reported greatly increased enemy radio traffic throughout the area, a sure sign something was brewing.

To Admiral Mikawa's staff it seemed clear: enemy task forces were moving in toward New Guinea to counter the

Japanese offensive there. Any activity down toward Guadalcanal was diversionary.

But Admiral Mikawa would not be diverted. The July 31 convoy to Buna had been broken up by American planes. The next big one, August 8, would have better protection. Destroyers and patrol craft were assigned to it. The main strength of the Eighth Fleet was held in reserve, at Rabaul and Kavieng, for the Milne Bay operations.

On August 6 the Guadalcanal garrison reported that all natives helping with the airfield construction had disappeared into the jungle during the previous night. This was not ominous. Native workers had been known to quit before without reason. That same day search planes reported to Admiral Mikawa that no enemy forces were present south of Guadalcanal. The work of the Port Moresby operation was pushed on.

chapter
3

The storm broke over Mikawa's head the next day at dawn: "0630. Tulagi. Enemy task force sighted."

Instantly Mikawa was engulfed in problems. He ordered the morning reconnaissance flight held, dispatched word to Cruiser Division 6 at Kavieng, and summoned air and naval staff officers to the command post. As they gathered the next report came in:

"Enemy task force of 20 ships attacking Tulagi. Undergoing severe bombing. Landing preparations under way. Help requested."

Complete surprise had been achieved; Mikawa was not prepared. His heavy cruisers had just departed from Kavieng, headed the wrong way—west. Led by his flagship, *Chokai*, the *Aoba* and the *Kako* had cleared Silver Sound not ten minutes earlier, en route for Manus Island in the Admiralties. The other heavy cruisers, *Kinugasa* and *Furutaka,* were under way for Rabaul. In the harbor he had only the light cruisers *Tenryu* and *Yubari* and a lone destroyer, *Yunagi.*

Even as he recoiled from the blow, in the very first moments a plan sprang to Admiral Mikawa's mind. He must attack, attack. It was the thing he knew, and the thing he did best. The audacity of the enemy was an affront to his command, to Japan. He would move swiftly to wipe out the insult.

His first order sent two Type-97 bombers off at 7:00 A.M. to search the sector 100–130 degrees from Rabaul, or straight down the Solomons chain to a distance of 700 miles, well beyond Guadalcanal. He was sure the landings must be strongly supported by aircraft carriers. No reports had mentioned them yet, but he knew they must be nearby; he had to find them. Pearl Harbor, Coral Sea, and Midway had proved the Battleship Age was over; the carrier was the key to this war.

Even as his reconnaissance flights left, Mikawa got confirmation. The commander of the Yokohama Air Group at Tulagi reported:

"All large flying boats burned as result of air attack."

The *Yunagi* was ordered to make full speed to intercept the *Chokai* and the other two heavy cruisers and escort them to Rabaul. (Mikawa did not know it, but the *Chokai* group had already turned back for Rabaul. They had intercepted the desperate messages from the Tulagi garrison and decided independently to race to support Mikawa.) The *Tenryu* and *Yubari* received orders to stand by to get under way by 1:00 P.M. for Tulagi. Mikawa meant to attack with every vessel he had. Until he could get there he used his planes.

As more reconnaissance planes took off Mikawa summoned his fighter squadron leader, Commander Tadashi Nakajima, and showed him the target on the map. Nakajima, veteran of air battles from China to New Guinea, figured the air distance in silent amazement. Nearly 600 miles to the target—and 600 back! Even if they could land at Buka on the way back, it would be the longest mission ever flown by Zeros.

"Take every Zero that will fly," Admiral Mikawa said.

But this was too much even for Nakajima.

"This is the longest fighter mission in history," he protested. "Not all my men are capable of it. Let me take only my best twelve pilots. They would have a chance of making it."

Admiral Mikawa, his hand steady but his eyes blazing, thrust out the latest dispatch from Tulagi:

"The enemy force is overwhelming," it said. "We will defend our positions to the death, praying for everlasting victory."

That was the last ever heard from the Tulagi garrison.

Nakajima compromised: 18 Zeroes for Guadalcanal. It was done, and he went out to face his pilots.

The final word from Guadalcanal was already in:

"Encountered American landing forces and are retreating into the jungle."

Nakajima briefed his men in solemn tones, and at 9:00 A.M. the flight was off, shepherding 27 land attack planes of the 4th Air Group. The fighter pilots were under strict orders to conserve fuel; there was no margin for weather, scarcely any for battle at the target. At 10:45 A.M. the last flight went off, 16 Type-99 carrier bombers, which couldn't possibly make Guadalcanal without staging through Buka.

Mikawa assessed his position. This was an attack in strength, not merely diversionary. It was a complete surprise and it was a serious menace to Japanese positions in the Solomons. It must be met with the full force of air and submarine countermeasures, but this was not enough. A bold offensive by surface vessels was necessary, to strike the enemy ships at night and destroy them. But who would command the force? He was the over-all commander for a vast area. Once the force set out it would be under strict radio silence. If he led the force he could neither receive nor send orders and intelligence. He should not leave Rabaul, but he was the most experienced officer present.

He had many other problems. There must be 2, perhaps 3 or even more, aircraft carriers in the attacking force. He had none. It was not reasonable to assume his planes, even with phenomenal luck, could eliminate all of them. Therefore his attack must be at night.

The garrisons at Guadalcanal and Tulagi must be reinforced at once. But the 17th Army staff soon settled that. Troops staging to New Guinea could not suddenly be diverted to the Solomons, not by any decision at the 17th Army level, anyway. Tokyo would have to order that.

In disgust Admiral Mikawa organized his own reinforcements, raiding the fleet and its shore forces until he had 410 men, armed with rifles and a few machine guns. With Lieutenant Endo in command, he put them on the transport *Meiyo Maru,* and ordered them to get away the next day, escorted by the supply ship *Soya* and the mine layer *Tsugaru.* (This force never had a chance. As it stood down St. George's Channel, on the night of August 8, barely out of the harbor, the S-38 [Lieutenant Commander H. G. Munson] fired two torpedoes and scored two hits. The *Meiyo Maru* sank with most of her men. The rest of the force turned back.)

The admiral had other troubles. Shortly after noon 13 B-17's raided Rabaul. Daylight raids were a novelty, and the Japanese officers and men ashore ran outside to watch. The cruisers, approaching Rabaul, saw the B-17's too, and were glad they had chosen Vunakanau airfield as a target. Sixteen B-17's of the 19th Group had left Townsville, Australia, refueled at Port Moresby, and arrived over Rabaul with the mission of pinning down aircraft that might be sent against the new beachheads. One B-17 crashed on take-off, 2 turned back with engine trouble, and 1 fell to enemy fighters over Rabaul. The B-17's claimed destruction of 7 enemy fighters in combat over Rabaul and a substantial number of bombers on the ground.

Mikawa was more perturbed by something else. His vessels had never operated together as a fighting force, had never even practiced steaming in column. Each commanding officer was a veteran, but night maneuvering in battle is difficult even when each commanding officer knows intimately the speed and characteristics of all vessels involved.

That wasn't all. Japanese charts of these waters were

far from perfect. Maneuvering at high speed in the darkness was extremely dangerous. Nevertheless, Admiral Mikawa was determined to strike. He radioed his plan to Tokyo, asking approval.

Admiral Osami Nagano, chief of the Naval General Staff, was staggered by the audacity of the plan, and opposed it immediately. This was not bold, it was rash. It would be foolhardy to send a small, unco-ordinated force racing through uncharted waters at night to hurl itself against a powerful enemy force backed by carriers. When Nagano was fit to talk again, his staff began discussing the proposal with him. Attack was the spirit of the Japanese Navy, some pointed out. The commander on the spot must know his situation best, others said. Admiral Nagano softened; what alternative was there anyway? If this salient was not smashed now it would imperil other operations already in train—New Guinea and New Caledonia—the strangulation of Australia.

As the *Chokai* entered the harbor at Rabaul, Admiral Mikawa received his answer: Execute operation as outlined. A short time later his planes began returning from the beachhead. They reported large fires at both Tulagi and Guadalcanal, enemy forces ashore on both islands, 3 heavy cruisers and 13 transports off Tulagi, destroyers and 27 transports off Guadalcanal, 60 to 70 planes over the ships. No carriers sighted.

Remembering Midway, Mikawa may have shuddered involuntarily. Where were the carriers? They could not harm him at night, but on his approach and withdrawal they could severely wound him. He would have to strike

26

a quick blow—in and out in the night. He gave silent thanks, in a negative way, to the naval disarmament treaties of the 1930's. Forbidden to take rank with the great naval powers of the world, Japan had turned to other measures. The answer to inferior forces was night torpedo attacks to whittle down the enemy so he could be attacked on equal terms or better in decisive day battles.

With the fanaticism of their race the Japanese had gone about night battle practice in the 1930's with the ferocity of the real thing. Ships were sunk in collision, men were lost without qualm; nothing was spared to achieve utter realism in war games. Knowing nothing of radar, the Navy developed powerful night marine glasses and combed the fleet for men with exceptional eyesight. These men were trained in special techniques until they could distinguish targets at 8,000 meters—over 4 miles— even on dark nights. It would never stand them in better stead than on the night approaching.

If the Japanese had a secret weapon at this stage of the war it was torpedoes. Between the wars a great battle had raged within the United States Navy until finally the side opposing torpedo tubes on cruisers had won. Not so the Japanese. Every cruiser carried torpedo tubes, as many as 8 on the heavy cruisers. The torpedoes them- selves were unsurpassed in any navy in the world. Since the early 1930's the Japanese had had a completely oxy- gen-fueled torpedo of 61 cm. (24 inches) diameter that could travel at a speed of almost 50 knots with a range of nearly 4 miles. This was the dreaded Long Lance torpedo, and when they hit the target with a 1,210-pound war head they exploded. This was more than could be said of early American models. The Japanese, using their torpedoes without stint in war games, had perfected the crews, and the weapon had become a thing of terror on the seas.

There was no question in Admiral Mikawa's mind that he went into battle with the best sailors and the best ships the world had ever seen. For ten years the weapon had been in the forge. The enlisted men, selected from the nation's fittest youth, had undergone rigors the like of which had never been seen in any navy. Driven and beaten, literally, by their officers, they had been tempered to a fighting edge. Month after month, seven days a week, they had trained in the frigid seas north of Japan. Time and again men were carried overboard in the raging ocean. No ship turned back. Men fell at their post from exhaustion, and were slapped back to sensibility. Not a word of this reached home, and from this system, strangely enough, the Japanese built an *esprit* and a competence that was to amaze the world.

Admiral Mikawa, of course, thought nothing of this as he prepared to go to sea. It was taken without saying. Out of the crucible had come a keen weapon, and he would use it with the skill expected of him. Before this engagement was over, the Japanese would rudely shake the enemy until he would look within himself to see where he had failed. It was truly a great moment in history. The first test of the United States Navy in surface battle since the Spanish-American War. They had a lot to learn.

At 4:30 P.M., followed by Rear Admiral Ohnishi and the rest of his staff, Admiral Mikawa boarded the *Chokai* in Simpson Harbor. His red and white striped flag was broken at the mast and he led the way out of the harbor— a samurai, off to battle.

chapter
4

Outside the harbor Admiral Mikawa ordered out the light
cruiser *Yubari* (Captain Masami Ban commanding) as
starboard screen, and placed light cruiser *Tenryu* and destroyer *Yunagi* on the port. Rear Admiral Mitsuharu Matsuyama, Commander, Cruiser Division 18, was in the
Tenryu, with his senior staff officer, Commander Tamao
Shinohara.

The group rounded Cape Gazelle, passing south of the
Duke of York Islands, and at 5:55 P.M. ordered zigzagging
commenced. At the same time Cruiser Divison 6, Rear
Admiral Aritomo Goto commanding in the *Aoba,* was
passing north of the Duke of York group, completing passage from Kavieng. The passage had been observed, but
not effectively. At 12:30 P.M., while passing Mt. Bong-
mut, highest peak on New Ireland, the warships were

sighted by B-17's of General MacArthur's command. But, as so often in those early days, the report lacked the vital information necessary for tactical value. And it was slow, taking nearly twelve hours to pass through tangled communications. When finally produced it said merely: "Six unidentified ships sighted by Forts in St. George's Channel, course southeast." It did not say whether they were friendly or enemy, sampans or battleships, or their speed. The Allies would learn, as the war progressed, that sighting reports must be far more informative and accurate; lives and ships depended on precision. Nevertheless, here was the first report, and it was only slightly more remiss than the ones which followed.

It was a beautiful evening at sea, still and clear, and spirits ran high on the bridge of the *Chokai*. The sword of the samurai was about to be unsheathed, and exhilaration ran through the crews of all the ships. The two forces rendezvoused shortly after 6:00 P.M., and Admiral Mikawa signaled: "Cruiser Division Six will place itself at the rear of the *Chokai*." At sundown zigzagging ceased and the line of ships steamed south through St. George's Channel. "Alert cruising disposition" was ordered for the night, and Admiral Mikawa gathered his staff in the chart room of the *Chokai*.

The main mission was clear: destroy the enemy force. But first the target must be reached. The run-in must be at night and torpedoes would be the main weapon, but all next day the force would be in the open; surprise could hardly be expected. Enemy planes would certainly report them, but Mikawa meant to press on and attack with vigor in the early hours of Sunday morning, August 9. Japanese audacity had paid high dividends thus far (always excepting Midway) and the quick, devastating thrust appealed to the Japanese Navy. A blade had been honed for just these tactics—the quick thrust, the stab at the enemy's vitals, the speedy withdrawal to prepare for yet another thrust. It was the code of the ancient warrior, applied to the sea.

Even as the staff conferred around the plotting boards the force was sighted again, this time by the old reliable U.S. submarine S-38, which the next night would sink the *Meiyo Maru*, rushing to Guadalcanal with reinforcements. The S-38 was seen from the Japanese task force, which turned east to avoid battle. No minor interruptions were desired at this time. Lieutenant Commander Munson, unable to maneuver into firing position, sent off his report by radio: "Two destroyers and three larger ships of unknown type, heading 140 degrees True, at high speed, 8 miles west of Cape St. George." Warning No. 2, and again inaccurate, though far better than the B-17 report. Perhaps because of failing light he had counted 5 vessels when there were 8, 2 destroyers when there was 1. The light cruisers could easily have been mistaken for destroyers, but at least this message identified them as warships and gave course and speed. It was an important sighting.

By 8:30 P.M. the Japanese force was well south of Cape St. George, and Admiral Mikawa ordered a sharp turn to the left. On course 80 degrees True he planned to pass north of Buka Island during the night, stay above Bougainville as long as he could during daylight, and cut south into the Slot through Bougainville Strait. He could have stayed north of Choiseul, but the passage into the Slot between Choiseul and Santa Isabel was imperfectly charted and he was unwilling to risk it at night.

As the day ended 4 submarines were also en route for the beachheads. At Mikawa's order the *I-121* left Rabaul at sundown, the *RO-33* was diverted from the New Guinea area, the *RO-54* was sheered off from its course up the east coast of Australia, and the *I-123* sailed from Truk. The plum trees were heavy with fruit, and Mikawa meant to pick them clean.

At midnight the Eighth Fleet was north of Buka, and two hours later changed course to the southeast to pass down the north coast of Bougainville. About this time the *S-38* made yet another sighting, its last. It reported a Japanese submarine 30 miles south of Cape St. George. It was the *I-121*, outbound for Savo.

Saturday, August 8, dawned clear and fine, and at first light Admiral Mikawa ordered the float planes catapulted from the cruisers. He was in radio silence now, and he needed to know what the enemy was doing at the beachheads. Starting at 6:25 A.M., the planes got away, one each from the *Chokai, Kinugasa, Kako,* and *Aoba.* The *Furutaka's* plane developed engine trouble at the last moment and did not get off. Sectors were assigned in 15-degree widths, from 70 degrees to 130 degrees True, each plane to search out 250 miles, jog 30 miles left, and return. As the planes were fired off, the crews cheered and waved their hats, their fighting spirits rising as battle neared.

To avoid detection, or concentration in case of bombing, Admiral Mikawa dispersed his vessels over the glistening sea to await the return of the planes. Here in these wide waters, out of sight of land, the warships frisked in the sun, the sailors hurrying about the decks preparing their ships for battle. Before the sun rose again they would have engaged the enemy, and excitement was mounting hourly. Confidence was high, although this was the first time the ships had operated together, and in fact they were only now getting a good view of each other.

All the vessels were old by warship standards, but heavily armed and at the peak of training and readiness. The *Chokai,* laid down in 1928 in the Mitsubishi yards, had been completed in 1932 but never modernized. A little over 600 feet long, she displaced about 10,000 tons and could make about 35 knots. In those early days, before American sailors had learned respect for the Japanese fighting qualities, the silhouette of a Japanese ship caused derision among them. The heavy, cluttered superstructure looked as if one thing had been piled on another, like innumerable tree houses, until the vessel would capsize or sink of sheer weight. The stacks, always dissimilar, seemed so strange as to evoke laughter. The *Chokai* was no exception. She had 1 fat stack forward, sharply raked toward the stern, and a slim stack rising straight behind it, so that the two nearly met.

Her main battery arrangement was no less odd, to American eyes. Instead of the usual 9 guns, in 3 turrets of 3 each, the *Chokai* had 10 guns, in 5 double turrets, 3 forward and 2 aft. The forward turrets were staggered, the center one higher than the other two. Her guns were 20-cm. (8-inch) 50-caliber weapons of very high muzzle velocity. The secondary armament consisted of 6 antiaircraft guns of 12 cm. (4.7 inches), 8 machine guns of 25 mm. and 4 of 13 mm. Amidships she carried eight 24-inch torpedo tubes. Her triple hull was girdled for 410 feet along the sides with 3- to 4-inch armorplate, and the main deck and turrets had 3-inch armor. All in all a formidable ship.

The other heavy cruisers, the *Aoba, Kinugasa, Furutaka,* and *Kako,* were well past middle age. The first two, sisters of the *Kinugasa* class, were finished in 1927, and the other pair, of the *Kako* class, in 1926. Their configuration also was quite strange, with twin stacks sharply raked, one fat and one slim, and six 8-inch guns mounted in single turrets, 3 forward and 3 aft. But they carried the same 8 torpedo tubes as the larger *Chokai,* and they had something else. Powerful 30-inch searchlights were mounted with each turret, or group of guns. The purpose of these would become apparent.

The *Yubari* and *Tenryu,* the light cruisers, were ancient. The *Yubari* was completed in 1923, the *Tenryu* in 1918 (correct!), under the 1916 building program. But these little fellows, rated around 3,000 tons, could still make over 30 knots with their 3 screws. The *Tenryu* had 3 stacks, straight and tall, and all of different diameter, the fattest one in the middle. To complete the dissimilarity, the *Yubari* had one funnel, a very fat one with double bent uptakes fore and aft. The *Yubari* had six 14-cm. (5.5-inch) guns, and the *Tenryu* four, with searchlights fore and aft. The *Yubari* carried four 61-cm. (24-inch) torpedo tubes (as big as the *Chokai's*) and the *Tenryu* had six tubes of 53 cm. (21 inch).

The lone destroyer, the *Yunagi,* finished in 1925, was

one of 9 boats of the *Kamikaze* class, named for elements of the weather. Her name meant "Evening Calm," hardly indicative of her design or mission. Her high bow and sharply raked stacks gave her a look of speed, and despite her age she could do over 34 knots on four screws. She, too, carried six 21-inch torpedo tubes, plus four 12-cm. (4.7-inch) guns and two searchlights.

Curious ships, all of them, but fanged like a tiger and far more deadly. One should not laugh at strange things.

About 10:20 A.M., with their float planes still away, the Japanese ships noted a Lockheed Hudson bomber circling high over them. It was a definite sighting, as the Hudson hovered overhead at least sixteen minutes before making off to the west in the direction of New Guinea or Australia. (We shall see later what happened to this sighting report.) Mikawa, distressed at losing surprise, turned northwest, back in the direction of Rabaul. About 11 A.M. another Hudson appeared, this time quite low, and Admiral Mikawa thought it was the same plane. (It was not, and this sighting report will be treated later also.) Shortly after the first Hudson had disappeared the search planes from the *Chokai, Kinugasa,* and *Kako* were recovered. They had not been far enough, and brought back little information. When the second Hudson appeared, ships of the Eighth Fleet opened main battery fire and drove it away, after which the fleet resumed course for Bougainville Strait.

The *Aoba's* plane returned about noon with the first full report. The pilot said he had seen a battleship, 4 cruisers, 7 destroyers, and 15 transports off Guadalcanal, and 2 heavy cruisers, 12 destroyers, and 3 transports off Tulagi.

This was a shock to Admiral Mikawa. His planes from Rabaul the previous day had reported sinking 2 cruisers, a destroyer, and 6 transports, and heavily damaging 3 cruisers and 2 transports. Pilots, it seemed, whether Allied or Japanese, were always overenthusiastic in reports of damage to the enemy. There were many more ships left in the invasion area than there should have been, had his pilots' reports been accurate.

But he did learn two things of great importance. First, the enemy's forces were split, part at Guadalcanal and part at Tulagi. That was encouraging, for instead of being inferior, Admiral Mikawa's force might be almost equal to, or even stronger than, either part of the enemy force. Second, no aircraft carriers were reported, though many enemy carrier planes were in the area. This was worrisome; the carriers must be somewhere in the area, probably south of Guadalcanal. Planes would make no difference in a night attack, but it was still a long time until sundown, and every hour brought him closer to the enemy.

Admiral Mikawa discussed this intelligence with his staff at lunch. He had been sighted and reported; the enemy had carriers and he had none; the enemy was stronger, but split. Planes from the morning attack had been sighted en route back to Rabaul, straggling in twos. or threes. This meant there had been heavy fighting over Guadalcanal. Admiral Mikawa was so worried he broke radio silence to ask Rabaul for information on the enemy carriers. A negative reply was sent, but he never received it.

Nevertheless, at 1:00 P.M. he made his decision: the attack would go on. He ordered speed increased to 24 knots and set course through Bougainville Strait. He cleared these waters at 4:00 P.M. and turned left into the Slot; he was committed. This was a bold move, and the Admiral was well aware of it. He took it without trepidation or hesitation; once decided, he moved forward with firmness and decision to strike a swift and terrible blow.

All afternoon Mikawa and his staff waited for word of the morning bombing runs, but no reports came in. Pacing near the radio room, talking with his staff, the Admiral finally decided to send the *Aoba's* plane off again. Late word of the enemy's disposition and of the damage he had suffered in the morning raids would greatly ease Mikawa's mind before the night battle. The pilot was ordered to fly down the Slot, spend not more than twenty-five minutes over Savo Sound, and return by twilight. It would be impossible to recover him after dark.

When he had gone (alas, he never returned), the general staff worked out the final operational order, and Commander Ohmae drafted it. At 4:20 P.M. Signal Order No. 25 was semaphored to all ships present:

1. During the night the cruising disposition will consist of a main body and a vanguard. The main body will be composed of *Chokai,* followed by Cruiser Division 6, with 1,000 meters between ships. The vanguard will be stationed 3,000 meters ahead of *Chokai,* and will consist of *Tenryu* and *Yunagi* to port, *Yubari* to starboard, separated by an interval of 6,000 meters.

2. Before the rush in, if enemy small craft are encountered, the vanguard will check them strongly while the main body heads southward.

3. At the time of the rush in, all ships will form battle column. Order of ships: *Chokai*, Cruiser Division Six, *Tenryu*, *Yubari* and *Yunagi*, with a distance of 1,200 meters between ships.

4. In the approach, the cruiser force will first pass south of Savo Island and will torpedo the main enemy force in the Guadalcanal anchorage, after which it will head toward the Tulagi anchorage to shell and torpedo the enemy. The cruiser force will then withdraw north of Savo Island. Each commanding officer will operate independently as regards run and torpedo firings.

5. As a means of recognition, each ship will display white sleeves on each side of the bridge. Each sleeve will be one meter in diameter and seven meters long.

6. Speed will be 24 knots at the time of the rush in.

An hour before sunset there was a final scare. A vessel was sighted hull down, far out on the starboard bow. Every gun in the task force trained out, ready to sink it if it was enemy. Lookouts at the masthead finally identified it as the seaplane carrier *Akitsushima*, of the Eleventh Air Fleet. She was bearing south to establish a seaplane base on Gizo Island, in Vella Gulf.

The sun set at 6:16 P.M. and darkness came quickly, as it does in the tropics. The Eighth Fleet, safe now from enemy reconnaissance, made final preparations for battle. All combustibles, depth charges, and loose gear were cleared from topside, and readiness Condition II was ordered in all ships.

Tension mounted in the ships. Some men wrote last letters home, enclosing a lock of hair or other personal memento. Some wrapped around their stomachs the cot-

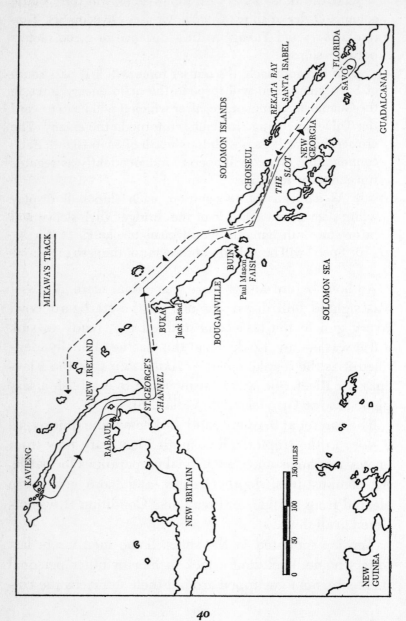

MIKAWA'S TRACK

KAVIENG

NEW IRELAND

RABAUL

ST. GEORGE'S
CHANNEL

NEW BRITAIN

BUKA

Jack Read

BOUGAINVILLE

BUIN

FAISI

Paul Mason

SOLOMON ISLANDS

CHOISEUL

REKATA BAY

SANTA ISABEL

THE
SLOT

NEW
GEORGIA

FLORIDA

SAVO

GUADALCANAL

SOLOMON SEA

NEW
GUINEA

0   50   100   150 MILES

ton band of one thousand red stitches, a powerful talisman to ward off enemy bullets. Enemy radio traffic was increasing sharply, and the strange jargon of war could be heard plainly. "Red base 2, red base 2, come in red base 2." "Deck clear for landing, deck clear for landing." Obviously, the carriers recovering planes.

At 7:15 flares were lighted, to guide the *Aoba's* search plane back, but it never appeared. Mikawa signaled his company: "Let us attack with certain victory in the traditional night attack of the Imperial Japanese Navy. May each one calmly do his utmost."

The staff gathered in flag plot and finally word came from Rabaul about 9:00 P.M. Planes of the Fifth Air Attack Force had sunk 2 enemy heavy cruisers, 1 large cruiser, 2 destroyers and 9 transports; a heavy cruiser and 2 transports had been left burning. Mikawa was greatly heartened; he had no way of knowing the reports were completely false. He was sure now his force was superior, and through his ships ran a thrill of victory.

With great confidence, supremely certain of the night tactics they had so arduously perfected, the Japanese sailed into battle. In high places in every ship, the finest eyes of the fleet peered into the night. Banners streamed from every bridge, and lookouts could identify every ship in the company, by silhouette and by red or white rings on the funnels. This night identification was uncanny, unique in the navies of the world, and it would pay stupendous dividends, shaming the enemy's early radar.

At 11:13 P.M. Admiral Mikawa led off with a tactic that would bemuse and confound the enemy. He launched 3 planes, one each from the *Chokai, Aoba,* and *Kako,* to lay course markers to guide the battle force in, to report the Allied disposition, and to illuminate the enemy when the signal was given. The catapult charges flashed in the night, and the 3 planes, old Type-94 float planes, were off on their mission. First Lieutenant Fumio Kiyose led the squadron, 3 men in each plane, and all were aware that after executing their part in the battle plan they could not be recovered. They would have to make their way back to safety as best they could—if they could. They welcomed this chance for sacrifice, and flew into the blackness in high spirits.

Cruiser Division 18 picked up the first marker lamp at 11:35 P.M., 30 miles off Cape Esperance. The Tokyo Express was on course and on time. Speed was increased to 26 knots, and all hands were ordered to battle stations at midnight. A light was sighted in the direction of Tulagi, the *Kako* reported fires on shore, and Rear Admiral Goto advised the sky was red over Tulagi, as from a large fire. At 12:40 A.M. the black dome of Savo Island loomed unmistakably 20 degrees on the port bow. Three minutes later every heart on the flag bridge fluttered as a lookout reported an enemy ship crossing the track ahead from right to left. The sighting was at an incredible 10,900 meters, over 5 miles, on a black, squally night.

Every eye on the bridge watched Mikawa—to attack, or not to attack?

"Left rudder, slow to twenty-two knots," he ordered. This was not the moment.

Officers and sailors watched in fascination as the vessel to starboard, now positively identified as an American destroyer, plodded steadily ahead, directly into their course. One sight, one sound showing she had discovered the Japanese force, and the destroyer would have been blown from the water. On the *Chokai* there was complete silence, and the hiss of the water past the hull sounded like a roar. Thirty seconds passed, a minute, it seemed forever. Then the destroyer, blind as a sleepwalker, turned away a full 180 degrees and started back toward Guadalcanal.

Unbelievable! The bridge sighed in unison relief and at the same moment a lookout reported, "Ship sighted, twenty degrees to port" and every head swung that way. It was another destroyer, north of Savo, but this one was showing her stern and steaming away, and not in alarm either. "Right rudder. Steer course one hundred and fifty degrees," Mikawa said calmly and automatically. The task force cleaved between the destroyers and south of Savo as smug as a fox already in the henhouse.

Commander Ohmae brought the chart and Mikawa hunched over it with great intensity. At 1:25 A.M. he ordered two signals: "Three heavy cruisers south of Savo Island, course two ninety True, speed eighteen knots." (The meeting would be nearly head on.) "Prepare to fire torpedoes."

The *Yunagi* dropped out of formation, cut speed, and turned back to keep an eye on the first destroyer. The rest of the formation upped speed to 30 knots and closed for the kill.

"Cruiser, seven degrees port," a lookout cried. It was a good 18,000 yards away (over 9 miles) silhouetted by the red glow of a burning ship behind it.

43

"Three cruisers, nine degrees starboard, moving to the right."

A parachute flare blossomed in the sky and suddenly Savo Sound was bright as noon. There they lay (in reality, 2 cruisers and a destroyer) at 8,000 yards.

At 1:33 A.M. Mikawa called the dice. "All ships attack!"

It was Sunday morning, August 9, 1942, just eight months and two days after another Sunday morning at a place called Pearl Harbor. Surely the enemy would not be sleeping twice.

chapter
5

Operation Watchtower came to life on a bright Sunday
morning in that boundless stretch of the South Pacific
near the point at which the Tropic of Capricorn crosses
the 180th meridian. As if by chance, here the armada
gathered on a sparkling sea and here was born the first
great amphibious assault of World War II.

It was not, of course, by chance. This reach of ocean,
far from land, had been chosen after thorough delibera-
tion, and the movement of these vessels had been or-
dained by the pinnacle of command. This was the opening offensive play, and it must succeed, even if the odds
were against it.

Operation Watchtower, the campaign against the
Solomon Islands, was conceived early in 1942, while the
United States Navy was still staggering backward from

the blows at Pearl Harbor, the Philippines, and the East Indies. Even as the Japanese rolled forward, across thousands of miles of ocean and over strange lands and islands scarcely heard of by Americans, Admiral King placed his finger on a map and said he wanted that spot—Tulagi. Tulagi? Where was that? It was near the southeast end of the Solomons chain, a few miles north of an island called Guadalcanal and within sight of a volcano top called Savo Island.

The Solomons. They sounded like Paradise; they were Hell. Ten degrees below the Equator, they were islands of swaying palms and blooming bougainvillea and mimosa. On soft, tropic nights the wind wafted flower perfumes far to sea, and by day coral heads and blue sea filled the eye with delight. And perhaps, back among the coconut palms, grass-skirted maidens, shy and giggling, waited for sailors who had never been west of Keokuk. Wait for us, maidens, wait for us.

And now on Sunday morning, July 26, 1942, the ships came in to the Koro Sea, 400 miles south of the Fiji Islands. First came the *Wasp*, all the way from the Mediterranean, a heart-leaping sight as she plunged in the swells, destroyers far off around her. In the train came the transports, the *President Adams, President Hayes, President Jackson*, the *Alhena*, and the *Crescent City*, loaded with Marines from San Diego. The *Saratoga* and the *Enterprise* stood in from Pearl Harbor, and with them the cruisers, the long, low greyhounds of the sea. The *Quincy*, recently in from the Atlantic, and the *Vincennes*, a veteran of the Doolittle Raid and Midway. Most beautiful sight of all was the *North Carolina*, the newest and most powerful battleship in the fleet.

They came from the west, too, destroyer-transports from Noumea with more Marines, and in early afternoon still more—Task Force 62.6, with 3 Australian cruisers in the van. From the yardarm of HMAS *Australia* flew the flag of Rear Admiral Victor Alexander Charles Crutchley, RN, commander of His Majesty's Royal Australian Squadron, bringing with him HMAS *Canberra* and *Hobart*, followed by the American cruisers *Chicago* and *Salt Lake City*, 9 more destroyers, transports, and 4 storeships. By nightfall it was a staggering sight—over 70 ships and 20,000 Marines, by far the most powerful striking force ever gathered under American command.

Shades of Dewey and Manila Bay. This was the first offensive thrust of the United States Navy since the Spanish-American War. In that "splendid little war" of 1898, the grizzled Dewey had taken an American fleet of 6 vessels into Manila Bay, passing Corregidor without a shot being fired, and finished off the Spanish fleet—all 7 vessels—before withdrawing to allow his crews to have breakfast. "You may fire when ready, Gridley," he had said, and the battle had opened at 5,500 yards. It was all over by noon, a smashing victory to start off the war. Would it be like that again?

Hardly. The Philippines lay thousands of miles off, and Allied forces could not even approach them. Corregidor lay in enemy hands, with the stillness of death, and it would be more than two years before MacArthur would wade ashore at Leyte and declare: "I have returned."

47

Like everything else, war had changed, and the enemy this time was no collection of rusting Spanish hulks.

Even before all vessels had arrived, Vice Admiral Frank Jack Fletcher called a conference on his flagship, the *Saratoga*. At fifty-seven, Fletcher probably had had more experience with the Japanese than any other American officer. He had been commander at the Battle of Coral Sea and at the Battle of Midway. Yet, like everybody else, he had never met a Japanese warship in surface battle. All his battles had been carrier battles, with the surface forces far out of sight of each other. But he had seen enough of the Japanese to have a well-grounded respect for them. He had lost a carrier in each battle—the *Lexington* at Coral Sea and the *Yorktown* at Midway. There were only 4 American carriers left in the Pacific and 3 of them were here; only the *Hornet* was missing. Admiral Fletcher did not intend to lose any more carriers; in fact, he may have been a little sensitive about it, particularly the *Yorktown*. That was the meaning of his announcement at this first conference—he would not keep his carriers at Guadalcanal more than 48 hours.

Rear Admiral Richmond Kelly Turner was stunned. So was Major General Alexander A. Vandegrift, USMC, Commander Ground Forces. Turner, beetle-browed and craggy of face, was fresh out from the States. Just a month younger than Fletcher, but two years behind him at the Academy (1908 to Fletcher's 1906) Turner had been chosen by Admiral King for a job new to the Fleet, Commander of Amphibious Forces, South Pacific. He was detached in Washington on June 13, learned of his assignment June 30 at San Francisco, stopped at Pearl

Harbor for quick conferences, and raised his flag at Wellington, New Zealand, on July 18.

Now, eight days later, he sat in the wardroom of the *Saratoga,* listening to Fletcher outline the plans. The carrier forces would go nowhere near the beachhead, but stand off to the south, on the underside of Guadalcanal, and provide air support from there. Fletcher, as Officer in Tactical Command, would be with the carriers. Turner would take the transports in, shielded by 8 cruisers and 18 destroyers, and Vandegrift would lead the Marines ashore. In command of the warships at the beachhead, second in command directly under Turner, would be Rear Admiral Crutchley. But he didn't even make the conference. Neither did Vice Admiral Robert Lee Ghormley, Commander, South Pacific Area and South Pacific Force. He was back at Wellington, far too occupied with command of the entire theater to get away for this rendezvous. He sent his Chief of Staff, Rear Admiral Daniel J. Callaghan.

There was little time for argument or consultation. Fletcher passed out his operations plan and discussed it, and that was that. There weren't even enough copies to go around, and Ghormley never saw one until the landings were a month old.

That's the way it had been for the past three months. Ghormley, a classmate of Fletcher's (standing twelfth in the class to Fletcher's twenty-sixth), had been in London since August, 1940, as Special Naval Observer. In this period "short of war" his job had been to offer Britain whatever help the United States Navy could prudently give. With America in the war this job was over and

Admiral Ghormley had flown back to Washington on urgent summons, arriving the night of April 17.

The next morning Admiral King received him and said, "You have been selected to command the South Pacific Force and South Pacific Area. You will have a large area under your command and a most difficult task. I do not have the tools to give you to carry out that task as it should be. You will establish your headquarters in Auckland, New Zealand, with an advance base at Tonga-tabu. In time, possibly this fall, we hope to start an offensive from the South Pacific. You will then probably find it necessary to shift the advance base as the situation demands, and move your own headquarters to meet special situations. I would like you to leave Washington in one week, if possible."

That was a long speech for King, but Ghormley was the one left breathless. He had been given the hottest potato in the fleet, and his friends soon told him about it. In the end, it took him two weeks to get out of Washington. The men he wanted for his staff were scattered from Washington to Australia, the latest charts he could find were British surveys of 1897 and German charts of 1908. From what he could learn, forces in the theater were slim and base construction was proceeding practically with hand tools.

"We were not even ready for defense, let alone offense," he wrote later, but there, too, he didn't know King. The admiral had long since divided the war into stages. The defensive-defensive was about over; the defensive-offensive would start in the Solomons, to be followed by the offensive-defensive and climaxed by the offensive-offensive, the smashing of Japan.

Admiral Turner was still in Washington, as King's Assistant Chief of Staff for Plans. Although he didn't know it yet, his position was unusual; he was planning an operation he would soon be ordered to execute. Admiral Ghormley dropped by to see Turner and urged him to reserve one Lion and one Cub for him on the West Coast. These were self-contained base units, a Lion being larger than a Cub. Four days later Ghormley was back, and this time he asked Turner to ship a Cub and a Construction Battalion (CB or Seabees) to New Zealand immediately. Neither request was granted, because they couldn't be —there weren't any available.

Admiral Ghormley left by train for the West Coast on May 1, and if he was depressed who can blame him? He didn't even have the shoestring for what was later dubbed "Operation Shoestring," the Guadalcanal landings. In San Francisco he picked up his chief of staff, Admiral Callaghan; his assistant chief, Brigadier General DeWitt Peck, USMC; his communications officer, Lieutenant Commander Louis M. LeHardy, and his flag lieutenant, Lieutenant Commander Jack W. Wintle. (In six months only Ghormley and Peck would still be alive, so vicious was the slaughter impending.)

They flew out to Pearl for five days of conferences with Admiral Nimitz, and were joined by Rear Admiral John S. McCain, who was the new Commander Aircraft, South Pacific Area. The staff hopped down through Canton and Suva, in the Fijis, arriving in New Caledonia on May 17, to find it in near insurrection. Admiral George Thierry d'Argenlieu had seized the island for De Gaulle and the Free French, and like his commander in chief he was sulky because he had not been consulted on South Pacific strategy. Ghormley, who was good at that sort of thing, mollified him and even got him to take a French force and occupy the Wallis Islands, just west of the Samoan Group. Admiral McCain set up headquarters in the USS *Tangier* at Noumea and made an extremely important move—he arranged to get the Australian Coast Watcher reports.

Admiral Ghormley flew down to Auckland on May 21 to open relations with the New Zealand authorities, and when he had a moment he set down his impressions of his long trip from Washington:

"The vast distances, the shortage of aircraft, the ease with which the Japanese could slip between defended points, the large size of many islands, the high mountains on most of them, the primitive state of the natives, the total lack of harbor or base facilities, the lack of cable and radio facilities, the lack of ships."

These things, he felt, were not understood in Washington, and indeed they were not. It was nearly 9,000 miles from Washington to New Zealand, and the transition from London to Auckland in six weeks was enough to stagger any man. But Ghormley turned to, and on June 19 activated his command.

Three weeks later he was ordered to execute Operation Watchtower, with target date of August 1.

What had happened? Admiral King had spoken of an offensive "in time, possibly this fall. . . ." But Admiral Nimitz had made a discovery: the Japanese had begun to build an airfield on Guadalcanal.

Ghormley, in dismay, flew up to Melbourne with General Peck to confer with General MacArthur and his chief of staff General Richard Sutherland, Rear Admiral Arthur S. Carpender, who was about to become MacArthur's naval chief, and Vice Admiral Herbert F. Leary. A few weeks earlier General MacArthur had reported that he could rush forces up and capture Rabaul, if the Navy would give him a few carriers.

Now, after the talks, Ghormley and MacArthur reported to the Joint Chiefs of Staff:

"It is our joint opinion, arrived at independently and confirmed after discussion, that the initiation of this operation at this time, without reasonable assurance of an adequate air cover during each phase, would be attended with the gravest risk. . . . It is recommended that this operation be deferred pending the further development of forces in the South Pacific and Southwest Pacific Areas. . . ."

In Washington, Admiral King snorted to General Marshall: "Three weeks ago MacArthur stated that, if he could be furnished amphibious forces and two carriers, he could push right through to Rabaul. . . . He now feels that he not only cannot undertake this extended operation but not even the Tulagi operation."

General MacArthur, according to his biographers, envisioned a supreme command for this entire corner of the Pacific, with one head (himself), and from this moment on felt he had lost the Navy.

Back from Admiral King on July 10 came the order: "Execute." They made few men tougher than General MacArthur, but they made one—King. "One of the great decisions of the war," said Navy historian Samuel Eliot Morison.

But it was simply not possible to meet the date of August 1. Part of the 1st Marine Division had arrived in Wellington as early as June. The transports dumped men and supplies on the pier and sailed off for Operation Torch, the invasion of North Africa. (Even King could not stand in the way of Torch, and the best he could do was save what he could for the Pacific.) New Zealand labor was costly and lazy, so the Marines loaded their own transports, combat style—each ship a complete unit with material ready to roll out in the order needed. The *American Legion, Fuller, Bellatrix,* and *Neville* took the first contingent aboard, and a second Marine contingent arriving in Wellington on July 11 completed the reloading in ten days. Six other transports, carrying the rest of the Marines, had sailed from San Diego on July 1, convoyed by the *Wasp* group.

D-Day had to be put back to August 7, and now on July 26 in the Koro Sea the men who were to do the job were meeting for the first time—some of them were, that is, for Admiral Crutchley arrived too late, the cruiser commanders were not invited, and 2 transports had not yet even made it from Pearl Harbor.

chapter
6

Turner, a blacksmith's son and a man of strong opinions, spoke out sharply at Admiral Fletcher's conference in the *Saratoga*. Withdrawal of air cover at the end of two days would jeopardize the whole operation. When the air cover left, the transports and the warships would have to leave too—the entire fleet. The transports and supply ships could not possibly unload in forty-eight hours. When the fleet withdrew the Marines would be left alone on a hostile beach, with whatever they had been able to wrestle ashore. Vandegrift joined in with Turner—after all, they were his men. Fletcher stood firm. He would not hazard his carriers beyond two days. In that time the Japanese could learn where he was, and submarines could converge on the area. Without doubt he remembered the *Yorktown*, picked off by submarines at Midway after the battle was over. Forty-eight hours; no more.

It is tragic, in retrospect, that Fletcher's decision was not appealed, although it probably would have availed nothing. Ghormley could not help, and Nimitz likely would not have. The almost unbreakable rule in command is: The commander on the spot knows the situation best, has the responsibility, and is not to be overruled except in most dire circumstances. Ghormley was out of the picture from the start. His orders brought him, quite unwarrantedly, the title of "Nimitz' errand boy," or "the traffic cop of the Southwest Pacific." The orders said, in effect, that task forces would be sent to him from time to time, with missions already assigned, and he was to order them to carry out their missions. This was precisely a case in point.

As he returned to his flagship *McCawley* after the conference, Admiral Turner caught a glimpse of the *Astoria* crossing the *McCawley's* bow, and he smiled sardonically. Three years ago, in the spring of 1939, he had had command of the *Astoria* on a solemn trip to Japan, returning to the homeland the ashes of Hirosi Saito, Japanese Ambassador, who had died in Washington. The *Astoria* had spent ten days in Yokohama, on a state visit of Oriental ceremony. Turner wondered what the Japanese had really been thinking, as his cruiser rode at anchor in the harbor. Captain Greenman, four years behind him at the Academy, had the *Astoria* now and it was just as well that neither of them knew what awaited two weeks from this day.

On Monday morning, July 27, the amphibious force moved north in the Koro Sea, and a strange sight it was.

Gay new cruise ships, the furniture gone from cocktail lounge and bar closed; 3 new President liners; the *American Legion*, a rusting and filthy Army transport dating from 1926; the swayback *McCawley*, an ex-British coal burner, most recently the *Santa Barbara* of the Grace Line; the new *President Jackson* and even the old *President Jackson* from 1921, now the *Zeilin*; and 4 liners finished just too late for the World War I, the old City liners of the Baltimore Mail Line—*City of Baltimore, City of Norfolk, City of Newport News*, and *City of Los Angeles*.

A thin, bespectacled youth named Richard Tregaskis was in the *Crescent City*, talking to the Marines and making notes for *Guadalcanal Diary*. Ralph Morse of *Life* magazine was in the *Vincennes*, and Joe James Custer of United Press in the *Quincy*. In the *Wasp*, congratulating themselves in the thought that they had the best seat for the impending battle, were Clark Lee of The Associated Press and Jack Singer of International News Service. The first amphibious operation of the war would be well covered.

But first there were the rehearsals on Koro Island in the Fijis, and they were "a complete bust," according to no less an authority than General Vandegrift. Closing in on the densely wooded little island, its volcanic peak towering 2,000 feet above them, the boats were hung up on coral reefs. Some broached, others were holed, and many broke down mechanically. On one transport alone a dozen boats were out of service, and the General dared not risk any more. But the carrier planes swooped in, the Navy poured on some gunfire, and some lessons were learned. It didn't look good, but that's the way it would have to be. The convoy sailed at nightfall on July 31, destination Savo Sound.

Late in the afternoon of July 31, Turner received Crutchley and Vandegrift aboard the *McCawley* for a final conference. All three outlined their plans—Turner for the whole operation, Vandegrift for the landings, and Crutchley for protection of the forces. The cruiser captains could not be included, and thus passed the last opportunity for some of them to meet Admiral Crutchley, their commanding officer, before battle. (Why Admiral Crutchley did not confer with his cruiser captains during the four days at Koro has never been explained.) For the captains of what became the Northern Force—the *Vincennes, Quincy,* and *Astoria*—the feeling of aloneness had already begun.

Tactical consideration aside, it was too bad the cruiser captains missed Admiral Crutchley, for he was a striking figure. A very tall man, of jovial countenance, he sported a "full set" of red beard and mustache that was the delight of all who contemplated it. In his summer whites, contrasting with his bronzed skin and set off with shoulder-boards and gold-braided cap, he made a dashing picture indeed.

But there was far more to the man than that, as attested by his decorations. Before he was twenty-five he had won the Victoria Cross (Britain's highest award for bravery), the Distinguished Service Cross, and the French Croix de guerre. With it all he was completely unaffected, a man of great charm and presence, frank and unruffled.

Admiral Crutchley, later Sir Victor by the Queen's Birthday Honours of 1946, was born in 1893 and as a boy went down to the Naval School at Osborne. A lieutenant in HMS *Centurion* at the Battle of Jutland, he later took part in those valiant British attempts to block the harbors of Zeebrugge and Ostend and bottle up the German U-boat fleets. He won the D.S.C. on the first attempt, the night of April 22–23, 1918, and when it failed he immediately volunteered for the second effort, May 9–10. He was First Lieutenant in HMS *Vindictive,* an old cruiser, when Commander Alfred E. Godsal took her in under heavy fire, attempting to sink her as a channel block.

Commander Godsal was killed almost at once, and his second in command fell severely wounded. Lieutenant Crutchley took command of *Vindictive,* and pressed on under murderous fire. When in position, the scuttling charges were detonated and he ordered his men to leave. With complete disregard for his life, he searched the cruiser with flashlight to see that all the wounded had been removed. He then jumped into Motor Launch 254 and took command of that vessel, the commanding officer being exhausted from wounds and the second in command dead. ML 254, loaded with wounded, was raked by shellfire and flooded in the forepart, but Lieutenant Crutchley refused to abandon her. Ordering weights shifted aft and organizing bailing brigades, he got her away. When HMS *Warwick* rescued them, ML 254 was nearly awash. No less than nine V.C.'s were awarded for these operations, of which none shone more brightly than Lieutenant Crutchley's.

Between the wars he rose steadily, and at the outbreak of World War II was captain of the battleship HMS *Warspite,* Mentioned in Despatches in the second battle of Narvik. In June, 1942, promoted to rear admiral, he had come out as Flag Officer Commanding the Australian Naval Squadron, the last Britisher ever to hold that command. As for nearly all other officers present, Operation Watchtower was his first chance at command of large units and he meant to have a whack at it.

On the way north, in complete blackout and radio silence, Admiral Crutchley completed his plans for disposition of the screening forces at the beachhead. Hunched over the desk in his cabin on the *Australia,* Crutchley wrote: "It will be my aim to meet the enemy to seaward of the area between Savo Island and Sealark Channel, and that the force engaging him shall remain interposed between the enemy and this area. It is expected that our extensive air reconnaissance will give warning of the approach of enemy surface forces."

In the disembarkation area, he said, destroyers *Ralph Talbot* and *Blue* would leave the formation one hour before sunset and "establish anti-submarine patrol and radar guard watch to give warning of approach of surface craft or submarines."

He gave them positions—the *Ralph Talbot* to the northwest of Savo Island, the *Blue* to the southwest—and continued:

"In the event of any enemy surface force being detected, immediate report is to be made, the force is to be shadowed and frequently reported, and when about to be engaged by cruisers, the destroyers in contact may be ordered to illuminate the enemy forces with searchlights."

How very correct it all sounded, and yet how very wrong it all turned out, for nothing happened according to plan on the night approaching. Admiral Turner thought well of the plans, and approved them, failing with all the rest to detect the faults so mercilessly exposed in battle. But it was a time of trying, and of learning, and the cost is often high.

On Tuesday, August 4, D-day minus three, Admiral Turner sent this message to all his forces:

> Publish to all hands X on August seventh this force will recapture Tulagi and Guadalcanal Islands which are now in the hands of the enemy X in this first forward step toward clearing the Japanese out of conquered territory we have strong support from the Pacific Fleet and from the air surface and submarine forces in the South Pacific and Australia X it is significant of victory that we see here shoulder to shoulder the US Navy Marines and Army and the Australian and New Zealand Air Naval and Army services X I have confidence that all elements of this armada will in skill and courage show themselves fit comrades of those brave men who have already dealt the enemy mighty blows for our great cause X God bless you all X R K Turner Rear Admiral US Navy Commanding
>
> Date 4 Aug 42
> TOR 1530

From CTF 62
To   TF 62

The weather was good (that is to say bad) during the last two days of approach, with intermittent rain and low overcast, and no enemy planes or submarines were sighted. During the night of August 6–7 the carrier task force, approaching independently from the west, cut across the path of the convoy and continued on along the south side of Guadalcanal.

Admiral Turner was for the last time seeing Admiral

Fletcher, the over-all commander, now bearing off to the east with the most powerful part of the force. Admiral Fletcher, destined to come no nearer than 200 miles to the beachhead and to quit the fight early, took with him the aircraft carriers *Saratoga, Enterprise,* and *Wasp;* the battleship *North Carolina;* heavy cruisers *Minneapolis, New Orleans, Portland, Atlanta, San Francisco,* and *Salt Lake City;* and the destroyers *Phelps, Farragut, Worden, MacDonough, Dale, Balch, Benham, Maury, Gwin, Grayson, Lang, Sterett, Aaron Ward, Stack, Laffey,* and *Fahrenholt.* The carrier planes would be some help to Turner —for as long as Fletcher allowed them to stay within reach—but the rest of the force could give him no support. Their only job was to protect the carriers.

The transports and screening warships moved around the western end of Guadalcanal, lookouts walking softly on deck, fearful someone might hear. In the very early hours of Friday, August 7, the long procession rounded Cape Esperance and split up to enter Savo Sound, the heart of the enemy camp.

Half the force passed outside Savo Island, entering by the north passage to face Tulagi. The other half steamed south of Savo and ranged themselves facing the beaches of Guadalcanal. Not so much as a signal light showed from shore. The approach had achieved perfect surprise, and at 6:13 A.M. the warships opened fire. It was the beginning of the Solomons campaign, the longest, bloodiest, and bitterest campaign in naval history. Before it was over, the very name of Savo Sound was transmuted into Ironbottom Sound, in grim memory of the ships that lay rusting on the coral 400 fathoms below.

chapter
7

At Guadalcanal, the landings went off with disarming ease. The vessels of Task Group X-ray approached the beach in perfect order and anchored at 6:50 A.M. A few moments later Turner gave the command: "Land the landing force," and the transports began lifting out boats. It was after 9:00 A.M. before the troops reached the beaches, but when they did they walked ashore without opposition and found breakfast still hot on the table at the Japanese airfield. The enemy had fled into the hills.

It was the same at Tulagi, where the troops went ashore with the loss of one man—a marine killed by an accidental discharge of a rifle. Once ashore, however, resistance developed almost immediately, and hard fighting began.

From the forces afloat, the *Quincy* opened the offensive

at 6:13 A.M., with a full salvo against the coast west of the landing beaches at Guadalcanal. Other cruisers and the destroyers joined in, firing on supposed targets ashore, and the destroyer *Selfridge* sighted and sank an enemy schooner carrying gasoline from Tulagi to Guadalcanal. There was no answering fire from shore, and the barrage was soon lifted.

Six float planes, 3 each from the *Quincy* and *Astoria*, were overhead for spotting, and 44 planes came in from the *Saratoga* and *Enterprise* for dive-bombing.

For communications, Admiral Fletcher had put radio groups from the carriers aboard the *McCawley*, the *Neville*, and the *Chicago*. Each group, which brought its own radio equipment, consisted of 2 officers and 2 enlisted men. With these Air Director and Fighter Director teams, air cover from the carriers could be called in when needed against the Japanese. Destroyer *Monssen* lobbed 60 rounds of 5-inch fire into Florida Island, west of Tulagi, and the antiaircraft cruiser *San Juan* and destroyer *Buchanan* laid 100 rounds on other points on Florida. Again there was no reply from the Japanese.

As the sun rose and the morning mist cleared, the landing operation, the first for Americans since 1898, proceeded in ominous calm. At 8:10 A.M., Radio Tulagi sent its last message to Rabaul: "The enemy force is overwhelming. We will defend our positions to the death, praying for everlasting victory." It had hardly cleared when shells from the *San Juan* smashed the station. Help, if it was coming, would have to come from Rabaul.

Paul Edward Mason, a bespectacled Australian planter with a most benign face, had been waiting many months for his chance. He was of the almost legendary force known as the Coast Watchers. When the Japanese overran the Solomons early in 1942, a few men stayed behind. Mason, a short, fair man in his forties, was one of them. He packed his radio into the mountains of southeastern Bougainville, overlooking Bougainville Strait, and waited for his chance to serve.

There were others like him, some on Guadalcanal itself, others on Malaita and Santa Isabel, ringing the theater of operations. Most were Australians, some were British, at least one was a woman, and all were volunteers, now in the service of the Australian government. Radio tied them together, feeding information to General MacArthur far to the westward in Australia, and southward to Vila, on the island of Efate in the New Hebrides. Hugh Mackenzie, erstwhile Australian Naval College student, rolling stone and planter, was at Vila as DSIO (deputy supervising intelligence officer), collecting information from the Coast Watchers and transmitting it to Turner's fleet at Guadalcanal.

On the morning of August 7, with the landings under way, Mason gave the first warning of reaction. High in the mountains he watched the Japanese planes flash by in the sunlight, then keyed a radio message to Malaita, 400 miles away, near Guadalcanal. "From STO. Twenty-four torpedo bombers headed yours." The STO was a code to establish the authenticity of the message. It was the first three letters of the surname of Mason's sister, Mrs. John Stokie. Malaita received the warning clearly, relayed it to Mackenzie, who passed it back to the fleet at Guadalcanal. On HMAS *Canberra*, the bosun piped:

"The ship will be attacked at noon by twenty-four torpedo bombers. All hands will pipe to dinner at eleven o'clock."

The Japanese began arriving shortly after noon, and there were two raids the first day. Radar on the *Chicago* picked up the first planes 43 miles out and the fighter-director team from the carriers, working on board the *Chicago*, called in planes from the *Enterprise* and *Saratoga*. The first attack was from high level, and did no damage. The second was by dive bombers, which scored a hit on destroyer *Mugford*, killing 22 men. In wild engagements, both sides attacking with great spirit but little skill, the Japanese lost some 14 bombers and 2 fighters, the Americans 11 fighters and a dive bomber.

The first day had passed in most encouraging fashion. Troops were solidly ashore at both objectives—Guadalcanal and Tulagi—the first enemy reaction had been turned back with minor loss; only one major problem was shaping up. The beaches were badly congested. Cargo and armament had poured ashore far faster than it was moved inland, and by afternoon 100 boats were landed but not unloaded, and 50 more stood off at the surf line, waiting a place to beach. The first good-sized intraservice row was under way. Captain Lawrence F. Reifsnider, convoy commander, believed it his task to land the goods, the Marines' task to unload it and move it inland. The Marines had other ideas; they were fighting men, not stevedores. They took their weapons with them and little else. By nightfall, the situation was entirely out of hand, and late that night Admiral Turner ordered unloading stopped.

Before sundown Admiral Crutchley ordered his night plan executed. Lieutenant Commander Joseph W. Callahan took the *Ralph Talbot*, a 1500-ton *Craven*-class destroyer, out on station north of Savo Island. His orders were to patrol a line running 071–251 degrees across the channel between Savo Island and Florida Island. On a clock face, it would be a line from about thirteen after the hour to seventeen of the hour. Commander H. Nordmark Williams, three years Callahan's senior at the Academy, took station with the *Blue* astride the channel south of Savo Island, somewhat farther west than the *Ralph Talbot* and on a course slightly more northerly, 051–231, or about eight after on the clock face to twenty-two of. All night long, the five-year-old sister ships were to cruise at 12 knots, back and forth in precise timing along their straight lines. In this way, Crutchley thought, nothing could enter the sound without alarm.

The picket destroyers had not been chosen by chance. Admiral Crutchley designated the *Blue* and the *Ralph Talbot* for this duty because, in training, they had shown the best surface radar capability of all his destroyers, consistently picking up a cruiser target at 7 to 10 miles. That capability could be vital in an operation of this kind. Unfortunately, their search runs were not co-ordinated and if both were at the extreme end of a search leg they could leave a hole as much as 25 miles wide in the screen.

Crutchley broke his cruisers into 2 forces (an attacker could not ask more). The reasons seemed sound to him. He felt heavy ships in groups of more than 4 were unwieldy at night. In addition, the *Australia, Canberra,* and *Chicago* had worked under him before. He knew them and their methods, so he kept them under his command as the Southern Force, and put them behind the *Blue*, nearest the Guadalcanal beaches. The other 3 cruisers—*Vincennes, Quincy,* and *Astoria*—he had never seen before. He decided to put them in a Northern Force and plug the north channel with them.

In his "Special Instructions to Screening Group and Vessels Temporarily Assigned," which Admiral Turner had approved, Crutchley wrote:

> It is my intention to divide [a dangerous word from the beginning of military history] into two groups the naval forces available to counter enemy attack with surface craft. Either or both groups may be brought against the enemy, depending on the size and composition of his force.
>
> *Australia* Group—*Australia, Canberra, Chicago, Self-ridge, Patterson, Bagley, Blue, Talbot.*
> *Vincennes* Group—*Vincennes, Quincy, Astoria, Henley, Helm, Jarvis, Mugford.*
>
> If both *Australia* and *Vincennes* groups are ordered to attack the enemy, it is my intention that *Vincennes* group shall act independently of the *Australia* group but shall conform generally to the movements of the *Australia* group so as to give greatest mutual support.

Further ensuring division, he directed that the *Vincennes* group stay north of a line from Savo Island cutting the Sound in half, and the *Australia* group stay south of the line. The isolation thus became total.

The eastern approach, via Sealark Channel, was guarded by forces under Rear Admiral Norman Scott, in the *San Juan*, and including the Australian cruiser *Hobart* and destroyers *Monssen* and *Buchanan*. The *San Juan* the only vessel present with the new SG surface search radar, was thus farthest from Savo Island. The *Ralph Talbot* and the *Blue* had only SC sky search radar. The Northern Force had no admiral present, only 3 cruiser captains. This disposition could not have been more fortuitous—for the Japanese.

Admiral Crutchley belonged to the old school—he issued no battle plan. It was sort of the "Well chaps, let's go" school, and it was not good enough any more. Battle had become far faster, more complex and more murderous. and it took more than guts and mass to win it. The situation at Savo was somehow mindful of Gallipoli, where General Sir Ian Hamilton, a man beloved by all, had given only the most general instructions to his juniors and then retired to his tent on the island of Imbros to await results. Here Admiral Crutchley had issued only the simplest instructions, mostly as to stations to be kept, and retired to his bridge to await developments. No one seemed to have realized that the posture of offense had slipped, quite subtly, to one of defense, and a quite bad defense at that. The defenders were close in, bunched in disconnected groups, having no clear idea of what was to come or what they were to do if anything did come. It was a perfect setup for murder.

But the first night it worked well; there was no opposition. Captain Frederick L. Riefkohl of the *Vincennes*, senior officer present in the Northern Force, selected a box patrol, about 10 miles on a side, and cruised at 10 knots, turning right 90 degrees about every half hour.

Behind him came the *Quincy* and then the *Astoria*. He was careful to stay north of the line.

Admiral Crutchley, in the *Australia*, led the *Canberra* and the *Chicago* up and down a straight line roughly parallel to the line dividing the two spheres of command. They steamed in column, 600 yards apart, and every hour reversed course.

East of these forces, Admiral Scott set the *San Juan*, *Hobart*, and the destroyers on a north-south course, plowing steadily back and forth through the night at 15 knots, Guadalcanal to Tulagi, back to Guadalcanal, back to Tulagi. Turn and steam, turn and steam. This force, containing the newest cruiser and destroyers, was destined never to be used during the night. The battle duly noted in the San Juan's log, the force plodded on in silence, uncalled on and uncalling.

For a set piece, it couldn't be beaten. All forces moving, on straight courses, back and forth, back and forth, like the parts of a giant steam engine. All night long they steamed in perfect formation, and no one interfered with anyone else, and everyone grew accustomed to the idea that this was working very smoothly. Looking back, years later, the military tacticians shuddered. What might have happened. What did happen!

At dawn on Saturday the eighth they broke formation and a busy day began. On Guadalcanal the Marines continued their advance and by afternoon occupied the airfield, later famous as Henderson Field. Sailors were assigned to the beach, and with the Marines helping, some cargo was moving inland. Tulagi had the same problems, complicated by severe fighting.

The next warning, Saturday morning, came from Jack Read, a blunt-spoken Australian with gray eyes and a cold manner. Hiding at the northern end of Bougainville, across a narrow strip of water from Japanese installations at Buka, he keyed out: "From JER. Forty-five dive bombers going southeast." The initials were those of his daughter, Judy. A half hour later the warning came back to Savo Sound all the way from Pearl Harbor. The transports stopped unloading and got under way. Cruisers and destroyers were deployed in a screen, and fighter planes from the *Enterprise* were summoned.

The first wave of Japanese planes came in just before noon, swinging over the eastern end of Florida Island and just above the water. They were met with a tactic first tried at Midway—8-inch gunfire from the cruisers, straight across the water in a devastating barrage. At least 17 planes were shot down and those that got through were riddled and groggy from the intense fire. They had scored 1 hit, on destroyer *Jarvis,* badly damaging the vessel.

Dive bombers came in a short time later and again took a severe beating. One staggered through the curtain of fire and, perhaps deliberately, crashed into the transport *George F. Elliot,* a venerable hulk dating from 1918, once known as the *City of Los Angeles.* At 100 feet out the plane wobbled from antiaircraft fire, at 50 feet it burst into flames, and at 1:20 P.M. it crashed into the starboard boat davit, exploding at the bridge. The blast cut the fire-main riser and ruptured a lubrication oil tank. Blazing oil cascaded into the engine room spaces and the fire was soon out of control. By 7:00 P.M. the transport was abandoned and the destroyer *Hull* fired 4 torpedoes

71

at her. She stubbornly refused to sink and through the night she rode, blazing fiercely, a funeral pyre visible for miles.

A dozen times that day, harried as he was, Admiral Turner reflected on what faced him. The forty-eight hours had nearly run out, the carriers would leave him Sunday morning. It was clear now that the invasion had gone well. All first objectives were in hand, the Marines were ashore and deployed. There still was no resistance of consequence on Guadalcanal, and the Japanese would soon be crushed on the Tulagi side. It had gone extremely well, except for one thing—unloading. Besides the squabble on the beaches, each air raid had cost precious time. If the carriers left—and Turner had no real hope they would not—Turner's force would have to leave also. But some of the supply ships had scarcely begun to unload. Thousands of tons of goods, ammunition, and supplies lay in the hulls and would never get ashore unless he could have a few more days.

Another problem was building up. Reports of Japanese ship movements were beginning to multiply.

From the first the Japanese had been under surveillance. General MacArthur's B-17's made the first sighting, discovering Rear Admiral Aritomo Goto leading 5 cruisers and a destroyer down from Kavieng to join Admiral Mikawa at Rabaul. This was at 12:30 P.M. August 7, only hours after the landing. But the message, which did not leave MacArthur's headquarters until nearly midnight, was utterly deficient for intelligence purposes. It said merely, "Six unidentified ships sighted by Forts in St. George's Channel, course southeast." This could, and did, mean nothing to Turner. The vessels, whatever they might be, were nearly 1,000 miles away.

The second warning came from Lieutenant Commander Munson in the submarine S-38, and reported "two destroyers and three larger ships of unknown type, heading 140 degrees True (southeasterly), at high speed, 8 miles west of Cape St. George." This could mean more to Turner. The vessels were definitely enemy, destroyer type and larger, moving out from Rabaul in the general direction of the Solomons. This was late at night on the seventh, still nothing to worry about.

The eighth was a different matter. Rear Admiral John S. McCain, Commander Aircraft, South Pacific, was at the conference on July 26 on the *Saratoga*. All land-based aircraft in this vast new area—Army, Navy, and Marine—had been placed under his command, and like everyone else at the conference he was scrambling to catch up with his job. His task for Operation Watchtower would be mainly long-range reconnaissance, from bases east of 160 degrees longitude. The line ran down through the center of Guadalcanal, and General MacArthur's planes, from Australia and New Guinea, would handle air search west of the line.

McCain, a tough little man looking a bit like Popeye the Sailor, was asked to put up B-17's from New Caledonia and Espiritu Santo—if the field could be made ready in time—and PBY's from Ndeni in the Santa Cruz Islands and from Malaita. No solid plans could be made, but they knew he would do his best.

Leaving the conference, he ordered the seaplane tender *McFarland,* under Lieutenant Commander John C.

Alderman, to Ndeni. The original plan had been to occupy Ndeni, but it was found to be far too rugged for airfield construction, and in addition was infested with malaria, a noisome island that was later abandoned. But the *McFarland* arrived August 5 and opened a base for 5 PBY's.

Malaita, a large and brooding island off to the northeast of Guadalcanal, was not much better. No American was known to have visited it since Jack London in 1908, whence he had fled in disgust from fierce storms and head-hunters. Now Commander Norman R. Hitchcock took the tender *Mackinac* up the back of the island and threaded his way into Maramasike Estuary on the southeast coast, through waters for which there were no charts. He opened for business with 9 PBY's on the morning of August 8. Their beat was to be north and westward, watching the sealanes down from the powerful Japanese base at Truk.

The plan was for MacArthur to watch the western approaches, and his B-17's were doing that August 7 when they raised Rabaul and spotted Mikawa's forces gathering from New Ireland—spotted them but failed, in the pattern of the day, to give adequate intelligence.

McCain's air search plan, to start August 8, called for 3 B-17's to sweep from Koumac, in northern New Caledonia, far up to the under side of the Solomons. PBY's from Espiritu Santo, Ndeni, and Malaita would search northward in the direction of Truk, and B-17's from Espiritu Santo would cover the Slot, but only up to the southeastern end of Choiseul.

On the way up to Guadalcanal with the invasion convoy, Turner became uneasy about this plan. Only the B-17's from Espiritu Santo were covering the Slot, the most obvious route for Japanese surface forces to rush down from Rabaul. The Slot was the outer limit for the Flying Forts search, and in addition they would reach it early in the morning, leaving these waters unguarded for the rest of the day. Turner's anxiety grew, and finally on August 7 he radioed McCain:

"The plan of search for August 8 does not cover sector 290–318 degrees from Malaita [the Slot]. Southwest Pacific [MacArthur] is responsible for this sector, but I consider a morning search by you is necessary for adequate cover."

There was no reply from McCain, and thus, on August 8, Turner assumed the search had been made. It had not. Nor did Turner know that the morning B-17's from Espiritu Santo had missed Mikawa's fleet—by 60 miles. Thus, on August 8, while Turner's forces wrestled with landing problems, fought off vicious Japanese air attacks, and Turner worried about the carriers pulling out, he could not worry about his most serious threat, because he didn't know of it. Admiral Mikawa, keen for battle, was making 30 knots down the Slot all afternoon under a burning sun. Not an eye was laid on him.

He had been sighted that day—twice—but again the chain of communications failed, and this time with most tragic consequences. Flights A16/218 and A16/185, a pair of Lockheed Hudsons of the Royal Australian Air Force, took off early in the morning of August 8 from Milne Bay, far out on the eastern tip of New Guinea.

The pilot of the first Hudson—his name now lost from

the records—flew off to the northeast and crossed Bougainville. Thirty miles off the northeast coast, near Kieta, he sighted at 10:26 A.M. what he believed to be 3 heavy cruisers, 3 destroyers, and 2 other vessels, gunboats or seaplane tenders. And there the lessons of air reconnaissance, so bitterly learned throughout the war, deserted him. His orders were to remain over target until recalled or forced to leave. He did not. He was to report immediately. He did not. He was to report contacts separately. He did not, but combined this report with one on a submarine sighting and attack he made later.

The second Hudson pilot was no less remiss. Thirty-five minutes later, at 11:01 A.M., he sighted 2 heavy or light cruisers and a third, unidentified, vessel. The canny Mikawa, waiting for his search planes to come back from Guadalcanal, was outsmarting the Allies again. He had split up his forces, so that the second Hudson had seen only part of them, probably the *Tenryu, Yubari,* and *Yunagi,* which had not launched planes. But it would have made no difference. This pilot, too, failed to report his sighting.

But the bad news was gathering like the virulent tropic storms in this part of the world and by late Saturday afternoon it began to break. The first blow, the expected one, fell at 6:07 P.M., when Turner's communications room intercepted the now-famous dispatch from Admiral Fletcher to Vice Admiral Ghormley.

"Fighter-plane strength reduced from 99 to 78. In view of the large number of enemy torpedo planes and bombers in this area, I recommend the immediate withdrawal of my carriers. Request tankers sent forward immediately as fuel running low."

As the message cleared his carriers were already heading south.

Turner was furious. Fletcher's concern had been growing all day. Not a Japanese plane or submarine had yet discovered where his carriers were hiding. The first day, August 7, hadn't bothered Fletcher. The initial Japanese reaction had been with high-level bombers over Savo Sound, and their aim was as bad as ours. No damage. It was true that some 16 dive bombers came in during the afternoon without warning, and one laid a 250-pound bomb on the *Mugford,* killing 22 men and damaging the destroyer. Altogether, Fletcher lost 11 F4F fighters and one SBD dive bomber, but at least 3 of his pilots were recovered.

The next day, however, most of the attackers were twin-engine Bettys, armed with those awesome Japanese aerial torpedoes. Seventeen of these planes were knocked down, mostly by ship's gunners in a battle wild with sound and fury. Ships churned around the Sound at high speed in violent maneuvers, and flak bursts at low level made the surface a caldron. Out of it emerged a clear victory for the sailor gunners. Fletcher lost another 9 planes this day, but that wasn't what really worried him. It was the torpedoes.

After the action, he advised Rear Admiral Leigh Noyes, commander of his air support force:

"This morning fighter section leaders contacted twin-engine horizontal bombers and similar engine torpedo planes. Seven torpedo planes burning on water. This section accounted for one torpedo plane and three bombers. Pilots' opinion some twin-engine bombers carrying torpedoes."

A little over an hour later he signaled Noyes again:

"Request any available information about attack this noon. Were planes actually carrying torpedoes?"

His forebodings were clearing rising. Without question he remembered Coral Sea and the *Lexington* trying to dodge all those fish (11 wakes in the water at one time). She couldn't make it and at least 2 got her, both on the port side. The crew fought magnificently, but internal fires and explosions were too much and finally she went down, with one tremendous terminal blast.

It was nearly the same with the *Yorktown* at Midway; her gallant crew was able to handle severe bomb damage, but then aerial torpedoes crippled her and finally submarine torpedoes killed her. Two mighty carriers gone, both to torpedoes.

It was hardly a surprise, when Fletcher again sent word to Noyes late in the afternoon:

"In view of possibility of torpedo plane attack and reduction in our fighter strength, I intend to recommend immediate withdrawal of carriers. Do you agree? In case we continue present operation, I believe same area should be used tomorrow as today. What do you think?"

Noyes replied, "Affirmative to both questions."

Fletcher did not consult Turner, the man closest to the battle, nor did Fletcher issue any orders to Turner during August 8. Fletcher had intercepted the dispatches warning of Japanese surface forces approaching, still he contemplated retirement.

Noyes may have agreed with the decision to run, others did not. Some senior carrier officers wanted to stay; the action was clearly intensifying, and the carriers would be needed more than ever. The phrase "in case we continue" showed Fletcher had not made a final decision; there was still a chance. They put forward their views, but they lost.

It was probably inevitable. Admiral Fletcher had been severely shaken. One does not lose two ships like the *Lexington* and the *Yorktown*—they were far more than ships, they were almost persons—without retaining scars. The United States had only 4 carriers left in the Pacific, and three of them were here under his command. He had a tremendous responsibility to protect them. At Midway the Japanese had lost 4 carriers in a few hours. What if their torpedo planes now discovered Fletcher's brood? By suppertime it was certain, and his message went off, "recommend withdrawal." The "recommend" was, of course, virtually rhetorical. He had already left, taking with him the strongest part of the fleet—a battleship, 3 carriers, 6 heavy cruisers, and 16 destroyers.

His critics later disparaged his reasons. Plane strength? Even with two days' losses he still had one more Wildcat than the total strength at the start of Midway.

Fuel? His engineering logs told this story: The *Saratoga* was burning about 116,000 gallons of fuel daily. On the night of the eighth she had 1,419,264 gallons in the bunkers, enough for more than ten days. *Enterprise* was using 1,300 barrels daily and had 16,534 barrels on hand, sufficient for at least twelve days. *Wasp's* records were lost when she was sunk, but she also had an estimated twelve days' supply. None of the destroyers was in critical need of fuel, and the cruisers were half full or better. Fletcher's main concern seemed not with fuel or plane losses. His anxieties came in a long, black shape, long and black with 1,200 pounds of high explosive in the war heads. At 8:00 P.M. the *Saratoga's* log recorded: "Task Force 61 withdrawing to the southeast, course 147, speed 15 knots, lat. 10-42S, long. 161-14E."

By that time he had had the Hudson's dispatch more than an hour. Turner had it too, and he knew he was in trouble.

Turner got the dispatch at 6:45 P.M., over eight hours after the sighting off Bougainville. "Three cruisers, three destroyers, two seaplane tenders or gunboats, course 120, speed 15 knots," it said.

Where had it been? When they put the story together months later it was nearly incredible. The Hudson pilot cruised on search four hours, finally landed in late afternoon, had his tea, then reported his sighting. This was only the beginning. From Fall River on Milne Bay the dispatch went by Australian Air Force radio to Port Moresby, then across the Coral Sea to Townsville, in northeastern Australia, by landline to Lieutenant General Kenney's headquarters in Brisbane, by hand across town to General MacArthur's headquarters, and finally by U.S. Navy landline to Canberra, where it was put on "Bells" to Pearl Harbor, and back to the fleet on "Fox." (Bells and Fox were, respectively, the regular Australian and U.S. Navy broadcasts carrying information and orders to vessels at sea.) Total elapsed time, sighting to beachhead—eight hours, nineteen minutes.

This sort of thing had been foreseen and the Navy had

set up special "Network E," which tied in all reporting points directly to Admiral McCain. Either Port Moresby or Townsville could have used "Network E." They didn't.

It wouldn't have made much difference anyway. When the dispatch finally arrived at the beachhead everybody, from Turner down, misinterpreted the meaning. Mikawa steamed on in bright sunlight, his ear to the radio, his eyes on the heavens. Nobody watching. He was incredulous; he even feared a trap.

By 8:00 P.M. Turner knew he had to move. A half hour later he called Crutchley and Vandegrift: Meet me urgently on *McCawley*. They prepared immediately to leave the scene of operations, one from the field, the other from the sea. At least one, Crutchley, was about to miss the battle of his life.

chapter
8

Later, they could not say for sure when they first knew it,
but for certain the fleet knew by midafternoon that the
Japanese were coming. Maybe they only heard rumors of
the Friday sightings and built them into a full-blown sea
story, or maybe they really did know something. The
records do not show it, but after all, records don't tell
everything. There are too many men who knew something was in the wind for one to believe that they all
made it up later.

Not only sailors knew it—they love to yarn—but officers knew it, Annapolis men, mature men, men of the sea.

They knew it even in the carriers. Clark Lee of The
Associated Press, heard it on the *Wasp* in the afternoon—
the Japanese were coming down with 2 or 3 cruisers and
a couple of destroyers. One of the *Wasp* pilots told him,

"Get your life jacket and helmet. Maybe we'll be taking off soon to hit those babies. Better be ready to take off with us if you want to see the fun." But the carriers turned away, and the planes never took off.

Captain Riefkohl knew it. "Fearless Freddie" the men called him. They liked Freddie, because it was hard not to like him. He was kind and friendly, perhaps a bit easygoing, but the *Vincennes* was a ship to match him. He was fifty-three then, thirty-one years out of the Academy, which he had liked immensely. Frederick Louis Riefkohl was the first man ever appointed to the Academy from Puerto Rico, where his father, Luis Riefkohl y Sandoz, was a wealthy planter. Young Fred went to school there and in St. Croix, in the Virgin Islands, before going on to Phillips-Andover and the Academy. It had nearly been MIT, until Governor Beekman Winthrop had stopped by the plantation and mentioned that Annapolis gave just as good an engineering degree and it was free. It was not the money alone that decided Luis, although that appealed to his thrifty Danish and German ancestry. At any rate, it was the Academy, and Fred never regretted it.

He had been on the track team and played class football. During World War I he was Armed Guard officer on the *Philadelphia* when she picked up a submarine contact in the Atlantic in August, 1917. A torpedo passed under the stern of his ship, his gun crew fired, at worst a near miss, and the submarine disappeared. Riefkohl was awarded the Navy Cross.

Later he was in radio communications, served in the Asiatic Fleet in the early 20's, and took his first command, destroyer *Smith Thompson*, in 1923. He had the *Corry* in 1926–28, and then served in the Caribbean, where his fluent Spanish was most useful. Later he was gunnery officer of the *New Mexico,* navigator of the *Omaha* and of the *Lexington,* executive officer of the *Nevada,* and finally in April, 1941, commanding officer of the USS *Vincennes.* She was a fine ship, a heavy cruiser of the *Astoria* class, in commission just over four years. The *Vincennes,* second of her name, was built at the Fore River yard of the Bethlehem Steel Company in Quincy, Massachusetts, and christened by Miss Harriet V. Kimmell, daughter of the mayor of Vincennes, Indiana. It was peacetime and the *Vincennes* was a peacetime ship, full of paint, linoleum, overstuffed chairs, curtains, and linens, things that made for a comfortable ship—and an eminently burnable one. But who thought of burning then; it was peacetime, and the United States Navy had never failed to give a good account of itself. For that they put on the main battery— nine 8-inch guns of 55 caliber, and a secondary battery of eight 5-inch 25's. One thing they left off—torpedo tubes. The battle had raged in the fleet for years, but then the "no torpedo tubes on cruisers" school had won. In the Imperial Japanese Navy they still carried torpedo tubes on cruisers. How quaint, those Orientals!

Fearless Freddie took his vessel to sea, and found her much to his liking. She was just under 600 feet long, of 9,400 tons, could do better than 30 knots, and held the sea well. We weren't at war yet, to be sure, but the crew was growing every day, now over 1,000 men, and at every yard the ship touched the workmen piled on more guns, more radio, more gear of every kind. She went into action right away—Bermuda patrols, convoys to Iceland—this was FDR and the "short of war" days.

When war came the *Vincennes* was off the Cape of Good Hope, in company with the *Quincy*, her sister, built in the same yard a year earlier. Their elder sister, *Astoria*, doyen of this cruiser class, was at Pearl Harbor. All the young officers on the *Vincennes* wished *they* were there, and Ensign Donald T. Dorris, a serious young man, wrote in his diary:

"There are no downcast faces on board the *Vincennes* over the prospect of a war with the Japanese Empire. Many of us would like for the *Vinnie Maru* to go from Africa to the Pacific on a raiding cruise. That would really be worth while."

He wrote as if in prophecy, and he was writing his own epitaph.

His wish was soon granted. The *Vincennes* joined the carrier *Hornet* off Norfolk, passed through the Panama Canal, and went into the yards at San Francisco to prepare for "a raiding cruise,"—Doolittle's Raid on Japan. After that came Midway, where the ship and crew got plenty of experience in antiaircraft warfare. She had still never engaged an enemy surface force, nor had a single man aboard her. One other thing—the *Vincennes* had last had night firing practice on February 28, 1941, seventeen months before Guadalcanal.

August 8 was a hard day on the ship, as had been the seventh. The men had been at general quarters since dawn, about 4:30 A.M., and they looked forward to nightfall and an end to the air raids. Once the black night of these latitudes closed them in, they would be safe. Topside men were exhausted from sun, and battle, and tension. Below decks, the black gangs, officers and men alike, were enervated from long hours on station and the intense heat of the buttoned-up ships, running up to 140 degrees in the firerooms. Once night fell, they would be safe, at least from air raids, and the men could open ship a little and go on deck. Many would sleep there.

Japanese surface forces were heading this way; everybody knew that. But they would not come tonight. You could tell, because there were no special orders for the night, and all the scuttlebutt was that they might be down the next day. More likely it would be just more air raids, because the dispatches already in mentioned seaplane tenders. Probably the Japanese were going to open up air bases nearer Guadalcanal, and pour in more planes.

The men thought so, and the officers did, from Turner down. Captain Riefkhol thought so, on the basis of early dispatches and no orders from above. They talked about it on the ships during the afternoon, and as Riefkohl finished supper Saturday night his radio officer, Lieutenant (j.g.) Harry L. Vincent, came to his cabin with another dispatch. It was much the same as the earlier one —cruisers on course 180, speed 15 knots, off Bougainville. It did not mention the seaplane tenders.

"Where do you think they're headed for, Scoop?" Captain Riefkohl asked. Riefkohl felt almost like a father to this youngster, thirty years his junior at the Academy. "Where do you think they're going, if they have AV's [seaplane tenders] with them?"

The two men bent over the chart and eventually agreed on Faisi, on Shortland Island, at the lower end of Bougainville. There was already Japanese activity in that area, and it seemed the most likely place at that time of day. From the reports, they would reach Faisi about 5:30 P.M., before nightfall.

"These fellows are putting their heads in the lion's mouth, Scoop," the Captain said. "Our carrier planes are going to get them there this afternoon." He didn't know Fletcher very well; the Admiral was already gathering in his planes and casting eyes southward.

"Of course, at twenty-three knots they could be here by early tomorrow morning," Riefkohl went on. "But I don't think so. If the carrier planes didn't get them today, we'll hear about it, and I haven't heard anything yet." "Scoop" Vincent, who knew everything that went on in the communications shack, hadn't heard anything either.

That settled that. Vincent went back to his watch, and Captain Riefkohl ordered the crew secured from general quarters. They had had over fifteen hours on it, and now was the time to give them some rest. There would certainly be plenty of action next day.

Just before sunset the screen forces resumed night stations, in the same formation as the previous night. In the Southern Force, Admiral Crutchley took station at the head of the column in his flagship, *Australia*, the *Canberra* fell in 600 yards behind, and the *Chicago* another 600 yards astern. Destroyer *Patterson* took station 1300 yards off the *Australia's* port bow, and the *Bagley* the same distance off to starboard. All were set for another night of steaming, back and forth, back and forth across the Guadalcanal beachhead. Keep the speed at 12 knots and reverse course every hour, just like a sentry walking his post.

In the Northern Force, Captain Riefkohl put the *Vincennes* at the head of the column, with the *Quincy* astern 600 yards and the *Astoria* bringing up the rear. Destroyers *Helm* and *Wilson* were out on the *Vincennes'* bows, and around they started on the box patrol: speed 10 knots, make a 90-degree turn every half hour, and be sure to keep station. There was a little trouble with the *Wilson* at first. She was replacing the *Jarvis*, severely damaged in the air attacks, and first went off to join the Southern Force. With a good deal of chatter on the TBS, she was brought back and assumed screening formation around the Northern Force.

Admiral Turner's summons by radio reached Admiral Crutchley about 8:30 P.M.

"Please come on board as soon as possible," it said. "I will send boat as soon as you approach."

Admiral Crutchley discussed the message with Captain Harold B. Farncomb, commanding officer of the *Australia,* and Commander G. C. O. Gatacre, Crutchley's Staff Officer for Operations and Intelligence. The implication seemed clear: he was to withdraw the *Australia* from the battle line and make for the *McCawley*. The withdrawal, criticized later, was sound from the standpoint of speed and safety. The *McCawley* lay off Lunga Point, some 10 miles east of the Southern Force's position, and the trip in a small boat, in these black and congested waters, would be slow and dangerous. It meant, of course, one less ship in the line, but apparently no action was considered imminent.

Admiral Crutchley ordered the *Australia* out of formation, and signaled to Captain Bode in the *Chicago* by blinker tube:

"Take charge of patrol. I am closing CTF 62 (Turner) and may or may not rejoin you later." This message would not be visible in the Northern Force, although by Admiral Crutchley's departure Captain Riefkohl in the *Vincennes* had become the senior officer remaining in the area. Captain Bode did not change position, but kept the *Chicago* at the stern of his column.

The command situation was now complete. Captain Bode was in command of the Southern Force, from the stern of his column rather than the head. Captain Riefkohl was in command of the Northern Force, and, quite unknown to him, now senior officer. Admiral Crutchley, over-all commander, had left the scene, leaving behind a broken and confused chain of command.

chapter
9

It was 9:23 P.M. when the *Australia* pulled out of formation, and the weather was worsening, with low clouds, patches of fog, and intermittent rain. The cruiser picked her way slowly through the destroyer screen around the transports and found the *McCawley*. Crutchley and Gatacre went across to her in a ship's boat and strode into Admiral Turner's cabin about 10:30. General Vandegrift did not arrive until nearly 11:15, looking more haggard even than Turner. He was under the impression that both Turner and Crutchley looked more tired than he.

During the day Admiral Turner had personally plotted and analyzed all dispatches reporting Japanese ship movements. In the first instance, at Koro, Turner had carefully studied Admiral Crutchley's instructions to the screening force, and had had his operations officer, Commander James H. Doyle, go over them. On the afternoon of the eighth, Turner got out the orders and again went over them thoroughly. At the conference that night Admiral Turner said he considered the orders excellent, that he felt all was in readiness, and that he hoped the Japanese would attack; however, he added, he did not believe they would. Instead, he believed the Japanese were setting up air bases at Faisi and at Rekata Bay.

Admiral Turner said he had considered two other actions—sending the surface forces out that night to attempt an interception, or sending the surface forces out the next morning after the transports had left. He rejected the first plan because it would leave the transports without protection. As to the second, it could be held in abeyance to see what the next day might bring.

Personally he felt the greatest danger still lay in air and submarine attack. Japanese plane attacks had been growing in intensity for two days, and intelligence on Japanese submarines moving into the area was increasing. Admiral Crutchley concurred, particularly as to the submarines. He had arrived in June from the Atlantic theater and was quite alive to the U-boat menace there. He had a healthy respect for enemy submarines, of whatever flag.

As to the transports, they would definitely have to be withdrawn first thing in the morning. The carriers had departed and the forces at the beachhead were now without air cover. The only questions were: Could enough supplies be got ashore by morning to enable the Marines to hold out for a time? Should the forces risk another day or so at the beachhead without air protection? General Vandegrift specified a few items he considered vital to the forces ashore, but there was general agreement that the transports would have to leave. The Marines would have to make do with what they had.

It was a grim prospect. Short of food, ammunition, and other vital supplies, the Marines would be open to increasing blows from the air bases being set up. General Vandegrift was dismayed, and Admiral Turner made pithy reference to Fletcher and the carrier boys leaving them "bare arse." Admiral Crutchley asked Turner what he thought of the reports of Japanese ship movements, and Turner replied he was sure they were headed for Rekata, so sure that he had asked Admiral McCain to bomb Rekata in the morning. "From now on," he said, "we can expect two torpedo attacks a day, instead of one."

What about surface attack? It was possible, Turner replied, but unlikely, and in any event his surface forces were disposed to his satisfaction to meet it. He could not know that at this moment Captain Bode, Captain Riefkohl, and nearly every other ship commander in the Sound was now or soon would be sleeping. It had been a tiring day; tomorrow might be worse—if it ever came.

The *Ralph Talbot* was on station, northwest of Savo Island, by a little after 5:00 P.M. A short time later, Ensign Ralph W. Kalish decoded one of the messages that said a Japanese force was headed for Savo, and took it to Lieutenant Commander Joseph W. Callahan on the bridge. The skipper read it, but gave no sign. Low clouds were making up over Savo, with an occasional flash of lightning, and it appeared certain there would be rain before long. The night was warm, almost oppressive, and patches of mist shrouded through the rigging now and then. The burning *George F. Elliot* gave the only light, far off on the Tulagi shore, and the only noise about the deck was the sound of the sea and the low hum of machinery. Lieutenant (j.g.) Russell E. Walton, a Reserve from Victoria, Virginia, had the 8:00 to 12:00 watch on the bridge.

Shortly before midnight, as he prepared to turn over the watch, an incredible sight startled all topside hands. A plane, not very high and showing a flashing light, passed directly overhead and on toward Savo Sound where the fleet lay. All men on deck saw it plainly, and the watch routed out Lieutenant Commander Callahan. At 11:45 the message went out by TBS: "This is Jimmy. Warning, warning, plane sighted over Savo Island heading east." The message, repeated several times, omitted only one salient fact—the plane was clearly identifiable as a cruiser type, a float plane.

Callahan repeatedly called the *McCawley*, 25 miles away, but could get no acknowledgment. Nor could he raise his squadron commander, Captain Cornelius W. Flynn in the *Selfridge*. Finally Commander Frank W. Walker in the *Patterson* answered, and said he would try to get the message through to Turner. There is some confusion as to whether he did. The *Ralph Talbot* log records: "It was later learned that this report reached the Task Force Commander at 0012 local time."

Admiral Turner, who had just bid farewell to Crutchley and Vandegrift, said the message never came to him.

In any event, many vessels did receive it. Captain Riefkohl, about to leave the bridge of the *Vincennes* at midnight, discussed the dispatch with his executive officer,

Commander William E. A. Mullan. One of his lookouts had also reported seeing a plane. Captain Riefkohl concluded it must be a friendly plane, perhaps coming in from the carriers with a message for Turner. How could he know—on this night when nobody told anybody anything—that the carriers were long since moving off to the south or that this was a float plane from a cruiser?

He and Mullan talked some more, mainly about the Japanese force approaching, and Captain Riefkohl said he believed they must have been destroyed (naïve thought) since he had received no word from Admiral Turner to be on the lookout for them. Had they been coming, he said, Turner would have warned him. Finally, the night being still, Captain Riefkohl retired to his emergency cabin and lay down in his clothes. He wanted to be ready for the morning.

On the bridge of the *Astoria*, Lieutenant Commander James R. Topper relieved Lieutenant Commander John D. Hayes just before midnight. The *Ralph Talbot's* warning had come through to them from the *San Juan*, or to be exact, the *Astoria* had heard the *San Juan* passing the warning to Riefkohl on the *Vincennes*. The *Astoria* skipper, Captain William G. Greenman, was told of the message. Greenman, fifty-three, had retired to his cabin, mentally and physically exhausted, and dropped off to sleep fully dressed. Hayes retired to his room and Topper paced the bridge. Off to the east he could see firing on Tulagi.

"The Marines are having no picnic there tonight," he remarked to his quartermaster.

"I feel sorry for them," the quartermaster replied.

Seaman Second Class James Stanley Carleton was on the deck above the *Quincy's* bridge when, about midnight, he thought he heard a plane. He told the battery officer, standing nearby, and the latter replied, "You probably hear No. 1 stack. They often sound like planes."

A long time later Carleton was pretty bitter about this, and in a report all survivors were asked to make he wrote: "An officer should not underestimate the ability of the men under him when reporting the sound of a plane. Because he did not hear it is no reason why it should be disregarded."

Carleton had no cause for concern. Many men on the *Quincy* saw and heard planes, and these reports came through to the bridge. The signal officer, Lieutenant (j.g.) Charles P. Clarke, Jr., then OOD, talked to the executive officer, Commander William C. Gray. Commander Gray pondered the matter and finally decided they must be friendly planes. No, he said, they would not go to general quarters; it had been a full day and everyone was tired. Captain Samuel N. Moore was sleeping and he was not awakened with this report.

On the *Blue*, that sleeping guardian of the south entrance, the *Ralph Talbot's* warning came through on TBS, and the *Blue's* air-search radar, installed three months earlier, picked up the bogey and tracked it across the Sound. Some of the lookouts even claimed they saw running lights.

This night surely must mark the death of innocence, the last stand of the credo: If you don't know what it is, assume it's friendly. All the ship commanders waited, and from the top there came—nothing.

chapter

10

Admiral Crutchley and Commander Gatacre left the *Mc-Cawley* just before midnight, taking General Vandegrift with them. He wanted to go to Tulagi and the admiral offered to put him on board the mine sweeper *Southard* for the passage. Visibility was bad, with rain clouds scudding in from the direction of Savo Island and lightning flickering around the transports off Tulagi. The *George F. Elliot's* fire glowed through the night. Crutchley's boat finally found the *Southard* and put the general aboard, but it was nearly 1:30 A.M. before they found the *Australia*. Just after Crutchley and Gatacre reboarded the cruiser the sky was brilliantly lighted by flares over Savo Island. They concluded at once that these must be enemy flares to illuminate the transports for submarine attack. There had been at least a half-dozen intelligence reports of Japanese submarines converging on the Guadalcanal area. Crutchley had been so sure of submarine attack that he had ordered all destroyers to make long-handled nets to scoop the burning flares off the water and douse them.

So sure was he now that the flares meant sub attack, or even night air raid, that he ordered the *Australia* to stay within the destroyer screen at the beachhead.

True to the code of the night, he told no one of this decision, and far away in the mist Captain Bode slept on in the *Chicago*, serene perhaps in the thought that his commanding officer was now back at the head of the column. Captain Riefkohl, off to the north on the *Vincennes*, couldn't know that Crutchley wasn't back because he had never known that he left. The two Forces steamed on through the night, the one cutting a nice clean square, the other a beautiful straight line. And nobody in command.

Across a short stretch of water, however, there was yet another force, and there someone *was* in command. It was old beady-eye Mikawa, and he didn't trust anybody. On the bridge, his knuckles white where his hands gripped the splinter shield, he listened as aides whispered in his ear the lastest word from his planes, via the radio shack. Beneath him, spread cross the water, he commanded 62 torpedo tubes, 34 big guns, and 37 smaller pieces. At a word from him this sleeping water would be blasted into a scene from Hell, and he was about to give that word.

In they went, breaths held in apprehension, past the *Blue*, over 50 Japanese guns trained on her, just waiting One sign, and she would be gone, but the destroyer's white wake fell behind her and she gave never a sign. Mikawa was incredulous; he *must* have been seen.

But he held his play until 1:05 A.M. when he ordered a slight change in course and the speed upped to 26 knots. It was a staggering risk he took. The passage between Guadalcanal and Savo was only 7 miles wide. For all he knew it could have been studded with mines, or a phalanx of torpedo tubes could have been waiting for him. The tension was terrible, but he pressed on. As the ships rounded Savo Island the admiral changed course to the eastward, entered the sleeping camp, and at 1:33 A.M. barked out the order: "All ships attack."

chapter
11

The *Chicago*, Lieutenant Commander Thomas D. Wilson on the bridge, recovered her float plane at 6:25 P.M. and a few minutes later formed up with the *Canberra* in night-cruising disposition, destroyer *Patterson* 1,300 yards out on the port bow and the *Bagley* in the same position starboard. The *Canberra* was in the lead, 600 yards ahead of the *Chicago,* and course was set for straight cruising through the night, from a point near the Guadalcanal beachhead up to the northwest toward Savo. Up near the lee of the tiny island zigzagging was ordered ceased around seven o'clock and the column reversed course back toward the beachhead. It seemed another night of routine patrolling, at 10 to 12 knots, ship darkened, Condition II set.

Admiral Crutchley on the *Australia* completed the

Southern Force when at 7:20 P.M. he brought her in and took the head of the column. By prearrangement she would reverse course about every hour, without signal, the other ships conforming. The night lay dark and lowering, without moon or stars, and now and then the vessels passed through heavy rain squalls, with spectacular lightning displays. The two days since the landings had been hard, and the off-watch men sprawled sleeping under gun mounts, turrets, boats, and overhangs, prefering rain to the heat in the steaming quarters below.

On the second outbound leg toward Savo the *Australia's* code room received and broke Admiral Turner's summons and sent it to staff quarters. Admiral Turner urgently requested to see Admiral Crutchley aboard the *McCawley*, at the beachhead, little more than 5 miles astern. Admiral Crutchley then made his decision, so unimportant at the time yet so fateful in retrospect; he decided to pull his cruiser out of formation, as was implied in Turner's summons. Admiral Crutchley thereby withdrew himself from one of the most vicious surface engagements of all time, the largest sea battle since Jutland, which he had *not* missed.

More important, his going weakened his force by one-third and left a welter of confusion in which there was no effective command, not only in the Southern Force, but also in the Northern Force, which knew nothing of his departure and through the night assumed him present and in command. It made fatal differences that he was not.

The *Australia* wheeled off to port and turned back for the beachhead. Admiral Crutchley had informed Captain Bode of the *Chicago* by blinker tube that he was leaving, directed Bode to take command, and said he did not know if he would rejoin formation that night. The ball had been passed, but it was a fumble.

"Ping" Bode (rhymes with toady, which he was not) was an aloof man, lacking a knack for friendship. Captain Howard Douglas Bode, fifty-three, son of a Cincinnati judge, possessed supreme self-confidence and in his mind there was no doubt that he would achieve flag rank. It was not to be. Life held for him the full measure of tragedy.

As captain of the *Oklahoma* he was ashore on the night of December 6, 1941. The next time he saw his ship she was smashed and capsized, her masts jammed into the mud bottom at Pearl Harbor, one of the first victims of the Japanese. He had every right to be absent from his vessel that night and his crew, under the executive officer, performed with intelligence and heroism. But to be so near a great event and have no part in it, to lose one's ship when absent from it...

His second chance had now come. In the annals of command it is written that the senior ship present takes the head of the column, overbearing reasons not dictating otherwise. Captain Bode did not take the head of the column, but directed the *Canberra* to lead, conducting the patrol and making course changes as previously ordered.

His reasoning was, at least, understandable. He said later that he decided against taking the head of the column for several reasons. Night maneuvering in close quarters, with ships blacked out, was dangerous. At the end of the northward leg he could order ships about, thus placing himself at the head. If Admiral Crutchley returned during the night, more maneuvering would be necessary to put the *Australia* in the van and the *Chicago* back at the tail end. He would stay where he was.

It was Captain Bode's decision, there can be no doubt of that. He was rarely one to consult his officers and this case was not an exception. There were doubts among some of his juniors, or so they said later, but Captain Bode was not a man to whom one made suggestions. Again the disputed Coast Watcher reports assume importance, for it is said now, by senior officers, that such a report reached the *Chicago* in the afternoon and a plot was made. It showed that a Japanese force, of inexactly known components, could reach Savo that night. And so, it was said later, there were head-noddings when the *Australia* left the formation and again when Captain Bode failed to take the lead position. Hindsight may have improved this recollection, but certainly Captain Bode's position, in the light of what was about to happen, would have been immeasurably strengthened had he seized command with a firm hand. He did not; in fact he lay down in his emergency cabin, and as he slept the night robbed him of the things he most wanted.

But if the Southern Force was leaderless, what of the Northern Force? Here now was the senior officer in the area, who would be the OTC, the Officer in Tactical Command. It was Captain "Fearless Freddie" Riefkohl, and he knew it not. In the rush of the operation he had never met his commanding officer, Admiral Crutchley, nor had either of the other two cruiser captains in the

Northern Force. They knew him only as a distant presence, assuming that orders would come from him and would be executed smartly. In this case no order came, either from Admiral Crutchley or from Captain Bode, classmate of Captain Riefkohl. The Northern Force sailed on in innocence, carefully boxing its square, with concern not to cut corners or break formation, unaware that now for a force of 5 cruisers and 6 destroyers, guarding the souls of 20,000 invaders, Captain Frederick Louis Riefkohl was the senior officer present. He went to bed also, as did Captain Moore in the *Quincy* and Captain Greenman in the *Astoria*. The fortress lay sleeping, the lines of command sundered as no enemy could have hoped for.

Admiral Mikawa did not ask, nor could he have expected, such confusion in the ranks of his enemy. It is hard to know what he did expect, but the important thing is that he was prepared for anything.

Safely past the *Blue* (both she and the *Ralph Talbot* were now heading away, opening wider the hole in the screen), Admiral Mikawa tensed as the minutes passed and it was 1:33 A.M. when he issued his battle order: "All ships attack." He could not have chosen a more perfect moment. In seconds an enemy ship was sighted, a destroyer far to port, creeping slowly westward under the lee of Savo Island. It was the *Jarvis*, her engines barely serviceable and her radio mute, creeping out of the area to salve her wounds. Torpedoes hissed into the water from several Japanese ships, but the gunners held their fire, mindful that the flagship had not yet opened fire. *Jarvis*, unable to return fire or give alarm, was spared this time (for a worse fate later), and the Japanese jugger-naut sailed by at 26 knots, closing on bigger game head on at better than 40 miles an hour. The destroyer *Yunagi*, Lieutenant (s.g.) Shizuichi Okada, thirty, in command, dropped off the tail end of the Japanese battle line to take care of the *Jarvis* and the *Blue*. The cruisers passed on and at this moment the destroyers of the Southern Force came in view. Reports by lookouts tumbled into Japanese centrals—destroyers ahead, port and starboard; cruisers dead ahead, two of them 12,500 yards and closing. Just three minutes had passed and Admiral Mikawa, his sturdy little figure rigid as a mast, barked, "Independent firing!" Torpedoes spewed from his ships and the orange flash of launching charges lit the night for an instant—but long enough. Overhead, at almost the same moment, flares burst into brilliant flower, and a lookout on the *Patterson* cried, "Ships ahead! Ships ahead!" The night, so dark and so quiet, was now to be ripped apart.

The *Patterson*, for one, was awake that night and in-stantly changed course, rang up 20 knots, ordered general quarters, and sounded the alarm to the sleeping fleet:

"Warning, warning. Strange ships entering harbor."

It was 1:43 A.M., and it was too late. The *Chokai*, in the van, was less than 5,000 yards away and opened fire, fol-lowed immediately by the *Aoba* and the *Furutaka*. The battle was joined, and even outpacing the gunfire ran the terrible torpedoes, silent and true and "hot." In the fore-front, by chance and by direction, lay not the *Australia*, not the *Chicago*, but the *Canberra*, Captain Frank Ed-mund Getting commanding. The Australian cruiser's gen-eral alarm was still sounding, her guns were still trained in and the crew running for battle stations when two torpedoes caught her flush on the starboard bow. The vessel staggered and a shudder ran all the way to the stern. In the same instant 8-inch and 4.7-inch shells began to fall with uncanny accuracy. The *Kent*-class cruiser, built on the Clyde and launched by Princess Mary, had come to the end of her road, just past her fourteenth birthday. The first blow had been the best blow, and she was doomed. "Ting" Getting, a warm and kind man, well loved in the fleet, did not live to know the fate of his ship.

Captain Getting had gone to his sea cabin shortly after midnight, leaving the vessel in command of Lieutenant Commander E. J. Wight as Principal Control Officer, with Sub-Lieutenant M. J. Gregory as Officer of the Watch. The *Canberra's* surface radar was in use and at intervals, despite interference from the surrounding land, picked up the *Blue* crossing the southern entrance to the Sound. No other ships showed on the radar screen, but just after 1:40 A.M. Lieutenant Commander Wight noted a flash under the loom of Savo. Almost at the same instant the *Patterson's* signal lamp began to wink out the warning message. Wight sighted 3 ship wakes south of Savo, moving to starboard, and cried out, "Alarm starboard, green twenty!" The *Canberra's* general alarm sounded and Captain Getting came tumbling to the bridge, followed quickly by the navigator, Lieutenant Commander J. S. Mesley, and the gunnery officer, Lieutenant Commander D. M. Hole.

"Port thirty-five degrees!" ordered Lieutenant Commander Wight, to unmask his guns. Lieutenant Commander Mesley ran to the voice tube and shouted down

to the plotting room, "Enemy report, two unknowns bearing three hundred, one mile!" There was no reply; a shell
had just torn through Plot, wrecking it. Mesley ordered
Chief Yeoman G. J. Gunthorp to run to the radio shack
with the warning; he arrived just after a shell had
smashed the transmitters.

Hardly had the ship begun to turn, on Wight's order,
than a torpedo wake, coming from port, passed close
down the starboard side.

"Hard a'starboard!" cried Captain Getting, and Lieutenant Commander Hole ordered, "Open Fire!" In an
instant the action had become intense. Two more torpedo
wakes were sighted, 2 brilliant flares blossomed overhead, 3 enemy vessels were sighted off the port bow, not
1,500 yards away. At this moment a full Japanese salvo
struck squarely on the bridge. Lieutenant Commander
Hole was killed instantly, Captain Getting fell mortally
wounded, and nearly every officer or rating on or near
the bridge was killed or badly hurt in one tremendous
burst. A second salvo, only a split second later, again
smashed the bridge and both engine rooms as well, cutting off all steam and power. In under two minutes at
least 28 large-caliber shells pounded the *Canberra*, all
square amidships, and she went dead in the water, blazing and already listing. So sudden and deadly was the
onslaught that her main guns were still trained in.

Commander J. A. Walsh, the executive officer, was at
his post in after control and there Sanderson, the captain's midshipman, found him. The captain was badly
hurt and would like to see him.

Commander Walsh ran forward, the shells still falling,

and paused only long enough to order bucket brigades formed. The upper decks were already ablaze. After a few ragged shots from the 4-inchers, fire from the *Canberra* had ceased and the vessel was perceptibly losing way. On the bridge, in a scene of carnage, Commander Walsh bent down to his captain and the captain acknowledged him. "Carry on," he said, and Commander Walsh began the fight to save the ship. Captain Getting, like his ship, lingered on, fighting for life, and Surgeon Captain Downward came to attend him. For short intervals Captain Getting was in command of his senses, and he asked about the crew and about the ship. But the moments came less often and soon he lost consciousness. Like the ship, he was barely alive.

chapter
12

The *Patterson,* first to sight the enemy, was also first to fire. After her radio warning, her signal lamps continued to blink out in the night, "Warning, warning," and she veered hard to port. The 5-inch batteries put up star shell and the skipper, Commander Frank R. Walker, screamed, "Fire torpedoes!" Bad luck, his order was lost in the crash of guns, although he didn't know it until much later. He came full circle at high speed, his 5-inch now putting out regular shells, but the tails of the enemy cruisers were already disappearing to the northeast. Commander Walker, who had saved his vessel at Pearl, knew he had 3 cruisers against him out there, but he was not a man to fear odds. He meant to attack with vigor, but he had started too late. At 1:55 A.M. a large-caliber shell struck in the gun shelter at No. 4 gun, and the ready ammunition went up in fire and smoke. It had taken the Japanese four minutes to blast him. Two Japanese searchlights had come on at 1:51, pinning him naked in twin cones of light from which his wildest maneuvers could not extricate him. He withheld his own searchlights, fearing to silhouette his cruisers, and in just four minutes the Japanese had found the range. The hit severed communications between guns Nos. 3 and 4 and the bridge, and except for a brief encounter with a friendly ship later in the morning, the *Patterson* was out of the fight. As they had with the other ships, the Japanese stabbed the *Patterson* and passed by, giving no time for retaliation. The *Patterson* ceased fire at 2:01, having expended 60 rounds of 5-inch and hit nothing. She paused now and from afar watched the battle pass to the north, meantime fighting her own fires and counting 3 men dead and seven missing.

The *Bagley*, out to starboard and thus nearest the foe, had a frustrating night.

Her lookouts sighted the Japanese cruisers a few seconds after the *Patterson*, but the *Bagley* gave no alarm. Commander George A. Sinclair, commanding a destroyer named for the only U.S. Navy officer lost in the entire West Indian phase of the Spanish-American war, ordered a sharp left turn to bring the *Bagley's* starboard torpedo tubes on range. Alas, the firing primers were not ready and he continued on full circle to try his luck with the port tubes. They fired and missed, and his chance was gone— the enemy was roaring off to the north. The Japanese had passed within a mile of him and disdained even to fire on him. The gunners were busy with fatter hens in the coop. The *Bagley* then bore off to the east, finally turned and headed for a destroyer rendezvous—in the wrong spot.

Only the *Chicago* was left, and it was now her turn. Her lookouts saw the orange flashes low on the water over toward Savo Island as the Japanese launched torpedoes. There was little reaction, except one man thought there might be a fire on the island. A minute later the first of 5 flares lighted the heavens, and soon the *Canberra* was seen to turn to starboard. Captain Bode came to the bridge, shaking off a sound sleep. He was just in time to get reports of 2 dark objects, 1 between the *Canberra* and the *Patterson* and another to the right of the *Canberra*. He ordered the forward 5-inch to train on the latter and prepare to fire star shells. This kind of thing, so common that night, was not going to be enough. Those Japanese torpedoes, already in the water, were racing down on him.

"Wake to starboard," cried the bridge lookout, and full right rudder was ordered. At the same moment the main battery control officer reported two wakes to port, and full left rudder was ordered. The *Chicago* would attempt to parallel the wakes, but it would not work. The first wake crossed the bow at 70 yards, the second at 20, and the third one didn't cross at all—it struck hard in the port bow at 1:47 A.M., the battle four minutes old. The blast tore a hole in the bow, like a giant shark bite, from 3 feet above the waterline to the keel and back to frame 4, 16 feet from the bow. Mangled steel plates, like flaps of skin, peeled off and slewed around to port, still attached to the hull. The bottom of the chain locker blew out and the anchor chains plunged downward.

A huge column of water shot skyward, deluging the

vessel to amidships and well above the foretop. The top
of the foremast whipped violently and the tip crashed
forward, fouling the radar fire-director for Turret I. Mercury sloshed out of both compasses, putting them out of
commission.

Simultaneous with the torpedo explosion, or possibly
an instant sooner, a 6-inch shell exploded high in the
starboard leg of the foremast, near the forward funnel,
showering shrapnel over the upper decks. Chief Boatswain's Mate Steve Balint, running for his battle station,
was cut down by a chunk of metal in the stomach. The
executive officer, Commander Cecil C. Adell, right behind
him, felt a hot stab of pain in his neck but stumbled forward. Balint lay crumpled on the deck, his body tightened
into a ball. Flying steel killed Seaman First Class Howard
M. Hatch instantly, and around the deck 23 other men
were injured, some seriously. Ensign Joseph R. Daly, a
Saratoga pilot, had been badly burned when his plane
crashed in the previous day's air battles. Picked up by the
Chicago, he was now wounded again by shrapnel in the
leg. Commander Adell crawled along the deck to the
amidships repair station, where Lieutenant Commander
Benjamin Oesterling, the ship's dentist, sewed him up—
without sedative. A jagged sliver of metal had passed
through his throat, between the jugular vein and wind-
pipe, damaging neither, but his right elbow was smashed.
It was too late to do anything for Balint.

The bridge meanwhile was having its troubles. The
same moment the *Chicago* was hit, the port 5-inch batteries got off two 4-gun salvos of star shell, followed by
the same salvo from the starboard battery. Not one ig-

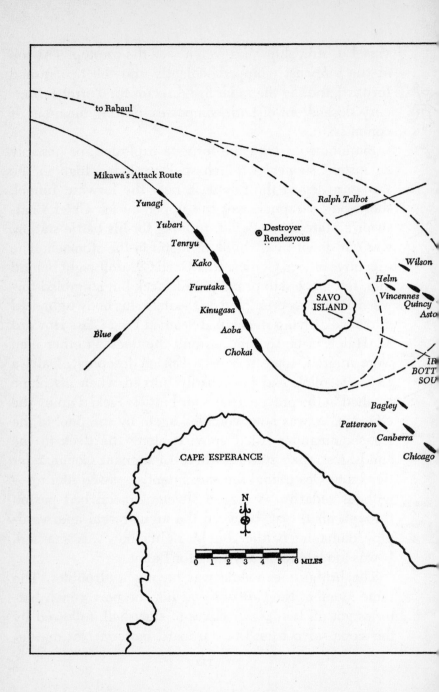

to Rabaul

Mikawa's Attack Route

Yunagi
Yubari
Tenryu
Kako
Furutaka
Kinugasa
Aoba
Chokai

Blue

Destroyer
Rendezvous

SAVO
ISLAND

Ralph Talbot

Wilson
Helm
Vincennes
Quincy
Asto

IR
BOTT
SOU

Bagley
Patterson
Canberra
Chicago

CAPE ESPERANCE

N

0 1 2 3 4 5 6 MILES

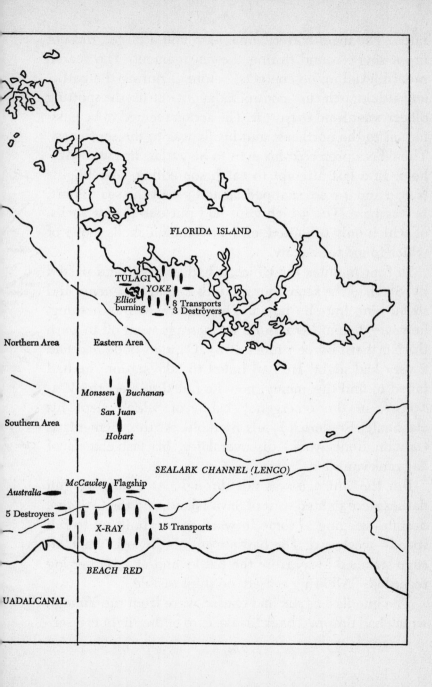

FLORIDA ISLAND

TULAGI
YOKE
Elliot
burning   ❙❙❙ 8 Transports
           3 Destroyers

Northern Area   Eastern Area

Monssen *Buchanan*
San Juan
Hobart

Southern Area

SEALARK CHANNEL (LENGO)

McCawley ▪ Flagship
Australia ◄
5 Destroyers
           X-RAY   15 Transports

BEACH RED

UADALCANAL

nited. The main battery, unable to find a target, did not fire a single round during the engagement. The search radar picked up no contacts, before or during the battle, and although the fire-control radar got one fix, the spotting officer was afraid to trust it. The action seemed to be passing off to the northeast and his fix was to the southwest. The officer preferred his eyes to his radar; fire was withheld. In a last attempt to catch something, searchlights Nos. 2 and 4 were snapped on and swept the sea to port. It was bare. The 5-inch guns had put out 44 star shells, of which only 6 ignited, and 45 common shells, none of which found the enemy.

In four minutes the *Chicago* had been hit and passed by. She had the same four minutes to find the enemy and strike him, but she failed. This failure was as nothing, however, to another failure: no message went off to warn the Northern Force 7 miles away. Captain Bode had had a very bad night. He had failed to take station; he had failed to find the enemy; now he failed to alert the *Vincennes,* in the emergency cabin of which slept his classmate, Frederick Louis Riefkohl. At this moment, as Captain Bode would discover later, his last chance of flag rank vanished.

But the *Chicago* was not through. At 2:00 A.M. gun flashes were sighted west of Savo Island, and the *Chicago,* despite weeping in some forward seams, built up to full speed—westward. The battle went northward. The *Chicago* steamed away from the battle, and at 2:05 her log recorded: "All firing ceased, no ships visible."

The gun flashes she had chased were from the *Yunagi,* which had dropped back to take care of the "light cruiser" sighted under the lee of Savo Island as the Japanese force raced in. This was the *Jarvis,* still limping out of the battle area. The *Yunagi* opened fire on her at 2:00 A.M. and claimed to have scored hits. The truth of this will never be known, because no one ever spoke the *Jarvis* again; a terrifying death awaited her next day. *Yunagi* sealed her fate when she reported to Rabaul that an *"Achilles*-class cruiser" was creeping toward Australia.

chapter
13

August 8 was a busy evening on the bridge of the *Vin-cennes*, climaxing two days of exertion and tension. The anxiety of completing a landing on a hostile shore far from base (thousands of miles farther than any previous such action in history) would have been enough to ener-vate the men. Here had been added the intense humidity of the tropics, the foreboding nature of these islands with unknown dangers in the jungled swamps and mountains, and, above all, the nature of the enemy. His vicious and unremitting air attacks through two days had done noth-ing to mitigate the popular picture of the Japanese— a fiendish Oriental without heart or moral code. Along with this there was, strangely enough, something of deri-sion at these little men who had the temerity to think they could contest on the field of battle with the United States

Navy. It was too early in the war to have discovered the true measure of the enemy—that he was, in fact, a very able fighting sailor, unorthodox according to American standards, one who could be beaten but should never be underrated.

After dusk alert, men of the fleet in the Northern Force had settled down to get what rest they could, for a repetition of the past two days' air attacks was expected the next day, repetition and probably intensification. But it was by no means sweet sleep for all hands. Condition II was set in all vessels, with slight modifications to meet local conditions. The captain or his executive officer had the bridge at all times, and the navigator or communications officer stood the OOD watch. Gun directors, range finders, and communications were manned, as were searchlights and radar. All guns of the main battery were loaded, with 2 guns in each turret manned, and all 5-inch batteries were loaded and manned, with half the heavy machine guns ready. All boilers were fired with steam on the line from half or more of them. In the *Astoria* it had been announced there would be no more surprise night-action drills, and that the next alarm would be real.

Nor was there any confusion about command. In the *Vincennes*, for one, the OOD had full authority to commence action without waiting for orders from Captain Riefkohl. He himself was on the bridge most of the evening, and from 7:00 P.M. on the TBS squawked continuously, if imperfectly, as Riefkohl sought to find out which destroyer was being sent him to replace the *Jarvis*, and to get her into position. It was the *Wilson*, and at first she had charged off as though to join the Southern

Force, had been dragged back, and was finally coaxed into position on the starboard bow of the cruiser column.

Atmospherics were freakish within Savo Sound (perhaps due to the surrounding mountains or the heavy clouds and rain squalls) and the stuttering TBS was further burdened with interference from other ships. Off to the northeast, near Tulagi, the destroyers *Hull* and *Dewey* chattered incessantly as they fought first to quell the fires on the *George F. Elliot* (futile), then to take off her men, and finally to sink her (also futile, despite four torpedoes fired by the *Hull*, only one of which exploded) as she blazed on through the night, a red and yellow beacon for the enemy.

During the night hours the general situation had been fully discussed on the bridge of the *Vincennes*. As far as Captain Riefkohl knew, Admiral Crutchley, from the *Australia* in the Southern Force, was in command of all the cruisers. There was no word from him, or from Admiral Turner, therefore the situation must be: Operations going well, nothing more to be expected before daybreak.

Of course, from the sighting reports of the previous day it was entirely possible that a Japanese surface force could arrive in these waters by 1:00 A.M., or any time thereafter. Captain Riefkohl knew this, as did every other cruiser captain who could handle a plotting board. The vessels would be alert through the night, but no such arrival could actually be expected or there would have been word from Crutchley or Turner or, in the last extremity, from the *Blue* or the *Ralph Talbot*, standing guard outside Savo Island with the latest search radar.

Shortly before midnight, when Captain Riefkohl was

thinking of a little sleep before the next day's action, the *Ralph Talbot*'s repeated alarm came through clearly on the *Vincennes*' TBS: "Warning, warning, plane sighted over Savo Island headed east." All eyes on the bridge turned to the speaker on the bulkhead, and as they waited first one acknowledgment was heard and then another. Or that's what it sounded like in the crackling interference. Captain Riefkohl was sure he heard Admiral Turner's flagship receipt for it, and he was positive the destroyer squadron commander had gotten it. As a matter of fact, neither of them received it then, and Admiral Turner said later that he never did receive it.

But the pattern of this night of missed cues was holding and no one queried Crutchley or Turner for possible interpretation or suggested action. They might have had a hard time finding Crutchley, who had just left Turner and gone off in the fog, leaving even Turner unaware of his whereabouts. But Turner was right there, on the *McCawley,* off the Guadalcanal beachhead, unaware of any planes over his command.

Captain Riefkohl did not let it rest, locally at least. He had the word passed around the ship and sure enough, one lookout reported he had seen the plane, showing a light. He was summoned to the bridge and the captain himself questioned him. All he could say was that he had seen it, briefly but surely, on the port quarter.

The captain, assured in his own mind that Turner knew of it, concluded that it must be a friendly plane. Such things were not unheard of. He knew instances where carrier planes had been sent in to drop messages, thus keeping the radio quiet and avoiding disclosure of a ship's position. They had all been in daylight, to be sure, but this plane was showing running lights and no enemy would be that foolish! There was no word from Turner. . . . Captain Riefkohl went to bed, removing only his hat.

He was no different from the others in command. Captain Bode had retired on the *Chicago*, Captain Moore on the *Quincy*, Captain Greenman on the *Astoria*, and Captain Getting on the *Canberra*. On the *Quincy* the hours before battle had been a welter of plane reports. Shortly after the *Ralph Talbot's* warning the *Quincy's* radar had picked up a plane coming in over Savo, and a few minutes later the bridge advised Control Forward to disregard this report. About 1:00 A.M. a plane was heard going forward on the starboard side, a half hour later it was aft on the same side, and a few minutes thereafter it was reported on the port quarter. All of this was relayed to the bridge. These reports were not the moonings of homesick sailors, dreaming on watch. Lieutenant Commander John D. Andrew, assistant gunnery officer, heard a plane at 1:00 A.M. and personally reported it to the bridge. He was outside the director tower then, but climbing to the top of the director he heard it again, and again reported to the bridge. Lieutenant (j.g.) Richard H. McElligott, in Sky Aft, three times heard planes and three times reported to Sky Control. Both Lieutenant Homer H. Nielsen in Control Forward and Lieutenant (j.g.) John D. Seal in Sky Forward heard planes three times. These were all Annapolis men, not Reserves just out of the insurance business. Ensign E. F. Shannon, Jr., also heard a plane, but he didn't know what time it was; his watch had stopped.

Destroyer rounds Savo Island at the southern end of the Slot with the tip of Guadalcanal at the left. On August 9 a Japanese task force slipped unnoticed through this 7-mile gap to sink 4 Allied cruisers in 40 minutes.

Savo broods over "Ironbottom Sound," graveyard of ships, as U. S. destroyers maneuver in tribute to the dead.

(upper left) Vice Admiral Robert Lee Ghormley, over-all commander of "Operation Watchtower," later dubbed "Operation Shoestring."

(upper right) Vice Admiral Frank Jack Fletcher, immediate commander of the Guadalcanal task force, whose carriers withdrew just before the Battle of Savo Island.

Rear Admiral Richmond Kelly Turner, who, aboard the *McCawley*, was the top commanding officer on the scene.

August 8, transports from which Marines were put ashore at Guadal-canal (left), just before Japanese torpedo bombers attack (below). ...Bomber in the center skims water through shellbursts.

Courtesy of S. O. Bulard

Official U. S. Navy Photo

(lower left) Transport *George F. Elliot,* set afire by crashing Japanese plane, burns out of control off Tulagi.

(lower right) Not all got away.... Japanese plane, one of those downed, burns on the water.

Courtesy of S. O. Bulard

Royal Australian Navy Photo

Before the
The four heavy cruisers

Official U. S. Navy Photos

USS *Astoria*, Captain William G. Greenman

HMAS *Canberra*, Captain Frank E. Getting

Royal Australian Navy Photos

holocaust.

and their commanding officers:

USS *Quincy,* Captain Samuel N. Moore

USS *Vincennes,* Captain Frederick L. Riefkohl

Rear Admiral Richmond Kelly Turner
and his flagship USS *McCawley*, . . .

. . . to which he summoned
Rear Admiral Victor A. C.
Crutchley, RN (left below),
and Lieutenant General
Alexander A. Vandegrift
(right below), USMC, for
midnight conference, un-
aware that Japanese force
was racing in for smashing
attack two hours later.

Rear Admiral Gunichi Mikawa, IJN, who led the daring night attack at Savo, and (below) the *Aoba*, one of his cruisers, at the end of the war, smashed in Inland Sea by U. S. Navy bombers despite her camouflage.

Official U. S. Navy Photos

Night spotter pilot, ready for take-off, inspired by Japanese propaganda: "We must just push on fighting to win this holy war at all costs, so that glorious success should be achieved."

U. S. Department of Justice Photos

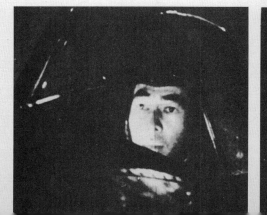

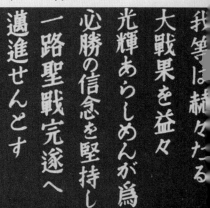

我等は赫々たる
大戦果を益々
光輝あらしめんが爲
必勝の信念を堅持し
一路聖戦完遂へ
邁進せんとす

Destroyer pickets USS *Blue* (above) and USS *Ralph Talbot* (below) failed to sight the Japanese force as it dashed into Savo Sound almost under the *Blue's* stern.

"Warning! Warning!" The Japanese force is finally discovered by the USS *Patterson,* which sounded the alarm to the sleeping cruisers.

 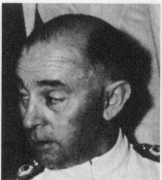

HMAS *Australia,* Rear Admiral Crutchley's flagship, which missed the battle, and her commanding officer, then Captain Harold B. Farncomb, RAN.

Japanese cruiser pilots, back from Guadalcanal beachhead, report U. S. force split, no carriers sighted.

USS *Quincy* caught in Japanese searchlights during the battle.

Twin weapons of terror: the searchlights, which left the enemy naked to the gunners, and the dread Long Lance torpedo.

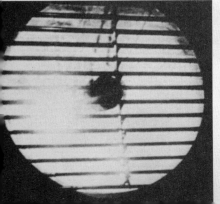

From a painting by Noel Sickles

USS *Quincy,* afire and sinking, keels over. In this wartime painting artist Noel Sickles shows the gaping torpedo hole in her bottom and captures the drama of men spilling into the sea.

Sunday morning

Official U. S. Navy Photos

(above) Lieutenant Commander Harry B. Heneberger, seventh in line of command and senior survivor of the *Quincy*.

(left) Sailors cutting away twisted bow plates of the USS *Chicago*.

at Savo.

Official U. S. Navy Photos

USS *Blue* (above) carrying survivors from the sinking HMAS *Canberra* (below). The burning Australian cruiser, with rescuing destroyer alongside, is seen from the passing USS *Chicago*.

Captain Howard D. Bode, aboard the USS *Chicago,* in command of the Southern Force, failed to stop the Japanese or to warn his Annapolis classmate Captain Frederick L. Riefkohl, commanding the Northern Force.

Official U. S. Navy Photo

Official U. S. Navy Photo

Captain Elijah W. Irish, who, as Lieutenant Commander, reached the bridge of the USS *Chicago* seconds before the torpedo tore a hole in her bow.

Royal Australian Navy Photo

Commander J. A. Walsh, who took over command of the HMAS *Canberra* when Captain Frank E. Getting was mortally wounded.

Admiral Ernest J. King, Commander in Chief United States Navy, . . .

. . . who asked Admiral Arthur J. Hepburn, the Navy's most senior officer, to investigate the Savo Island debacle, . . .

. . . and Commander Donald J. Ramsey, aide to Admiral Hepburn in the inquiry.

Sunday morning, the fleet driven from the beachheads, Marines on Guadalcanal look over the silent Sound toward Savo Island.

Lieutenant Commander Topper (Annapolis '24) had taken the bridge of the *Astoria* just before midnight, relieving the engineering officer, Lieutenant Commander John D. Hayes (his Academy classmate). Hayes told him of the *Ralph Talbot's* warning, and that Captain Greenman had been advised. That was all, and Topper went about filling out his report. The night was dark and overcast, visibility about 10,000 yards, with occasional light rain, and heavy clouds over Savo and toward Guadalcanal to the south. Topper dutifully noted in his report that the washroom and toilet drains were open, ventilation open to the living spaces, and all hatches above the second deck closed except "those necessary to permit limited traffic." The watch settled down for a routine night.

Along about 1:20 A.M. the Northern Force cruisers opened up again on the TBS, this time on a course change. The *Vincennes* had gotten a fix on Savo Island and an island to the north in the Florida group, disclosing that the formation was slightly off course toward Florida. (The overcast was pretty thick toward Savo and on down to the south, but visibility was good northward.)

The executive officer of the *Vincennes*, Commander Mullan, ordered the word passed on TBS to the other ships that the regular 1:30 course change from southwest to northwest would not be made until 1:40. But there was trouble again on the TBS. The *Astoria* heard the message clearly, but the *Quincy* and the *Wilson* had trouble getting it, and there were requests for repeats, then the repeats, and again requests and repeats. It was as bad as a party line in the farm belt, but finally the *Vincennes* made the turn about 1:40, the *Quincy* two minutes later, the *Astoria* bringing up the rear at 1:44.

In the midst of these messages the TBS operator on the *Vincennes* got one other message, by far the most fateful of the night. It was at 1:43 A.M. from the destroyer *Patterson* and it said: "Warning, warning, strange ships entering harbor." There was one difficulty: in the confusion of the course change the message was never relayed to the bridge of the *Vincennes*. The *Astoria* did not hear it at all, and on the *Quincy* the message reached the bridge but was never relayed to gunnery. The *Australia* did not hear it because she had no TBS. The chain had broken not in one link, but in nearly all. The cruisers steamed northward at a quiet 10 knots, following each other like ducks across a barnyard. Not a man aboard felt alarm.

No word came from the south—nothing from Admiral Turner, nothing from Crutchley, each silently watching the action; nor from Captain Bode, who was even then emerging from the holocaust. No one thought to warn the Northern Force, yet at this moment the Japanese force was roaring down on the sleeping cruisers, appetites whetted and gun crews keen from the action in the south. It had been slaughter.

chapter

14

Crutchley and Gatacre, on the bridge of the *Australia*, had changed their views. When the flares overhead were followed by gunfire, they began to think it might be a surface action. As the gunfire increased and steady salvos were discernible, all doubt vanished—it *was* a surface engagement. What to do?

First off Crutchley radioed Turner that a surface engagement was under way near Savo Island. (This was no news to Admiral Turner, who could see the gun flashes himself.) Then Admiral Crutchley decided to do one other thing—wait. He was confident his 5 cruisers and 4 destroyers near Savo could handle any force the Japanese might send in. He also felt it would be madness to charge into a night battle without knowing what was going on. Placed as he was, he could at least help guard the transports. He decided to sit there until he could find out what was happening. He never found out, at least not *that* night.

Admiral Mikawa, having finished off the Southern Force in exactly six minutes, now ordered a turn to the northeastward and raced down at 26 knots on an even fatter target. His men, many half naked, their bodies glistening with sweat, worked smoothly and fervorously to reload torpedo tubes and replenish gun chambers. In the turn, the only flaw of his night's operation, if flaw it was, occurred: the force split. The tail of the Japanese dragon broke off. The *Furutaka*, with the *Tenryu* and *Yubari*, found herself cutting in close to Savo Island, while the mighty *Chokai* led the *Aoba, Kako*, and *Kinugasa* further to the east. The cause of this split was never settled, but the result was dramatic. Now it was a two-headed monster, both heads speeding north with the Americans squarely between. The *Chokai's* giant searchlights snapped on and there in the beams lay three American cruisers, all guns trained in. Again Mikawa gave the order, and again the Japanese guns and torpedo tubes delivered destruction in staggering force.

Lieutenant Commander Cleaveland F. Miller, officer of the deck in the *Vincennes*, hesitated a few moments, but finally decided to call Captain Riefkohl. The captain had retired only forty-five minutes before, after nearly twenty-one hours on the bridge, but there was definitely gunfire off to the south and Lieutenant Commander Miller felt the captain should be told. Captain Riefkohl picked up his binoculars and hurried to the bridge, just forward of his emergency cabin. The general alarm was already sounding.

From the bridge he noted the low clouds to the south and shrouding the top of Savo Island. To the south of Savo, 3 or 4 star shells hung in the sky, and still closer to Guadalcanal there were flashes that appeared to be 5-inch fire. Commander Mullan, preparing to leave the bridge to take charge of gunnery in Battery II, said he thought the firing near Guadalcanal was probably ships of the Southern Force firing on Japanese positions on the island. Captain Riefkohl thought it more likely to be the Southern Force firing on an enemy destroyer trying to sneak into the Sound. He wanted to be most careful to avoid firing on his own ships to the south, and at the same time he had no intention of being drawn down there, thus leaving the northern passage unguarded. He ordered his group to increase speed to 15 knots—he didn't want too much speed because he felt he was in good position to counter any incursion from the north. Even when the enemy searchlights came on—he saw 3, picking out first the *Astoria,* then the *Quincy,* and finally his own ship— Riefkohl was not alarmed. He assumed it was from the Southern Force searching for enemy ships and he ordered Radio to instruct them to "Turn those searchlights off of us. We are friendly." He also ordered speed upped to 20 knots. His radar reported a range of 8,250 yards on the right-hand searchlight, and his main battery trained on it, but it was already too late; astern of him the *Astoria* was in battle.

Lieutenant Commander Topper had just completed the *Astoria's* turn when he felt an underwater explosion which he thought to be a destroyer dropping depth charges some distance away. He may have been right, for the Japanese cruisers, unlike the American, carried depth charges in addition to torpedoes and were exploding them in their race through the Sound, taking no chances that American submarines might be inside the islands. There were none, as it turned out, the nearest being hundreds of miles off on patrol near Truk and the Bismarcks. Topper asked his talker to tell Central Station to be on the alert, and the reply came back that they were very much alert and had felt a slight shake.

Thinking a submarine might have gotten through the screen and be heading for the transports, Topper went out on the starboard wing of the bridge. Lieutenant (j.g.) N. A. Burkey, Jr., the OOD, came out too, but said he had heard nothing. Just then Signalman Second Class W. A. Fletcher on the signal bridge reported hearing a plane. Topper cocked his head but could hear only his own blowers. Up ahead all ships seemed to be on proper station and the *Vincennes* opened up on the TBS again, this time about the 2:00 A.M. course change.

At that moment a lookout somewhere on the ship called over his phones that star shells were exploding on the port quarter. Topper ran to the door of the pilothouse and told Burkey to summon Captain Greenman. At the same time he saw the "star shells," which he recognized immediately as aircraft flares, about 5,000 yards away. As he peered to port he was astonished to hear his own main battery fire a full salvo. He could see no ships and had given no order to fire, nor had he ordered general alarm sounded, yet it was clanging throughout the ship.

As he dashed into the pilothouse he ran into Captain Greenman, whose first questions were: "Who sounded the general alarm? Who gave the order to commence firing?"

Topper said he had not and had no idea who had.

"Topper," said Greenman, "I think we are firing on our own ships. Let's not get excited and act too hastily. Cease firing."

Topper fully agreed with his captain, who was quite calm, and passed the word, "Cease firing! Cease firing!" In the brief moments since Captain Greenman had been roused from heavy sleep, he had noted 2 full salvos from his own ship, flares off the port quarter, and searchlights to the south. He thought immediately of an enemy submarine on the surface. In another instant he would be disabused of all misconceptions.

Who had ordered the firing and the general alarm? It was Lieutenant Commander William H. Truesdell, the gunnery officer, who had already had a busy night. When he came on watch he found that his main battery fire-control radar was not working. He was furious. The main battery radar aft had been out of whack for weeks with a short circuit in the transformer. That one couldn't be fixed until they returned to Pearl Harbor, but this one could, and would. A striker felt his way into the chiefs' quarters and on the second try roused Chief Radioman John J. Datko, Jr.

"Commander Truesdell says to fix that radar right away," the striker said, and Datko rolled out. He had been working on it the previous evening, finally got it so there was half a horizontal picture, and gave up until he could work on it in the daylight. Now he was hurrying back to complete the job (and, incidentally, save his own life, as it turned out). He found the radar officer, Ensign Raymond G. Herzberger, Jr., and they opened up the spares locker and got busy. They found the trouble (bad tubes) about 1:45 A.M. and in a few minutes Datko had it fixed. By this time the harbor was lit up like the Fourth of July and Datko went out to the rail to watch the show.

Lieutenant Commander Truesdell tested his radar on the ships ahead and found it working just as his phone talkers reported star shells in the sky. Truesdell went outside and, like Topper, spotted them immediately for what they really were, airplane flares.

"All stations alert," he barked, and immediately ordered general alarm sounded. It was simple to him: if they were flares they were enemy, and they *were* flares.

Within seconds the enemy began firing, and Truesdell saw the first salvo fall ahead of the *Astoria,* short of the *Quincy* and *Vincennes.* He called the bridge and requested permission to commence firing. No answer.

"Commence firing," he ordered, just as his spotter reported, "Cruisers of *Nachi* class! Cruisers of *Nachi* class!" Off went the 2 salvos that unsettled Topper and Greenman, and down came the word to Truesdell, "What are you firing at? Cease firing!"

"Japanese cruisers!" he shouted, adding, "Request permission to resume firing." As the talker on the bridge relayed the word to Captain Greenman it came out, "Mr. Truesdell said for God's sake give the word commence firing." Captain Greenman hesitated no more: "Commence firing!" he barked, for at that moment he had seen splashes of an enemy salvo falling short of the *Vincennes.* In less than sixty seconds on the bridge he had been shaken completely awake. "Full speed ahead," he ordered, and a slight left turn to keep out of the *Quincy's* fire path.

"Our ships or not, we've got to stop them," said Captain Greenman, with still a nagging doubt that this was the enemy. "Go to your post, Topper," he said, and Topper dashed for Central Station, out into the swirling traffic around the bridge house as men on watch ran for their battle stations and off-watch men raced to their posts.

Electrician John J. Fowkton, asleep on the main deck to escape the intense heat inside the ship, was awakened by the commotion and rolled over in time to hear someone ask Electrician's Mate First Class Lloyd E. Williams, "What do you make of it, Willie?"

And Willie replied, "Looks like they're firing at us."

He was right. The first 2 Japanese salvos had been short and ahead, the third 500 yards short, the fourth 200 yards short, and the fifth—bull's-eye, amidships, and the Jap gunners, once on target, never let up. The salvo amidships hit the tenderest spot on these old-style cruisers—the planes, catapults, and hangars, with their stores of gasoline, oil, and fabric. As fire broke out amidships the second salvo struck Turret I, silencing it forever; and with frightening speed successive salvos struck the bow, the gun deck, and then the bridge.

In the few seconds intervening, Captain Greenman had caught sight of the *Quincy* and *Vincennes* ahead, both already afire. As he grasped this, a shell tore through his bridge, instantly killing the navigator, Lieutenant Commander William G. Eaton, and the chief quartermaster. The *Astoria*, coming up to full speed now, was drawing ahead of the *Quincy* and Captain Greenman ordered a

129

further left turn to get out of her way. At the same time a hit on the starboard side of the bridge felled the signal officer, Ensign T. Ferneding; the helmsman, Quartermaster First Class Houston E. Williams; and Boatswain's Mate First Class Julian Young. The latter, badly wounded, struggled to his feet and threw the wheel over to the left.

Captain Greenman realized he was losing speed, although he had ordered full ahead, and he rang up the engineering officer, Lieutenant Commander Hayes. There was more trouble below than he knew. Hayes advised him that he was even then abandoning the after engine room, due to fires overhead, and for some reason the boiler rooms could give him steam for only 8 knots. At this critical time, from 2:01 to 2:06 A.M., Japanese shells were raking the ship from the foremast aft.

Young, at the wheel, whispered he was getting weaker and couldn't hold on much longer. Quartermaster Second Class R. A. Radke, who had the watch, stopped tending the wounded and took the wheel; there was no control and he so advised the captain, who ordered steering shifted to Central Station.

Topper, racing down from the bridge, had scudded into Central Station as metal showered around him, and a minute later a heavy hit close by shattered instruments and set off alarm bells. Then the reports flowed through the ship in a steady stream: Turret I hit, No. 2 engine room full of smoke, several big hits aft, fire-main risers carried away, no water topside and no communications with after battle dressing station, Marine compartment being abandoned due to heavy smoke, No. 1 fireroom direct hit, No. 2 being abandoned. Topper could watch it all in his mind, and he could do nothing.

Fighting to keep alive, the *Astoria* was also trying to fight the Japanese force, but she never really had a chance. Truesdell's first 2 salvos from the 8-inch main battery, before the incredible (to him) order to cease fire, were not full salvos. Each of the 3 turrets fired, but not all of their guns. The first salvo was probably 6 guns out of the 9, the second likely 8. As Turret I reloaded the first of the Japanese shells found it, and an 8-inch armor-piercing projectile tore a hole in the faceplate, followed by 2 more shells on the barbette. Almost every man in the turret was killed instantly, and only luck prevented a far worse toll. Powder bags were being passed up the hoist, but the door at the top into the turret had not yet been opened. Had it been, an explosion inside the turret might have torn the ship apart.

Turrets II and III, their communications and control torn asunder, went to local control and continued firing raggedly, the third salvo getting off 6 barrels, and then 2, 6, 5, 3, 3, 6 again, and finally 5, 3, and 3. The last one, the final blast from the *Astoria*, got off from Turret II only because the communications officer, Lieutenant Commander Walter B. Davidson, climbed up in the trainer's seat, coached the turret onto a searchlight target and fired. Captain Greenman saw it get away and he thought he saw it hit, but the Japanese were gone now, and he was left with a blazing ship, out of control. A few moments before he had barely avoided collision with the *Quincy*, ablaze from bow to stern, as she passed down his side. It was a sight he never forgot.

chapter
15

The *Quincy* was running in very poor luck that night. The *Patterson's* warning of strange ships in the Sound came through to the bridge, but it was never passed to Lieutenant Commander John D. Andrew, the assistant gunnery officer, who had the watch in Control Forward. The first he knew of it was when searchlights came on and a full Japanese salvo fell just short of the *Vincennes*. Then general quarters sounded from the *Quincy*, on orders of Lieutenant Commander Edward E. Billings, supervisor of the watch. Lieutenant Clarke, being relieved as OOD, sent a quartermaster to rouse Captain Moore, and Lieutenant (j.g) J. M. Baldwin ordered the bugler to blow general quarters.

Clarke had a glimpse of 3 cruisers and a destroyer, obviously enemy, since 1 silhouette showed 3 turrets forward, something no American cruiser had. Captain Moore arrived on the bridge just as star shells arced over his vessel, lighting it up. Searchlights picked out the *Quincy* from the west, and Captain Moore ordered, "Fire at the ships with the searchlights on!" Almost immediately, on second thought—they might be friendly forces —he ordered the Quincy's recognition lights turned on. Junior officers argued the folly of this, but it really made little difference—the *Quincy* was soon bathed in her own fires, far stronger than any recognition lights. Which way could he turn, Captain Moore asked, and Clarke told him, twice, to turn right.

The shot was falling heavily, and from the bridge they saw the *Vincennes,* a flaming torch. Clarke jammed on a helmet and rushed out onto the starboard wing of the *Quincy's* bridge. Light gunfire was coursing across the signal bridge and he fell to the deck, pushing Chief Signalman F. C. Szoka with him. Clarke crawled around to the port side in time to see the port plane catch fire on its catapult.

"Shoot it off," the captain roared, but it was too late. Amidships was already ablaze and shells were falling in a drumfire around the bridge. A shell, 5-inch or larger, tore straight through the bridge house, killing the executive officer, Commander William C. Gray; the navigator, Lieutenant Commander Edward C. Metcalfe; and the damage-control officer, Lieutenant Commander Raymond H. Tuttle; fatally wounding Captain Moore and Lieutenant Commander Billings, and crumpling the bridge phone talker. Lieutenant Commander Billings staggered onto the wing, the side of his face shot away.

Lieutenant Clarke grabbed him, but he said, "I'm all right, I'm all right. Keep calm, everything will be all right. The ship will go down fighting."

Lieutenant (j.g.) J. H. Mee, Jr., and Lieutenant (j.g.) Douglas C. Skaife, felled in the bridge house by the blast, came to in time to hear Billings' words. Mee looked around the bridge house. All were dead in there, he thought, except Captain Moore, who was slumped to the right of the wheel. "Transfer control to Batt II," the captain said, adding something about "beach the ship," and then he expired in Mee's arms, or so Mee believed. A few minutes later, Lieutenant Commander Andrew, all his turrets silenced, all his communications lost, arrived on the bridge to ask instructions. A lone quartermaster, surrounded by bodies, was spinning the wheel, trying for a port turn.

"The captain is dead," he said. "He told me to beach the ship, but I can't steer." Just then Captain Moore half rose from the deck, collapsed, and died. (His body was washed up on Savo Island, and weeks later natives led a Marine party to a grave where they had buried him. One of the natives was wearing the captain's Annapolis class ring.)

Soon after Lieutenant Commander Andrew had noted the splashes forward toward the *Vincennes,* Lieutenant Commander Harry B. Heneberger, the gunnery officer, arrived to relieve him in Control Forward. Running across the deck, Lieutenant Commander Heneberger had made a curious discovery. The noise was terrific, but the surprising thing to him was that he could see the enemy shells coming toward him—luminous black shapes in the air, glowing orange. He had never realized before that you could see shells coming at you. Andrew quickly briefed Heneberger, but even before the red lights blinked on to show that the main turrets were ready the *Quincy* received her first hit. It was on the 1.1 mounts aft, and set the fantail afire. Then the ready lights came on and the first main battery salvo lashed out, a full 9-gun salvo to port at a 6000-yard range. But the Japanese force was moving fast—the *Quincy's* first range had been 8,400 yards, the first salvo at 6,000 yards, and now the targets had passed astern. Turrets I and II could no longer bear on target until the *Quincy* came around to starboard. Control was quickly shifted aft to Director II so Turret III could fire, but it was too late. Turret III had already been hit and jammed in train. Control was shifted back to Forward, but time was running out—Japanese shells raked the entire length of the *Quincy*. Two more salvos were fired from her Turrets I and II, then II was hit, exploded, and burned out. Turret I followed a moment later, put out of action with a fire in the upper powder room. Communications from Gunnery were cut off, and Director I jammed. A shell had cut away the forestay—a cable guying the mast—and it had snarled around the Director preventing it from turning.

After the shooting Lieutenant Commander Andrew ran to the bridge, where he found his captain dead. The Japanese had passed by and the battle was over for the *Quincy*. Afire and out of control, she narrowly missed the *Astoria,* as she passed alongside in a mass of flame.

On the *Vincennes* the situation topside differed little from that on the *Astoria* and on the *Quincy*. Captain Riefkohl was undecided from the start. Watching the gunfire off his port, in the direction of the Southern Force, he waited for word from Admiral Crutchley. He would have been astounded to know Crutchley was nowhere in the vicinity. Believing he was, however, Captain Riefkohl felt he was in an excellent position to go to the aid of the Southern Force. He thought for a moment of having the *Bagley* illuminate southward, but hesitated to do it without orders for fear he would silhouette Crutchley's forces dangerously. If Crutchley wanted illumination, surely he would order it. No order came and no illumination was made. Riefkhol thought, too, that the action to southward might be a diversion to draw him down while an enemy force entered north of Savo to attack the Tulagi transports. Should he throw his ships across that channel to block it? Should he go southward to give aid? No orders came, but very shortly his dilemma was resolved for him.

A searchlight picked out the *Vincennes* from the port quarter. That would be the Southern Force, he thought, and sent his message telling them to get the searchlights off his vessels. He got his reply in armor-piercing shells, ordered a swing to the left, and caught the second salvo aboard. One shell pierced the armored tube of the conning tower, severing every communication channel on the bridge. Another struck the soft belly amidships, setting the planes afire and providing a marker no enemy could miss. As the *Vincennes* swung to port, Riefkohl noted that the *Quincy* was also afire, and he ordered hard right to get away from her. The turn was too late. Torpedoes slammed into the *Vincennes*, hitting Nos. 1 and 4 firerooms, while 8-inch shells cut into the main steam lines, the fire mains, and the main battery control. The after director was blown entirely off the ship.

A hit on the bridge killed Lieutenant Commander Miller, standing not ten feet from Captain Riefkohl, and shrapnel sliced through the bulkheads, killing two men on the other side of the pilothouse.

An intense barrage of Japanese shells was falling now, from both the eastern and western groups of ships, and at least two, perhaps three, torpedoes from the *Chokai* finished the job. The *Vincennes* was dead in the water.

Below decks on all three cruisers it was hell. On the *Astoria*, Lieutenant Commander Hayes, off watch since midnight, was roused from his cabin by a flashlight in his eyes and Machinist's Mate First Class J. W. Bengal telling him "the shells are sure flying up there." The engineering officer immediately went below. Even as he did, a hit above the engine room sent flame spurting down the exhaust trunks, filling the room with smoke and fire. Then there was a hit above No. 2 fireroom, and the officer in charge ordered it evacuated after the steam line was cut in to the forward engine room. Before the men left there was a tremendous blast in No. 1 fireroom and the bulkhead bulged. There were no survivors from No. 1 fireroom.

Lieutenant Commander Hayes remembered passing the electrical officer, Lieutenant (j.g.) J. T. McNulty, on watch in the log room, but he was never seen again. Nor was Ensign F. M. Long, the engineering OOD, who never reached the after engine room.

The carnage below was swift and terrible. Starting at

2:00 A.M. the shells fell steadily and the *Astoria's* engineering areas blinked out in succession: No. 2 fireroom first, followed by the after engine room, No. 3 fireroom, No. 4 fireroom, and finally the forward engine room. When the bridge called down to ask what speed could be made the answer was simple—none. By 2:25 A.M. all men had to be ordered out from below. Many, like Lieutenant Herbert F. Carroll, Jr., the assistant engineering officer, Lieutenant (j.g.) G. W. Thompson, the A Division officer, and Machinist E. F. Kyne, never made it.

Chief Water Tender M. K. Smith, in No. 3 fireroom, ordered his men to light off the two boilers, secured hot earlier in the evening. As steam was coming on the line the tremendous blast in No. 1 fireroom sent shrapnel flying through No. 3. Hot metal slashed through the gauge board, and smoke sent some men gasping on the floor plates. Smith ordered his men out, but the port side was afire and the hatch at the top of the starboard ladder was jammed. Smith pushed it up about 3 inches and could see that a grating from the machine shop, which had been blasted loose, was blocking the only exit. He shouted and flashed his light, but no one heard him and he fell back into the fireroom exhausted. Others scrambled up the ladder and, a long time later it seemed, someone came through the passage and said, "Take it easy, I'll see what I can do." He struggled with the grating, the hatch moved a few more inches, and the men pushed from below almost enough to raise the deck itself. Finally the hatch was open 12 inches or so, and one by one the trapped men squirmed through. Those who were unconscious were lifted and pushed through the hatch like cooked spaghetti. Forward the passageway was blocked by fire, aft by bodies—thirty or more. Finally a scuttle was opened to the well deck above, and the men escaped —into a sea of flame.

No. 4 fireroom was worse. A hit in the uptakes loosed smoke and fire and Water Tender First Class John Larru advised the forward engine room the men would have to leave. Stay, he was ordered. A second hit set off a bad fire in the uptakes and the room glowed bright pink. No order was needed this time. The men who fled up the starboard escape hatch were never seen again. Larru and those who went up the port side survived.

In the control engine room, water, smoke, and shrapnel came through the blowers, the lights went out, steam pressure dropped, and everything stopped. In the eerie darkness Chief Machinist's Mate C. D. Weaver suggested they get the men out. Chief Machinist R. L. Davis agreed, and Chief Water Tender Sidney Provost led the way. Blindfold drills paid off. Provost and Machinist's Mate First Class C. F. McIntosh, who knew the engine-room spaces better than any rating, led the men through the darkness to the mess deck and out onto the fantail.

Lieutenant Commander Hayes, prowling below, found a violent blaze in the boilermaker shop, and fire in the blower trunk. He went back to the engine room, ordered all men out, and started out himself. Somewhere he passed out, but came to later on the main deck aft. Chief Machinist Davis found Chief Machinist's Mate H. F. Ray lying in the mess hall and carried him out to the fantail.

chapter
16

The *Quincy's* luck was as bad below decks as above. The watch started quietly, with Ensign Abe Francis Cohen, four years out of Annapolis, in Main Control. About 1:40 A.M. he heard what he thought was a clanking noise alongside the engine room, and sent his pump man to check. Nothing out of order was found, but a moment later Cohen heard the same noise, this time louder. It sounded as if the *Quincy* had grounded or hit a submarine. Cohen called the bridge and told Lieutenant Baldwin that something was definitely wrong outside the hull. "I'll check it now," Baldwin said, but he never called back. In a few minutes general quarters sounded.

Cohen quickly went into action. Light off boilers 5 and 6, he ordered, and start the second forward generator, cut in main feed pumps, and secure all hatches. Machin-

140

ist A. C. Brooks relieved him promptly, and Ensign Cohen climbed to his battle station in No. 1 mess hall, directly over the engine room.

The engineering officer, Lieutenant Commander Eugene E. Elmore, arrived from his cabin and Cohen told him what had happened. It was now nearly 2:00 A.M. and heavy firing could be heard all around. Lieutenant Commander Elmore said he would go below, and they broke Condition Zed to open the hatch for him. He climbed down, followed by Machinist Brooks. The hatch closed behind them and neither man was ever seen again.

Small hits could be heard overhead, fore and aft, and finally a tremendous blast rocked No. 2 mess hall. Ensign Cohen opened the door and looked into a caldron. His men ran for RBA (rescue breathing apparatus), opened the door again, and moved in. Fire and smoke were intense, but soon some wounded staggered out bleeding and choking, a couple of them dragging a shipmate. They wanted to get him to the after-battle dressing station, but the journey was too late for him. They tried anyway, for themselves, but No. 2 mess hall was impassable and fire blocked their forward passage. Then a great shudder ran through the *Quincy* as a torpedo exploded under them. Water Tender First Class Lynn Sullenberger opened the escape hatch to the well deck, but flames belched downward on them and he slammed it shut. "You can't get forward; the Marine compartment and sick bay are all shot to hell," someone said.

So Ensign Cohen tried the well deck again; it was the only way. He fought his way onto the well deck, through the fire and carnage, and then went back for his men and got them all out.

No. 1 fireroom got off easy. There was a hit around 1:50 A.M. and a minor flareback from the boilers, but the men finally got the fires going. There was a second hit shortly after 2:00, and all fires went out when the fuel suction stopped. Tubes snapped in No. 2 boiler and water poured into the firebox. Nothing more possible, Water Tender First Class L. M. Smith led his men out.

No. 2 fireroom filled with smoke about 2:03, and the feed lines, shaken loose by blast, began to leak at all flanges. The feed pressure dropped and the port bulkhead began to leak. One boiler was cut off as water rose to the firebox, and by 2:17 the second boiler had to be secured. Water Tender First Class Henry J. Monsimer ordered everyone out at 2:19.

In No. 2 engine room a heavy explosion snapped the straps supporting the main steam line and it vibrated wildly under pressure. Fortunately it did not rupture. Chief Machinist's Mate Harvey A. Storey noticed the fire pumps running at full speed, but there was no pressure on the line. The main steam pressure on the port line dropped to zero (it was ruptured somewhere), communications ceased, and the ship began to list to port. All machinery stopped and Storey opened the hatch to No. 2 mess hall. The fire was fierce and he quickly slammed it. Storey then led his men up the escape hatch to the well deck. Lieutenant (j.g.) A. S. Maxim had ordered the men out and when they had protested he had said, "You go first, I am senior." His body was never found.

No one knows what happened in No. 1 engine room.

There was not a single survivor except a messenger. He left the compartment at 2:25 A.M. on orders from Lieutenant Commander Elmore to go to the bridge and report the ship would have to stop.

Little is known of what happened below decks in the *Vincennes*, particularly in the forward end, as there were few survivors. Besides the steady rain of shell, at least 2, and perhaps 3, torpedoes from the *Chokai* hit No. 4 fireroom, and a fish from the *Yubari* slammed into No. 1 fireroom. There were no survivors from that compartment. Men in the after engine room followed the battle by scraps of talk over the phones, in their gauges, and through the phone calls to other rooms forward—calls that were never answered.

The first hit in No. 4 fireroom was quickly reported to Lieutenant Edmund P. Di Giannantonio, assistant engineering officer, in the after engine room. "Tell them to abandon the space and make sure they close the hatches," he called to his talkers, who passed the word. A moment later the men below knew instantly when the *Vincennes'* planes had been hit; heavy white smoke and sparks came down the blower ducts. "Shift to exhaust blowers," Di Giannantonio said calmly, and a few minutes later the room was clear. Then came the report that the well deck was aflame. The only escape trunk from the after engine room led to the well deck.

"Forget it," the lieutenant said. "The men up there will take care of it." A dull thud far forward shook the ship. "Another torpedo," said Chief Machinist's Mate William R. Baker and Lieutenant Di Giannantonio nodded.

Up to this time steam pressure had remained normal. Now it dropped, and the lights went out. The emergency lights came on and the talker said No. 1 fireroom had been hit. No word from Nos. 2 and 3, but they must still be there, as the steam pressure returned to normal. Full ahead, came the bells from the bridge, but in another minute they rang full astern, then the engine-room telegraph indicator went out of control, swinging rapidly from full ahead to full astern. The lieutenant called the forward engine room, and Lieutenant F. C. Wilson, Jr., the officer on watch, said the bridge had been badly hit, but the last he had heard was flank speed. Di Giannantonio turned to his throttlemen and passed the word, and as they executed it his talker reported "They passed the word to abandon ship."

This seemed incredible to Di Giannantonio. Here, far below the water line in the stern everything seemed nearly normal: pressure was good, there was no smoke or fire, and it was impossible to imagine the devastation throughout the rest of the ship. Nevertheless, the men began automatically to secure when the word came, "Belay that last order."

That was more like it, Lieutenant Di Giannantonio thought, but at that instant an explosion more violent than any before shook the *Vincennes*. She throbbed and quivered, and began to list and settle. The end was coming quickly. Not one fireroom answered the phone, nor did the forward engine room. A tremendous explosion blew out the lights aft, and when they came on Di Giannantonio noticed his men below on the lower grating. They were covered with soot, and their eyes and teeth gleamed up at him like those of minstrel men. "Anyone hurt?" he cried, and Baker shouted, "Everyone okay."

Then a shell hit directly overhead, a steampipe burst and a terrible hissing filled the compartment. Baker turned a valve and stemmed it, but there was no longer any question: it was time to get out. Almost for the first time they noticed the *Vincennes* had a bad list to port, and when they tried the port hatch it was jammed. There was one door left, and every man in the engine room stared at it. Would it open?

In dead silence they watched as one man climbed the ladder, undogged the hatch with great care and slowly pushed. The door opened as if newly oiled, and one by one the men climbed out on the well deck. It was ablaze, but they stepped out into it. Last 3 up were Chief Machinist's Mate Baker, Ensign N. W. Carter, and Lieutenant Di Giannantonio.

chapter
17

The *Quincy* suffered most terribly, on a night when suffering was common, and her ordeal pointed up the faults of practices then in use. The weakest point of every cruiser that night was the well deck where fabric-covered planes (old-style SOC-3 biplanes), gasoline, and oil were concentrated virtually unprotected. In each case the well deck went up in a flash early in the engagement, not only setting dangerous fires amidships but silhouetting the ships and giving enemy gunners and torpedomen an aiming point they couldn't miss.

Quincy had 3 planes in the open, 1 on each catapult and 1 on the deck, plus 2 more in the hangar, and to make the night's work easier for the enemy each plane was fully fueled with 135 gallons of aviation gasoline. (The *Astoria* and *Vincennes* crews drained their planes each night; the

Quincy did not, arguing that draining and refilling not only took two hours but made the planes useless during the hours they were empty. Actually it made little difference; planes on all 3 cruisers seemed to burn with equal ferocity.)

Action on the *Quincy's* well deck was intense but brief. As general quarters sounded, Aviation Machinist's Mate Second Class F. B. Forbes and Gunner's Mate Second Class R. D. Byers ran into the "silo" at the base of the starboard catapult. The phone talker already had orders from the bridge—"Warm up the planes," but even as Byers struggled into his flashproof clothing (it saved his life later) the order was countermanded. The tiny silo was jammed now. Lieutenant (j.g.) L. H. Reagan and Lieutenant (j.g.) H. W. Smith, who had been sleeping under Turret I, ran in to put on their flying suits. Lieutenant (j.g.) E. L. Kempf and Lieutenant (j.g.) T. A. Chisholm arrived from their cabin already dressed for flying, and Lieutenant (j.g.) P. E. Webster pushed in to say the fantail had been hit and he wanted the bridge informed. The word was passed and Webster dashed out again, to his death. A few seconds later the port catapult was hit by a 6-inch shell and the *Quincy's* fate was decided. The plane flared up with a whoosh and everyone on the well deck scattered. Byers ran to the starboard catapult and trained it out over the water. Lieutenant Chisholm dashed for the hose reel and Painter First Class Tom J. Appling for the foamite hopper, but a wing dropped off the burning plane and set fire to the plane in the well deck. Fuel spilled across the deck and flashed off as an arson job would.

There was never any hope of containing the fire. Flames cut off the foamite hopper and the hose was sliced by shrapnel. Where a whole piece of hose could be found the hydrants issued only a trickle of water or none at all. Great clouds of gas fumes came from somewhere (several of the aviators said later they thought the Japanese might be using gas shells). To add to the horror, a shell fragment cut the steampipe leading up the forestack to the ship's whistle. The pipe ruptured with a great noise and boiling water rained down on the well and boat decks, providing a choice of death—burning or scalding. Byers went over the boat deck, dragging Seaman First Class James F. Chadwick, whose ankle was smashed. Lieutenant Chisholm pulled out a man with a broken leg. Lieutenant Smith and Marine Lieutenant F. S. Aldudge carried Aviation Machinist's Mate Second Class Andrew J. Simko to the rail and dropped him over, although he didn't want to go. Lieutenant Kempf climbed to the gun deck, found it a shambles of broken guns and broken men, and ran to the rail choking from gas fumes. Byers hopped from the starboard catapult to the spud locker, over to the top of the movie shack, and up to the gun deck. In seconds the well deck was cleared of the living, leaving only dead and a great fire raging with a hot water fountain spraying down on it.

Turret II was the first of the *Quincy's* main battery to go. A direct hit caused it to flare and no other word was ever heard from it. Turret I followed quickly. Chief Turret Captain John J. Connolly was sleeping under it at general quarters (good protection from rain squalls). The turret was quickly manned and got off three salvos, fast and without much aim, before a heavy explosion outside sent flames leaping as high as the pointer's port. Smoke and fumes filled the turret and Master Gun Captain Henry M. Grice called out, "Is there fire in the upper powder room?" A second hit, and Connolly shouted, "Where's the fire?" There was no answer, but the gun chamber was a mass of flame. Connolly set off the alarm and turned on the sprinkler. No water. Men spewed from the turret, driven by flame and fumes, and as they crawled away Turret II exploded in a heavy blast, blowing some of the men over the side.

Turret III functioned perfectly on the first salvo, then the power failed. A terrific hit almost directly under him nearly threw Boatswain's Mate First Class H. L. Berg from the pointer's seat. He was not hurt, but his instruments were smashed. Fire broke out in the upper powder-handling room, and Chief Turret Captain C. L. Kendrick ordered it flooded. Auxiliary power came on, but the turret would not turn; the explosion had jammed it at 190 degrees. As the motors strained to turn it the overload switch blew out. Lieutenant (j. g.) Robert M. Jacobs, the turret officer, ordered the magazines secured and all men below to come to the gun chamber. Fire broke through the blower in the upper handling room, and the voice tube told him of another fire behind the powder hoists. There was a list to the ship now and Jacobs talked with Kendrick as to the best course of action—to stay in the turret or abandon. A big lurch to port settled the question, and the men scrambled out, horrified at the devastation they saw.

If one place on the *Quincy* was worse than another it

was the gun deck. The 5-inch batteries there were ordered to put up star shells for illumination of the target, and actually got off several rounds, set at 25.6 seconds. Then the Japanese gunners, by now solidly on target laid on a barrage which smashed the 5-inchers and virtually decimated their crews. Gun No. 6 was hit first, and called for 5 replacements. Gun No. 2 was blasted next and all men were knocked off the mount. The gun captain, Boatswain's Mate First Class E. T. Bryant, pulled one of his men clear and tried to round up enough of a crew to man the piece again, only to have another hit again sweep his loaders off the deck. He and the only man left, Gunner's Mate Third Class Patrick Drum, fought to man it themselves. Drum loaded and Bryant pointed, but before they could get on target smoke and flame drove them off. As they raced past Gun No. 4, they saw the crew there in a heap, clothes torn off and scalding water showering down from the ruptured whistle pipe. Wooden rafts were burning and the deck was ablaze from end to end. Bryant knifed down a floater net and plunged over the side hugging it to him. Behind him there was nothing but flame and death, all guns smashed.

Across the entire superstructure, men were learning some hard lessons. Life jackets were securely tied in bundles, high off the deck to keep them out of traffic. Floater nets were lashed in their baskets high up on bulkheads, and rafts were secured atop gun turrets. Now that it was needed, all lifesaving gear seemed to be stowed where least available in emergency. Men scaled flaming bulkheads and turrets, slashing at the lines to free rafts and nets. In some cases they succeeded, but many a man could get no life jacket, net, or raft.

The medical staff had its own horrors. Chief Pharmacist's Mate John J. Mahan reached to open the medical locker in Battle Dressing I. A shell hit nearby put out the lights, shattered glass, and blew the handle off the locker. Fumbling in the dark Mahan forced the locker open with his knife, set up a lantern and pulled out dressings for Lieutenant Wilfred W. Forbes, the *Quincy's* junior medical officer. Forbes had treated only three or four men, mostly bad shrapnel slashes, when water and smoke and exploding 1.1 ammunition forced them from the compartment. The doctor ran to the 3rd Division compartment where a man was trapped in smashed lockers and bunks. Water was already ankle deep, but they wrestled the man loose and started him for the deck. Mahan stepped on the fantail, skidded in oil and blood, clawed his way back into the compartment, and helped Dr. Forbes move the wounded outside. The ship was already ablaze and there was nothing more that could be done.

Sick bay, with Lieutenant Commander C. F. Morrison in charge, was hit early. The lights went out, and in the darkness and choking smoke men screamed in agony. There was no help for them. Those who could, cleared out and struggled to the rail or lay gasping on the coamings. On the gun deck Pharmacist's Mate Third Class Merlin J. Schwitters worked as fast as he could against the stream of men lacerated by shrapnel, but he was confronted with a river of blood and he ran out of tourniquets trying to stem it. The able men were wonderfully helpful, dragging or pulling the injured to the rail, beating out flaming clothing, tying off spurting arteries with shoe-laces, shirts, or handkerchiefs.

On the *Quincy's* main deck near the captain's entrance the dental corpsman, Pharmacist's Mate Second Class Paul W. Scott, lay with his leg torn off at the thigh. Facing him, feet braced against the bulkhead, was Lieutenant Walter A. Hall, Jr., the ship's dentist. Hall, badly wounded himself, had pressed against his own stomach the bloody stump of Scott's leg, trying in desperation to stop the flow of blood. It was heroic but futile, and both perished.

In Radio I the supply officer, Lieutenant Commander Bion B. Bierer, Jr., heard the first salvo and asked, "What was that?"

"Somebody dropped his watch," said Chief Radio Electrician William R. Daniel.

Radioman Second Class D. R. Caylor rushed in to report, "We've been hit! The superstructure's afire!" "Nuts," said Daniel, just as a shell crashed through the bulkhead and exploded over the workbench. Sparks and shrapnel showered around the radar, and through holes in the bulkhead the men could see flames leaping on the forecastle. Lieutenant Earl E. Ordway, the radio officer, arrived from his cabin as a shell crash put out the lights, jammed the door behind him and cut all communications. Suddenly he remembered, vividly, personally decoding the previous day the reports of the Japanese force heading toward Guadalcanal. It came to him then, as it did to many others, that the cruisers should never have been bottled up inside Savo but patrolling outside. It was somewhat late for such thoughts.

Lights were still on in the *Quincy's* coding room, but a

shellburst shattered them along with the furniture and equipment. The men in there crawled bleeding into Radio I and huddled on the deck with the rest of the radiomen, but as fire below heated the deck they began to choke. Lieutenant Ordway stuffed the code books into the safe and locked it, discovered he had missed a set of coding wheels and opened the safe again to put them in. Last word on the phones was, "The fantail is on fire." It was time to go, and they forced the door with their shoulders, pushing aside a body that had fallen in the passageway.

Daniel, all out of wisecracks now, ran to Radio II with Caylor, but they couldn't stay long. Shells rained around, all circuits failed, and gas was coming from somewhere. Daniel led them up through the smoke-filled compartment above and out on deck. He helped Caylor to start down a line hanging over the side, and told him to catch the first raft coming by.

On the deck were Lieutenant (j.g.) Roland Rieve, the radar officer, and Lieutenant Commander Heneberger, who had climbed down from the bridge. "What's the score?" Rieve asked, and when the gunnery officer didn't hear he shouted, "Are we abandoning ship?" Heneberger said he didn't know. Chief Radioman N. F. Dostal came along and said, "Come on, Mr. Rieve." "Coming," Rieve replied, and they skidded into the water as the ship took a sharp list.

Although he did not know it, Heneberger, the seventh man in line of command, was now the *Quincy's* senior survivor. Carried away in the tragedy on the bridge, or sealed in compartments below, were the captain, executive officer, navigator, first lieutenant, engineering officer, and watch supervisor. The last word Lieutenant Commander Heneberger, or anyone else, had heard from the bridge was, "We are going down the middle. Give them hell!" It had sounded like Captain Moore.

What actually happened was that the *Quincy*, blazing and out of control, passed dangerously near the *Astoria*, veered to starboard, and limped a short distance toward Tulagi before she sank in 500 fathoms. It was 2:35 A.M. and the battle was just one hour old.

chapter
18

The *Vincennes,* pounded by shells as few other ships in history, lasted about eighteen minutes. The first salvo whistled in about 1:51 A.M. and each shell, it seemed, had been intelligently aimed at a vital spot. One clipped the bridge and killed Commander Miller, others hit the carpenter shop (always a fine spot for fires), the hangar (best fire spot of all), Batt II, directing guns, and the antenna trunks, severing all communications. Short of an open magazine hit no attacker could ask more. Out went radio and searchlights, battle phones, and power on the turrets; the fire mains ruptured and the planes went up in a bright blaze amidships. In one salvo the Japanese had set a fire to aim by and the ship was slashed to less than 50 per cent efficiency.

She still had steam, and Captain Riefkohl ordered 20

knots and a course change to the left, turning down to help his friends in the Southern Force, should they ask him. They never did, and furthermore they never told him anything. How could he know he was now heading down between 2 enemy columns just waiting to smash him? But they were, and they did.

While she lasted, the *Vincennes* got off a second main salvo and Lieutenant Commander Robert R. Craighill thought he saw the target turn and disappear out of control. It was the *Kinugasa* and she was hit all right, but not that badly. The Japanese searchlights snapped off, but not for the reason the Americans thought. They thought they had shot them out, but the truth was the Japanese were now on range and needed no more light.

Salvo after salvo slammed into the *Vincennes*, 8-inch, 5.5-inch, 4.7-inch, and even machine-gun fire from somewhere. Fire broke out in the movie locker, the cane fender storage, and the searchlight platform.

In forward battle station Commander James D. Blackwood had a Negro mess attendant on the table, sewing up his jaw, when a 5.5-inch shell exploded in the room. Dr. Blackwood, twenty-two years in the Navy and a fine old gentleman in his sixties, was killed instantly along with every member of the medical team around him. The mess attendant bounded from the table holding his jaw together with his hand and ran from the room with only a leg scratch.

Captain Riefkohl, frantic now with fire raining in from both sides, turned hard right again. Trying to escape, he rang for 25 knots, but the speed never exceeded 19.5 and in the turn 2, perhaps 3, torpedoes slashed through the port side. A hit in main battery control aft killed Lieutenant (j.g.) Victor J. Fama, the control officer there, hits were scored on Turrets I and II, and it was not yet two o'clock, the battle less than nine minutes old.

Steering power failed in the pilothouse and control was shifted to steering aft. A forward steam line burst with a terrible hiss and Boatswain C. F. Baker flooded down the forward magazines. Captain Riefkohl tried a frantic left turn by stopping the port engine, but there was no response. He sent a messenger, who never returned.

Shortly after 2:00 A.M., by some miracle the main battery got off two more 6-gun salvos, their last, firing at a searchlight which did not, however, go out. Two more searchlights picked out the burning *Vincennes* and the shells fell without mercy. The forward director jammed in train, and shells hit the machine shop, forward mess hall, starboard catapult tower, well deck, and radar room. The *Vincennes'* colors were carried away by shot, and Captain Riefkohl, unaware that the age of gallantry had ended, ordered another set hoisted. Chief Signalman George J. Moore and a chief quartermaster, risking life in that hail of steel, raised a new set on the starboard yardarm, using the last remaining halyard.

The Japanese gunners were delighted. They thought it signified an admiral's flagship, and they redoubled their fire. In one last great blast shells smashed Turret II, top and side, and silenced every last gun in service. Lieutenant Commander Robert Lee Adams, the gunnery officer, was forced to report, "Captain, we have absolutely no guns to fire with. Everything is out."

"All right," the captain replied, "you tell the men to get

down below from exposed positions and see if they can seek cover." Captain Riefkohl never forgot his men, and he ordered messengers sent along decks and below to order the men out—those who were left.

The slaughter finally ceased and the *Vincennes* was left alone to die. The list increased steadily between 2:15 and 2:30, and the captain ordered all life rafts put over the side. The wounded were helped into life jackets. Lieutenant Commander Samuel A. Isquith and Lieutenant W. A. Newman, medical officers, stayed on duty at aft and amidships dressing stations until the end. It was not long in coming. Captain Riefkohl gave the order to abandon ship about 2:30 A.M., and was washed off an upper deck about 2:40. Ten minutes later the *Vincennes* sank, only a mile or two from her sister, the *Quincy*. When they drew up the *Vincennes'* List of Known Hits later, it showed at least 56 large-caliber hits and many more probables, not to mention at least a half-dozen torpedoes.

The *Astoria* died a stubborn death, in two distinct phases. Early in the battle the ship had been cut in half by fires amidships and by the severance of communications. As far as Captain Greenman knew there was no one alive aft, and he feared the worst. But many other things demanded his attention.

While the fiasco of "Commence firing," "Cease firing," "Commence firing," was being enacted on the bridge, there was no lack of action elsewhere. In Turret II, Ensign Raymond C. McGrath, just out of the Academy, got the word on his phones, "Flares on the port quarter. The *Australia* is firing." (The *Australia* did not fire a shot that night.) Turret II got off three salvos and then heard a terrific jolt (Turret I was finished, temporarily). Turret II fired again, despite failures in the powder and shell hoists, but then came to the limit of train to port and had to swing around to starboard. On the fifth salvo only the left and center guns fired, but then she got off 3 barrels, 2 again, 3, and another 2. She was done, as main battery control and Director I were out, due to smoke and shell. McGrath ordered the trainer to bear on what he thought was an enemy to port—it was the *Quincy*—and fortunately all power failed in the turret. Men were fainting now from smoke and fumes, and McGrath led them out. Ordered back to flood the magazines, he led his turret captain and gunner's mate to the control panel and pressed the buttons. Nothing happened, and finally they went below and opened the valves by hand.

On Spot II, Fire Controlman First Class W. W. Johns somehow missed the word to evacuate. He picked up a target at 4,000 yards—a searchlight—and turned to find himself alone. A sight setter and trainer appeared from somewhere, the ready lights went on for Turrets II and III, and Johns fired—a 6-gun salvo. A second salvo was fired, but the third time only Turret III light came on and that was fired. A Japanese cruiser appeared, but at that moment the Director jammed, Turret III reported no power, and Plot said it was abandoning due to smoke. Johns quit then and took his men out.

The record of the *Astoria's* 5-inch guns told her story. No. 1 got off twelve rounds, No. 2 one round before the barrel was hit, No. 3 six rounds, No. 4 ten rounds before the ready service ammunition blew up, No. 5 six rounds, No. 6 seven rounds before its ready service exploded; No.

7 after seven rounds was hit by a shell, and No. 8's ready service went up on the tenth round. Altogether, 8 guns and only 59 rounds, a tribute to the power and accuracy of Japanese gunnery.

Lieutenant Donald E. Willman, putting on his phones in Sky Forward, heard the bridge say, "Don't fire, they may be our own ships." It was too bad, because there was very little time this night and such confusion cut it even shorter. When he received the order, "Commence firing," he was able to get off only 2 to 4 rounds before his Director was smashed and he had to abandon it. He started down among his 5-inchers to tell them to go to local control, but an explosion broke his arm and cut his leg and he fainted. Lieutenant R. G. McCloy was there, bloody and dazed, and finally a 5-inch battery officer, Lieutenant (j.g.) Vincent P. Healey saved the gunners, Willman rousing long enough to give permisssion to abandon the gun deck.

In Sky Control, Seaman First Class Lynn F. Hager had the bridge phones on his head and the first words he heard after the erroneous "cease fire," were, "Fire every damn thing you've got." The last order he heard was, "Get those damn searchlights." Between those two orders, seemingly only minutes apart, lay the whole battle.

Lieutenant George M. K. Baker, Jr., the radio officer, reached Main Radio just as the lights went out. He snapped on the battle lanterns and in their light read a contact report that had just been decoded. It placed the Japanese force of 3 cruisers and 3 destroyers, previously reported earlier in the evening, slightly farther south of Bougainville. He had no time to reflect on this, or even to remember the contents exactly, for the force had now arrived, and to verify this sent two 8-inch shells into the *Astoria's* radio room. One pierced the bulkhead near the door to the communications office, the other passed through an armored door into the coding room, exploding in a blinding orange flash. The rooms were instantly a shambles of blood and bodies, smashed desks and chairs. Of those not yet dead, Radioman Third Class Joseph T. Muskus lost a leg, Chief Radioman Samuel R. Gladden was terribly wounded, and Electrician C. F. O'Neill was hit. Chief Pay Clerk B. Q. Swinson put a tourniquet on Muskus' leg and gave him a hypo. There was nothing to be done for Gladden, but he wanted a cigarette, so Swinson lit one and put it in his mouth.

Two more shells hit Radio I, followed by another pair, and then a final one. The room was shot to pieces now, and all the able-bodied could do was move the (hopeful) wounded out to the deck, where they might have a chance.

It was much the same everywhere topside, the shells boring in relentlessly with a roar like an express train. The highest intensity came between 2:01 and 2:06 A.M., and thereafter the shelling tapered off until 2:15, when it stopped as suddenly as it had begun.

Lieutenant Commander Truesdell, coming out of Director I, saw nothing but fire topside. Appalled, he worked his way through fire and bodies to the bridge and told Captain Greenman he should leave, the ammunition room directly over his head was afire. Very well, said Captain Greenman, he would take station forward of Turret II on the communications deck, and he wished all wounded men to be brought down to the forecastle. Truesdell offered to search all topside stations and assure that all men still alive were brought out. Lieutenant Commander Topper reported there seemed to be no fires below the *Astoria's* second deck, and Lieutenant Commander Hayes said the engineering spaces were watertight. There was just a chance the ship might be saved. As to what was happening aft, Lieutenant Commander Hayes said he had no idea, but he assumed the ship was afire to the stern.

It was not quite as bad as that. Commander Frank E. Shoup, Jr., the executive officer, leaped from his bed at general quarters and ran aft, putting on his pants and shirt over his pajamas. At his battle station, Batt II, he found only his talker, Quartermaster Second Class J. U. Walker, and no one else ever arrived. Shoup saw nothing to starboard, but stepped out on the port-gun platform in time to greet an arriving shell, which blinded him temporarily and burned his hands and face. Almost immediately the boat deck, well deck, and gun deck were hit and broke out in flames. The ship's boats began to burn, and Walker reported he had no contact with the bridge. The announcer system went dead and suddenly Batt II was on fire, with flames blocking both ladders down to the fantail.

Fire was driving all men from the mainmast section and they scrambled down as best they could. Monkey lines had been rigged aft of the machine-gun platform and finally Shoup and Walker went down that way, satisfied that all living and wounded who could be moved had escaped the caldron.

Machinist's Mate First Class O. S. Sells was saved only

by the intrepidity of his shipmates. They saw him pinned under the whaleboat davit, surrounded by fire and apparently dead. Then his hand moved. Shipfitter First Class C. C. Watkins raced in, followed by Shipfitter Third Class Wyatt J. Louttrell and Water Tender Second Class Norman R. Touve. Standing in flames they forced the davit up and pulled Sells free. On the way out of the flames they picked up Fireman Second Class J. R. Bene and dragged him to the fantail too. Those who saw it were awed by the courage of these men.

Forward, Captain Greenman was under increasing strain. He had noted that the *Astoria* now had a list of some 3 degrees. It might mean only that the after magazines had been flooded, but more likely that some part of the hull was open to the sea. Fires were raging unchecked, with every fire main ruptured. By 3:00 A.M. some 400 men were gathered on the forecastle, about 70 of them wounded and many dead.

A bucket brigade was organized, with the faint hope that the fire might be forced back amidships, but flames belched from every passageway and ventilation duct. The main fear was the 5-inch magazines. Captain Greenman was satisfied that the 8-inch magazines had been flooded, but if the 5-inch went up every man on the forecastle might be blown to bits.

The bucket brigade, dipping water from the sea, worked slowly aft on the starboard side of the gun deck, and a gasoline handy-billy pump was rigged, but its puny stream seemed ludicrous against the wall of flame. Fire had now reached the lower ammunition hoists, and 1.1

and 5-inch shells could be heard exploding below. Any moment might bring real disaster.

Captain Greenman dared not delay longer, and ordered the *Bagley* to be brought alongside. The destroyer, reached by blinker earlier, had been ordered to stand by. Eerie lights blinking from the forepeak of the burning cruiser signaled the *Bagley* to approach and Commander Sinclair brought his vessel in to a very smart Chinese landing (bow to bow, like mare and foal nuzzling). The ships were lashed together and the transfer began, the wounded being lifted across first. Able-bodied men followed, and finally Captain Greenman and his officers jumped into the destroyer, leaving the *Astoria,* they thought, for the last time. It was 4:45 A.M.

As the *Bagley* cast off, flashing lights winked out from the stern and for the first time Captain Greenman learned that men were alive back there. The *Bagley* signaled them that they had been seen and would be picked up later. The destroyer, jammed with wounded and shipwrecked sailors, backed off slowly, and began pulling from the sea dozens of men who had been forced off the 3 cruisers. A soft rain began to fall and it seemed to Captain Greenman, as he looked at his ship, that the fires amidships might be dying. Thus ended Phase I of the *Astoria's* ordeal.

chapter
19

Admiral Crutchley was having a frustrating morning. Leaving the *McCawley* just before midnight after his conference with Turner, Crutchley offered to take General Vandegrift to his boat, and together they boarded the admiral's barge. The night was dark, with patches of fog, and the barge searched over an hour before it found Vandegrift's mine sweeper and put him aboard for his trip to the Tulagi beachhead. It was 1:30 by the time the barge found the *Australia* and put Admiral Crutchley back aboard his flagship. Only a few hours remained before dawn and the admiral decided to spend the rest of the night near the transports at the Guadalcanal beach and reform his forces about 5:00 A.M. There is no record that he communicated this decision to anyone.

He heard the reports of planes over Savo Sound, and

about 1:46 A.M. aircraft flares brightened the sky over the transports. A few moments later there was a burst of what Admiral Crutchley took to be light fire, as though a ship were engaging the flare dropper. This was followed by heavy firing. Within five minutes heavy gunfire had broken out and he believed (according to his report later) that the *Vincennes* group must be coming into action against an enemy being engaged by the Southern Force. He felt it impossible that any enemy force could break through into Savo Sound undetected, and if it did his 5 cruisers were adequate to deal with it. He complained, rather wryly: "I was in complete ignorance of the number or the nature of the enemy force and the progress of the action being fought."

Even the one order he issued went awry. Sometime during the battle he ordered destroyers not in contact with the enemy to concentrate on him in his position off the beachhead. Night of fiascoes! At least 5 destroyers which received this, including the *Wilson, Helm, Bagley, Selfridge,* and *Mugford,* thought it referred to Part 6, paragraph d, of Crutchley's night instructions, and went charging off in the opposite direction to concentrate 5 miles northwest of Savo Island. The trouble lay in scrambled codes. None of the destroyers could make out the position given in Admiral Crutchley's order, because it was a cipher from the General Signal Book reciphered into the signal cipher then in force. Each destroyer assumed independently that the position must be the one given in his night orders, which said: "If ordered to form a striking force, all destroyers under Desron 4, less *Blue* and *Ralph Talbot,* concentrate under *Selfridge* 5 miles northwest of Savo Island. In the event of contact with enemy surface units, the Striking Force will at once attack with full outfit of torpedoes and then maintain touch from the westward."

Vain hope! Even now, Admiral Mikawa's force was streaking out of Savo Sound, giving the *Ralph Talbot* hell as it passed. When the destroyers did arrive, at the wrong rendezvous, there was nothing there.

In a desperate attempt to find out what was going on Admiral Crutchley radioed the *Chicago*, the *Vincennes*, and Admiral Scott in the *San Juan* group: "Are your groups in action?" There was, of course, no reply from the *Vincennes*, already smoking and dead in the water. The *Chicago* replied cryptically, "Were, but not now." Scott replied, a little more fully, "This force not in action. Appears to be surface force between Florida Island and Savo." Crutchley continued his efforts, but could not raise any cruiser of the Northern Force. The *Quincy* had already sunk, the *Vincennes* would follow at any moment, and the *Astoria* was being abandoned.

At 2:42 A.M. Admiral Crutchley asked the *Chicago* to "report situation." The *Chicago*, for reasons never fully explained, had continued on a straight course westward after her sharp and damaging encounter with the Japanese force, and had gone out beyond Savo Island before turning back. At 2:45 she replied to Crutchley's request for information with: "We are now standing toward Lengo on course 100." Not a word yet of what had happened, but four minutes later she amplified: "Chicago south of Savo Island, hit by torpedo, slightly down by bow. Enemy ships firing to seaward. *Canberra* burning on bearing 250 five miles south of Savo. Two destroyers standing by *Canberra*." At 3:10 A.M. Crutchley made his first report to Turner: "Surface action near Savo. Situation as yet undetermined." This was scant news to Turner, for he already knew something was going on out there but, like Crutchley, had little idea what it was.

Destroyer *Blue,* guardian of the southwest passage, was in somewhat the same position—an interested but noninquisitive spectator. Unaware that a powerful Japanese force had passed close off her stern, the *Blue* continued her monotonous passage back and forth across the channel. Lieutenant (j.g.) Milton I. Moldafsky, who had the bridge, summoned Commander Williams, sleeping in the radar room, as soon as the flares were sighted over the Guadalcanal beachhead. They heard the gunfire which broke out soon thereafter and it was obvious that a heavy engagement was under way. All hands watched it with great interest and even the medical officer, Lieutenant Donald L. Martinson, on watch in the wardroom, strolled out to the deck occasionally to speculate on "who was firing on whom."

The *Blue's* executive officer, Lieutenant Commander Richard S. Craighill (Academy '32), had more than an academic interest. His brother, Lieutenant Commander Robert R. Craighill (Academy '30), was on the *Vincennes.*

On the bridge of the *Blue* it was decided to keep station, as per orders, until instructed otherwise. One or more aircraft were noted overhead, flashing red and white lights which were assumed to be signals of some kind. For thirty minutes the firing was intense, but around

2:15 it suddenly ceased, and just about this time the *Blue's* attention was diverted. For the *Blue,* which had missed the entire enemy fleet going by, had sighted a tiny schooner to the south, going east along the Guadalcanal coast. The destroyer overhauled the boat and passed close aboard. She seemed to be a typical native inter-island craft, and harmless, and she was passed without hailing.

Just before 3:00 A.M. another ship was sighted, and an exchange of blinker tube signals showed her to be the destroyer *Jarvis,* outward bound. Seriously damaged in the air attacks the previous day, she was limping along at 8 knots, trailing a long slick of oil. Turner had ordered Lieutenant Commander William W. Graham, who once had served under Captain Bode on the *Chicago,* to wait for an escort and depart via the east channel. Apparently Graham never received these orders and was now departing alone, by the west channel, heading for Sydney and the destroyer tender *Dobbin.* Commander Williams blinked out that the *Jarvis* was trailing oil, and Lieutenant Commander Graham replied that he knew it.

"Are you all right?" the *Blue* asked, and the *Jarvis* replied, "Affirmative." She was never seen again.

The *Blue* resumed patrol. Her report summed up the night's activities: "This vessel took no offensive measures, inflicted no damage to enemy and sustained no loss or damage." No hits, no runs, one error.

The *Bagley,* unscathed in her brief brush with the Japanese force, steamed eastward as the enemy raced northward. Approaching Admiral Crutchley's position, the *Bagley* heard his order to rendezvous. Unable to make out the position given, Commander Sinclair ordered the *Bagley* to head for the position given in pre-battle instructions and turned directly away from the *Australia*. The *Patterson*, the other destroyer of the Southern Force, did not hear the admiral's order and remained in the area of the battle.

In the Northern Force, the destroyer *Helm*, Lieutenant Commander Chester E. Carroll, had very bad luck. Ostensibly guarding the port flank of cruisers, she missed the entire battle. Lying somewhere between the Northern and Southern Forces, she was passed by the enemy at such great speed that she never found a solid target. Churning about hopefully, she fired only 4 rounds from her 5-inch batteries, and none of her torpedoes.

The *Wilson*, Lieutenant Commander Walter H. Price, had better luck, despite a somewhat humorous start (the hands fell off the clock on the bridge when she fired her first salvo). Nevertheless she began firing enthusiastically at 1:49 A.M., upon seeing the first of 3 large searchlights. She picked the one farthest to the right and opened at 12,000 yards, firing southward over her own cruisers. Maneuvering to keep her batteries unmasked and avoid other ships, she fired steadily until 2:06 A.M., getting off 212 rounds of 5-inch. Her enthusiasm was commendable, but the battle seemed extremely confused to her and it is not known whether any hits were scored. In one tense moment she nearly collided with the *Helm*, Lieutenant Commander Price ringing up 30 knots and swinging the *Wilson* hard left to avoid a crash.

Both the *Helm* and the *Wilson* heard the call from Crutchley, and they too bore off in the wrong direction, passing entirely around Savo Island to the south and winding up far out in left field. There they stayed until 5:35 A.M., when ordered back.

The *Bagley,* somewhere in the same area, became curious long before that and started back for the battle area. It was then she found the burning *Astoria,* about 4 A.M., and commenced rescue operations.

During the battle some of the transports had gotten under way, without orders, churning about in the dark and narrow waters. Only the most skillful ship-handling and a full measure of luck averted collisions, but for a while the night near the beachheads was full of eerie shapes, moving in and out of the gloom. On one occasion a great ship loomed out of the night and trained her guns on the *Hopkins.* Commander William H. Hartt, Jr., commanding the mine-sweeper group from the *Hopkins'* bridge, grabbed the transmitter from his phone talker and barked out: "This is Hartt; for Christ's sake *don't.*" The other ship bore off into the night.

During the evening of August 8, Admiral Fletcher's carriers steamed steadily southeastward, away from Guadalcanal, and by early on the morning of the ninth, about the time the battle opened, were nearly abreast the far end of San Cristobal Island. Fletcher paused here a few hours, making a dog-leg turn to the right, and when still no word had come from Admiral Ghormley turned his task force back toward Guadalcanal. It is not clear what Fletcher had in mind, but at least he knew something was going on at the beachhead. Admiral Turner had radioed him: "Surface attack on screen, co-ordinated with use of aircraft flares. *Chicago* hit by torpedo, *Canberra* on fire."

Captain Forrest Sherman of the *Wasp* had an air group especially trained in night operations. He asked Rear Admiral Noyes, commander of the air-support group, who was on his carrier, for permission to use it. Captain Sherman suggested that his carrier and a few destroyers continue northwestward at high speed to help Turner. At the worst his planes might catch the Japanese homeward bound. Had Sherman known it, this was Admiral Mikawa's greatest fear of the night, but the Japanese commander could have relaxed. Admiral Noyes said no, three times, and refused even to forward the request to Admiral Fletcher.

As for the latter, word finally came through from Ghormley at 3:30 A.M.—permission to retire granted. (Admiral Ghormley wrote later: "When Fletcher, the man on the spot, informed me he had to withdraw for fuel, I approved. He knew his situation in detail; I did not.") With permission granted, Fletcher hesitated no more. He turned southeastward again and steamed on all that day and until Monday afternoon, when he met his tankers off northern New Caledonia. Thus the Japanese escaped air harassment before the battle, during the battle, and after the battle.

The battle had, in fact, gone miraculously well for Mikawa. As he rounded the northwestward curve passing out of action, the Japanese admiral could count the following damage:

Shell splinters from a near miss by the *Chicago* had wounded two men on the *Tenryu* about 1:51. The *Kinu-*

gasa had been hit in the starboard side near the water line, probably by the *Patterson*, at 1:56, flooding a storeroom. A second hit later by the *Vincennes'* second salvo had damaged the port steering control room, but she was by no means severely damaged and had suffered 1 killed and 1 wounded.

The *Aoba* had taken a hit in a torpedo-tube nest, burning it out, but the fire was quickly controlled. The only serious hit was that suffered by the flagship, *Chokai*. She was struck at 2:05 A.M. by 3 shells from the *Quincy's* main battery. Two of them struck in flag plot, killing 34 men and wounding 48, and burning all her charts. The other struck near the aviation crane. Had the 2 shells that hit flag plot landed 15 feet forward, Admiral Mikawa and his staff might well have been wiped out. This would have been a severe personal blow, but would hardly have affected the outcome of the battle.

As Admiral Mikawa drew away from the Northern Force, he ordered firing ceased at 2:15 A.M., and he was now faced with the decision whether to continue the battle or withdraw. The discussion with his staff was brief. There was no doubt that the transports now offered a tempting target. Against this was the fact that the Japanese force was in bad disorder (the *Chokai* had wound up the battle in the rear of the formation, instead of at the head); charts had been destroyed; dawn was not far off and American planes would certainly attack with vigor while he himself had no air cover. Captain Kenkichi Kato, executive officer of the *Chokai*, was among those in favor of returning. The American cruiser screen had been badly damaged, the transports awaited, he argued. Admiral Mikawa hesitated. It was a tempting prospect, but there was too much against it. At first light he could be found by Fletcher's planes, found and slaughtered. At 2:23 A.M. Admiral Mikawa gave the order: "All forces withdraw."

The decision was wise, in the Japanese view. It was now nearly 2:30 A.M. Mikawa had smashed the American force in accord with the Japanese Navy's doctrine of "decisive battle." His own force was scattered and would take some time to reassemble; daylight would be here soon. American carriers were 100 miles south of Guadalcanal. Their planes would certainly be out at dawn in pursuit. Only by leaving now would Mikawa have a chance of getting away. In addition, his forces, though virtually unscathed, had been through a major engagement in which the main batteries had fired 1,020 rounds and launched 61 torpedoes. He would withdraw.

In the future years there was frequent assertion by American authorities that Mikawa had come to get the transports, had left without them, thus this was an American victory. It was extreme good fortune that the defenseless transports were not molested, but the fact is Mikawa did not come only to get the transports. He came as a fighting force to smash the enemy's fighting force, and that he did. As to the American carrier forces, which weighed very heavily in his deliberations, he could not possibly have guessed that they had fled the field. He would have been foolhardy to make any such assumption. Mikawa was not concerned with the American ground forces; his Army advised him they would take care of the U.S. Marines. So the *Chokai* blinked out: "Force in line ahead, course 320, speed 30 knots."

There was one more matter to be settled on the way out; the *Ralph Talbot* stood in the way. After giving warning a few minutes before midnight of planes over Savo, the destroyer had, like the *Blue,* continued patrolling her assigned channel. Off to the southeast she had watched the pyrotechnics with interest, though with no full appreciation of the great battle in progress. But at 2:17 her turn came. As the *Yubari* came out of the main action, followed by the *Tenryu* and the *Furutaka,* her searchlight stabbed out and pinned the *Ralph Talbot.* The Japanese opened fire at 7,000 yards and the first salvo was short.

Lieutenant Commander Callahan, noting green dye splashes, believed they were friendly forces. (It seemed that no one this night could quite comprehend that an enemy juggernaut was loose in its midst.) Callahan ordered flank speed and zigzagged off to the northwest, crying out on his TBS, "You are firing on Jimmy. You are firing on Jimmy." He turned on his masthead recognition lights, merely whetting Captain Masami Ban's appetite, and the *Yubari* obligingly stepped up its fire. The second salvo was over, but on the third he had the range and fired 8 more salvos, 2 of them hitting the wildly maneuvering *Talbot.*

One shell hit the No. 1 torpedo tube, killing 1 man and blowing another overboard. Another exploded inside the wardroom, killing the doctor, Lieutenant E. N. Kveton, and an enlisted man he was treating. One moment the sailor was sitting in the captain's chair while the doctor bent over him, cutting away his shoe. The next, in a bright orange flash, they disappeared in a burning room.

The *Ralph Talbot* got off 4 torpedoes; all missed. Still another Japanese shell hit 5-inch gun mount No. 4, blasting the crew. For Coxswain W. B. Cobb luck had run out. He had been blown overboard from the *Mugford* when the destroyer was hit by a Japanse dive bomber two days before. Rescued by the *Ralph Talbot,* Cobb volunteered as first loader on her No. 4 gun. Again he was blown overboard, and this time he did not come back. Other Japanese shells found the destroyer, one holing her below the water line, and only a rain squall, mercifully closing in, saved the *Ralph Talbot* from a pounding as terrible as the cruisers got. Abruptly, the battle was over, and the *Ralph Talbot,* in flames and listing badly, was dead in the water. The Japanese juggernaut raced on, homeward bound, picking up the *Yunagi* as she came around the west side of Savo Island.

The Imperial Japanese Navy's doctrine of the slashing night attack had been executed with brilliance, courage, and élan. It remained to be seen if the second phase of that doctrine—the daytime follow-up, with now superior forces—would be executed.

chapter
20

By 3:00 A.M., more than 1,000 men were in the water, mostly from the *Vincennes* and the *Quincy,* beginning a second struggle for survival. Free now from the terrible shelling and fire aboard their ships, they faced dangers, real and imaginary, which to many of them were worse than those they had faced aboard ship.

Some were wounded or dying, others in deep shock and thus immune from further suffering, but many were unscathed, miraculously, or with minor cuts or burns they had not yet taken account of. Real fears included sharks, numerous in these waters, and being run down by vessels in the dark or blasted by depth charges from destroyers hunting submarines. The imaginary fears, far worse, lay in the unknown, for all the dark and unidentified shapes in these mysterious waters might be Japanese, with trigger fingers ready to machine-gun survivors. Or worse, take them prisoner. The land held no promise, for Savo Island had never been penetrated and might be full of savages, Japanese or native, while Guadalcanal and the Florida group were in confused battle with no firm lines drawn.

The *Quincy* went down with a hiss and a rumble as the sea quenched her fires, and in the oil and debris around her perhaps 600 men struggled for survival. With the great light of the fires gone there was only blackness and shouting, whistles shrilling, and here and there a flashlight beam. But all noise stopped quickly, the lights went out, and the whistles were stilled as officers and CPO's took charge of little knots of men. It was dangerous to give away position while the seas might still be hostile and a whistle or a light might bring not rescue but death or capture. From then on the only noise was depth charges as the destroyers chased "sub contacts," or rifle and machine-gun fire as the destroyermen fought off sharks or what passed for sharks. A lot of unsuspecting ammunitions cans got sunk that night.

Lieutenant Commander Andrew assembled around him a nest of rafts and nets containing 75 to 100 men, including Lieutenant Commander Bierer, Lieutenant McElligott, and Ensign Cohen, the latter already beginning a night of heroic acts outstanding on a night when such deeds were commonplace. On one trip he swam away and came back with Lieutenant (j.g.) Robert M. Jacobs, the 3rd Division Officer, and on another he brought in Lieutenant James C. Smith, Jr., A Division Officer, and 3 men. Time after time during the dark hours he left the security of the nets to swim into the night when a shout or a moan identified a shipmate in trouble.

Off to the west the *Vincennes* blazed for ten minutes or more and then she was gone, but in the south the *Astoria* burned with great fury, her ammunition exploding through the night in a spectacular display of fireworks, and many of the *Quincy* men feared they would drift down into this holocaust. Discipline, however, was established early in most groups, generally by an officer or senior enlisted man, and here and there smart cracks testified to the American capacity for humor under any circumstances.

A petty officer called out to a fireman, "Hey, Mack, you can't go on liberty without dress blues," and another shouted, "Where's your liberty pass?"

"Remember that ten bucks you owe me? Well, forget it."

But there were grim times, too. Chief Boatswain's Mate G. J. Strobel did what he could for Seaman Second Class Samuel A. Blaser, whose back had been punctured by a shell fragment. Blaser, with wonderful courage and determination to survive, talked quietly through the night of his mother, and Strobel talked with him and attempted to tend his wound. Just before dawn Strobel got him aboard the *Ellet,* but he died within an hour and was buried at sea the next day from the *American Legion.*

Lieutenant Rieve took charge of 15 men in his group of rafts and nets. Chief Signalman Szoka, in charge of 3 nets, saw a destroyer approach, but would let his men give no sign until the vessel blinked out, "Are you drifting?" He flashed back, "Three *Quincy* nets with wounded," and the *Ellet* picked them up, shortly before dawn.

Ensign H. I. Hill, Jr., just out of Annapolis, gave his life jacket to a man who had none, and the rest of the night swam ahead towing a raft. Lieutenant (j. g.) H. W. Smith, an aviator, signaled a destroyer when dawn disclosed it as friendly, and again the *Ellet* came to the rescue. Lieutenant Donald R. Levy swam to meet it and pointed out a raft containing many wounded. A sailor from the *Ellet* dived overboard and carried a line to the raft, so those men might be picked up first.

Chief Water Tender Earl O. Spalding, weak from wounds, asked Fireman Second Class William H. Stolz to stay with him during the night, and acknowledged later he could not have survived without Stolz's help. Lieutenant Clarke noted his binoculars were dragging his head down and slipped them off and let them sink. He swam to a screaming man, fought with him, and finally wrapped him in his own life jacket and quieted him. Later he climbed on a raft, rallied a group about him, and near dawn allowed one of his men to signal a destroyer. "DD 398," the ship replied, and sent over a boat; it was the *Ellet* again, and Lieutenant Clarke went to the bridge to lend a hand while one of his quartermasters took the wheel and a signalman took the watch on the signal bridge.

Storekeeper Second Class William Metz of the *Quincy* found himself in the *Ellet's* engine room.

"Where were you guys last night?" he asked a fireman, and the fireman replied, "Right here watching the whole thing, but we couldn't tell who was who."

Lieutenant Hopkins and a small group were determinedly paddling toward Savo Island, ready to take their chances, when the *Ellet* came by to retrieve them. Lieutenant Ordway had the same idea, swimming with Chief Radioman Ellsworth D. Miller, who helped him support wounded Signalman Third Class Leonard A. Joslin. Along the route they found a floater net, still tightly tied in a bundle, and finally got it open. They put Joslin in the net, along with a badly wounded *Astoria* man (how he got out toward Savo nobody knew), and held them up until rescue came.

Boatswain's Mate First Class H. L. Berg, in a web of floater nets, cans, and wood, rode herd on 30 men, including one with a foot nearly torn off and another with a broken leg and with bad burns on his hands. Fighting started around the rim, and Berg finally swung a board over his head shouting, "I'll kill the first bastard who causes trouble." They quieted down then, and Berg held them together until the *Wilson* picked them up at 8:45 A.M.

A sailor swam up to one group, towing a body in a life jacket and calling, "Is there a doctor in the house?" Dr. Forbes responded and pronounced the man dead. "Thanks," said the sailor, "I wanted his life jacket," and began picking out the knots of the tie strings. With great good cheer, he freed the body, which sank, and wrapped the kapok around himself. Chief Radio Electrician Daniel, of a philosophical bent, witnessed the occurrence and in later years told of it many times with a sardonic smile.

Between dawn and 10:30 A.M., the *Wilson* and the

Ellet picked up several hundred men from the *Quincy.* The able-bodied were taken off to the crew's quarters for rest and a shower, clothes, coffee, and a cigarette. The wounded went to the wardroom until there was no more space, and then into offices and cabins or anywhere they could rest until a doctor or pharmacists mates could get to them. Burns and noncritical shrapnel wounds were most numerous, but there were also amputations, broken limbs, severe bleeding, skull injuries, and internal damage for 1, or sometimes 2, doctors, who moved without pause from one emergency to another. In the background some corpsmen performed medical miracles without benefit of license.

The *Vincennes* men were succored mainly by the *Mugford,* which swept up more than 400 men from the water, and the *Helm,* which rescued over 170.

When the *Vincennes* was near the end, Captain Riefkohl told those around him, "Pass the word to stand by to abandon ship," and they called it out for anyone who might hear. He sent his chief yeoman, Leonard E. Stucker, aft and his Marine orderly, Corporal James L. Patrick, forward with the word. Earlier he had sent a messenger to the engine room with the message for Lieutenant Commander Bisson to "get his people out if he can give us no power," and a similar message was sent to Damage Control. In both cases events were marching too fast for compliance, and neither the engineering officer, Lieutenant Commander John K. Bisson, nor the damage-control officer, Commander Raymond A. Hansen, survived.

In the moments left to him Captain Riefkohl looked about. The bridge was frightfully torn by shellfire, the charthouse was wrecked, and his emergency cabin a shambles. He climbed to the gun deck, and Stucker and Patrick reappeared. Together they were washed over the side from the No. 4 gun. They came upon a raft quickly, and in it was the Negro mess attendant, Morgan C. Sykes, who had survived the operating-room blast, still holding his smashed jaw together with one hand. Through the night he used his other hand to assist where he could.

Captain Riefkohl left his raft and swam to nearby groups reassuring the men and offering help where possible. He found no hysteria and gave orders to bring the rafts and groups together. The captain first considered paddling toward Savo, thought better of it, and told the men to remain quiet and await developments. The *Mugford* and the *Ellet* came by soon after dawn, but dashed away to chase a sub report, leaving their boats behind.

If all the reports could be believed, Savo Sound was jammed with submarines that morning, and the blast of depth charges rocked the harbor throughout the night. In fact, there was no submarine within a hundred miles, Japanese or American.

Commander Mullan, the *Vincennes'* executive officer, was placed in a boat, along with 3 enlisted men, all of them seriously wounded, and finally the *Helm* arrived, back from her false rendezvous. By 9:00 A.M. most of the swimmers were safe aboard ship, Captain Riefkohl being picked up about 8:30 A.M. by the *Mugford*. Last man to leave his raft was Sykes, still holding his jaw. But, as with the *Quincy*, there were many men missing, and among them the captain's orderly, Corporal Patrick. Riefkohl had seen him in the water and believed him unhurt, but others said later he had internal injuries.

Among the Academy men who perished were Commander Hansen ('22), Lieutenant Commander Miller ('29), Lieutenant Commander Bisson ('30), Lieutenant Irving G. McCann, Jr. ('35), Lieutenant (j.g.) Raymond J. Murray ('40), Ensign Alexander Butsko, who graduated twelve days after Pearl Harbor, and Ensign Arthur Diirck, exactly one month out of Annapolis. There were many others, too, who had long called the *Vincennes* home. Machinist Edward W. ("Pops") Forster, aboard since the vessel was launched, was rescued by the *Mugford,* died on the transport *Barnett,* and was buried at sea. He had planned to retire in 1940, but the war had kept him on and claimed him, at fifty-seven. Machinist Simon L. Sersain, twenty-five years at sea, was not seen again, and many young reserves went with him, including Lieutenant (j.g.) Victor J. Fama, twenty-six, remembered as the ship's chess and checker champion; Lieutenant (j.g.) James B. Ginty, twenty-six, an accountant from Holy Cross, leaving a son he had never seen; and Ensign John Wahl, twenty-seven, who, recalling the tyranny his parents had known in Europe, had written his young nephew, "I am here so you will not have to put on a uniform."

Three Marine aviators, aboard to fly over the beaches as gun spotters, gave their lives instead on the *Vincennes.* Second Lieutenant Carl I. Schuessler, twenty-five, of Columbus, Georgia, a Sewanne graduate who had gone on to an Episcopal seminary, was last seen firing a machine gun from his plane on a catapult. Dying with him were Second Lieutenant William P. Kirby, twenty-six, of Emmett, Idaho, and Second Lieutenant Jay C. Griffith, twenty-one, a Dartmouth man from North Brookfield, Massachusetts.

Of the 24 Negroes aboard the *Vincennes,* 9 perished.

The top command of the *Quincy* was taken by death when the shells smashed through the bridge early in the engagement. Captain Moore ('13), was mortally wounded, and his executive officer, Commander William C. Gray ('21), was killed outright. The navigator, Lieutenant Commander Edward C. Metcalfe, and the damage-control officer, Lieutenant Commander Raymond H. Tuttle (both '22), perished with another classmate, Lieutenant Commander Elmore, the engineering officer.

In all, this terrible night claimed 370 officers and men from the *Quincy.*

chapter
21

The fight to save the *Astoria* began about daylight when the *Bagley* returned to the burning hulk and placed her bow to the stern of the cruiser. Captain Greenman jumped to the deck of his vessel and was greeted by his executive officer, Commander Shoup.

"I think we can save her," Shoup said, and the engineering officer, Lieutenant Commander Hayes, backed him up. The list of 3 degrees to port had not increased in three hours. Hayes said he had been able to enter the after engine room and No. 4 fireroom, and if he could get some power to work the fuel and feed pumps he might get up steam.

Captain Greenman ordered a special party of about 300 selected from his men in the *Bagley*, including electricians, ship fitters, water tenders, and other specialists.

Every *Astoria* officer who was able volunteered. All other survivors were placed in the *Bagley*, which backed off and departed to take them to the *President Jackson*. It was 6:00 A.M. and time for the effort to save the ship.

The fires, except those in the wardroom area amidships, were subsiding, and by climbing over the wreckage on the gun deck it was now possible to reach the forward part of the ship. Men were put to work here with buckets and ammunition cans to attack the fire. The handy-billy pump, rigged on a raft alongside the ship, was started up again.

Lieutenant Commander Topper, the damage-control officer, took a party below and they picked their way through dark and torn compartments, their battle lanterns shining eerily in the smoking and blackened interior.

Working from the bow, fire amidships kept them from going farther aft than Turret I, but from the stern they were able to work forward to No. 1 fireroom. Three 8-inch shells had holed the hull, just above the water line: one near the hangar, another below the galley, and a third at No. 1 fireroom. The latter 2 had torn through the second deck, 1 making a hole 4 feet in diameter. There were many smaller holes, but the 3 big ones could mean trouble; if the ship heeled even a little, more water could pour unchecked into the engineering spaces and fill the hull fatally.

Lieutenant Commander Hayes reported he could make steam only in No. 4 fireroom; Nos 1 and 2 were cut off by fire, and the uptakes for No. 3 had been ruptured.

It would be a desperate, almost hopeless, gamble, but Captain Greenman decided to make the try.

Lieutenant Commander Benjamin Coe brought his destroyer, the *Hopkins,* near about 7:00 A.M. and asked if he could be of assistance. Greenman said he would like to try to ground the *Astoria* in the shallow water near Guadalcanal. If they could make it, it would be easier to fight fires and those gaping holes near the water line might be kept above water. Coe agreed to make the try, but with misgivings. The *Astoria* was six times the size of his *Hopkins,* and was afire, listing, and dead in the water.

The *Hopkins,* a World War I four-stacker, backed down on the *Astoria,* stern to stern. Hose and another handy-billy pump were passed over to help in the battle against the flames. A power cable was also found, to be spliced into the *Astoria's* electrical system, but it turned out to be useless for it was 120 volts against the *Astoria's* 240-volt system.

The towing cable was made fast at both ends, and Coe sent his executive officer to the *Hopkins'* fantail to telephone reports to the bridge. The destroyer began to move forward slowly, the cable tautened, and it seemed the *Astoria* would begin to move. But the *Hopkins'* towing cleat, welded to the deck, began to tear away from the vast weight of the water-logged cruiser.

The *Hopkins* backed in again, and this time the cable was passed around the destroyer's after deckhouse and shackled back on itself. If anything went now it would be the whole deckhouse. The *Hopkins* took up the slack again and began to apply power. The battered old cruiser, burning like a firepot, began to move and a cheer went up from her decks. Coe crossed his fingers and rang for more power. The cable held, the deckhouse held, and the *Hopkins'* screws beat the water to a fury. Slowly, very slowly, the tow picked up speed, from 1 knot to 2, then 3. Minutes passed and the *Astoria* men began to take heart.

Salvage parties below decks had nearly finished their work, plugging the big holes with mattresses shored with heavy timbers. These patches would never hold in heavy seas or against severe water pressure, but the sea was calm and if they could reach shallow water there was still a chance. Greenman was encouraged enough to have the *Hopkins* radio Admiral Turner that if he could get power for the fire pumps he might yet save the *Astoria*.

Turner ordered the *Wilson* over and she came alongside the starboard bow and pumped water on the fires for about an hour. But around noon both the *Wilson* and *Hopkins* were ordered away. The *Wilson* went off to transfer her more than 200 survivors to the *Hunter Liggett* in the transport area, and the *Hopkins* to rejoin her group, for they were forming up for the flight from the beachhead. The *Buchanan*, a new *Bristol*-class destroyer, arrived about 11:30 A.M. to relieve the *Wilson* in fire fighting, and Captain Greenman was told the transport *Alchiba* (ex-*Mormacdove*) would be sent to tow.

But time was running out. The list had been increasing slowly, despite the best efforts of Lieutenant Commander Topper and his men working below to plug holes. Fires still raged amidships, and shells exploded frequently. About 11:00 A.M. a very heavy blast was heard below, apparently aft of Turret II, and sickly yellow gas bubbles came to the surface on the port side near the magazines.

Topper ordered his men out from below, and went aft to confer with Captain Greenman. Climbing over the gun deck he looked down at a mark he had put on the hull; the list had increased 12 inches.

As he reached the fantail the list was increasing even more rapidly, and from below came the unmistakable rumbling of bulkheads collapsing. Commander Shoup was there and he, too, told the captain that it was time to go. There was no question of it; the vessel was heeling rapidly, and they all knew that the port side patches had given way. Greenman ordered the *Buchanan* aft to pick up his salvage parties, but even before she got there men were spilling off the deck, now canted 30 degrees. At this moment the *Buchanan* was ordered away to chase yet another sub "contact." She put over her 2 boats and threw rafts into the water for the *Astoria* men before departing, and the *Alchiba,* steaming in close, took over the rescue operations.

Greenman called out the fateful words, "Abandon ship!" and all hands still aboard went over the side. Most of them made it to the *Buchanan's* boats standing about 300 yards off; the *Alchiba* picked up the rest. In the tradition of the sea, the captain was the last to go, following Commander Shoup from the vessel, which now had a list of 45 degrees. The *Astoria* turned on her port beam, settled slightly by the stern, and quietly sank at 12:15 P.M., last of the 4 cruisers to go.

The *Canberra's* fate had been settled as early as 5:00 A.M. by a dispatch from Admiral Turner: the *Canberra* must either be ready to join him at 6:30 A.M. for the flight from Guadalcanal, or she must be destroyed. Since she was dead in the water and burning fiercely, this left no choice. Commander Walsh, executive officer, commanding in lieu of his mortally wounded captain, ordered the vessel abandoned.

The *Patterson* had been alongside since shortly after 3:00 A.M., on orders of Captain Bode of the *Chicago*, fighting fire and aiding the wounded. At 5:15 A.M., Commander Walsh having made his decision, Commander Walker of the *Patterson* called in the *Blue* to help evacuate the cruiser. In light rain, with visibility under 1 mile, the *Blue* steamed slowly in, her boats out to pick up men already forced into the water. The cruiser, listing 15 degrees, was burning smartly amidships.

A few moments after calling in the *Blue*, and before she arrived, the *Patterson's* lookouts reported "strange ship on the port quarter." The *Patterson* immediately challenged this vessel with the blinker tube recognition signal, but there was no answer. Commander Walker cast off his lines and pulled away from the *Canberra*, prepared for battle with the new intruder. The last strange drama of this weird night was about to be enacted.

The *Patterson* challenged twice again, with still no reply, and then snapped on her searchlight. The other vessel instantly opened fire on the *Patterson*, and Commander Walker ordered his 5-inch batteries to reply. Poor marksmanship paid off for once, for the other vessel was the *Chicago*, badly shaken by the night's events and now obviously on a hair trigger. Her 5-inch guns Nos. 1 and 3 on the starboard side, belatedly assuming that any strange vessels must be enemy, had opened fire without orders. The officer in charge immediately ordered cease fire, but

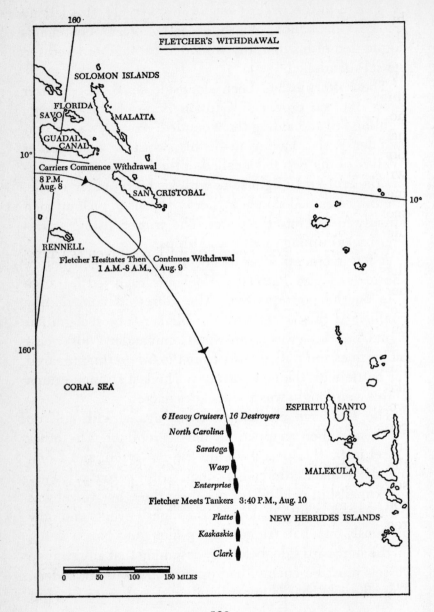

FLETCHER'S WITHDRAWAL

160

SOLOMON ISLANDS

FLORIDA
SAVO
GUADAL
CANAL

MALAITA

10°

Carriers Commence Withdrawal

8 P.M.
Aug. 8

SAN CRISTOBAL

10°

RENNELL

Fletcher Hesitates Then Continues Withdrawal
1 A.M.-8 A.M.,   Aug. 9

160°

CORAL SEA

ESPIRITU SANTO

6 Heavy Cruisers 16 Destroyers
North Carolina
Saratoga
Wasp
Enterprise

MALEKULA

Fletcher Meets Tankers 3:40 P.M., Aug. 10

Platte
Kaskaskia
Clark

NEW HEBRIDES ISLANDS

0   50   100   150 MILES

192

by this time the *Patterson* was already replying. With this, the *Chicago* resumed fire with both 5-inch and 1.1-guns.

Just as a serious engagement loomed, Commander Walker had misgivings. His searchlight, in the bad visibility, revealed something familiar in his opponent's silhouette, and he ordered cease fire, after his 5-inch guns had shot off 3 salvos. He flashed the emergency recognition signal and although, to Captain Bode, it was the wrong one, the *Chicago's* skipper also ordered cease firing. The battle of friendly forces was over, with no hits scored on either side. It seemed a fitting epitaph to a night of confusion.

The truculent *Patterson*, first to have given warning that night of enemy ships in the harbor, now returned to her job of clearing the *Canberra* for destruction. The *Blue* tied up on the port side of the cruiser and the *Patterson* on the starboard.

The *Canberra's* seamen, many wearing pajamas and thus a strange sight to American sailors who slept in their skivvies, refused at first to leave their vessel until the wounded were taken off. This being the natural procedure anyway, the burned and maimed Australians were trundled over the rails into the American destroyers, and the able-bodied followed. The *Patterson* took aboard some 400, including about 100 wounded; the *Blue* took some from the stern and then shifted to the bow to receive more. Just before 7:00 A.M. the vessel was cleared and the destroyers moved off to deliver the refugees to the transports, the *Patterson* taking hers to the *Barnett* and the *Blue* unloading onto the *Fuller*.

The way was now clear to execute Turner's order to

destroy the *Canberra,* and the destroyers moved in for the coup de grace. But even this was not easy. The *Selfridge* fired 263 rounds of 5-inch shells into the burning ship and the *Ellet* added 105 more, and still she was afloat. The *Selfridge's* faulty torpedoes either refused to explode on contact or erratically avoided the hulk, one exploding 5,000 yards beyond her. Finally one from the *Ellet* struck home and shortly after 8:00 A.M. the *Canberra* sank. Many an Aussie cried as she went down.

One more cripple, the *Ralph Talbot,* remained in need of help, but no one knew it, or even knew where she was. Dead in the water and with her radio room shot away, the destroyer drifted west of Savo Island, out of view of the rest of the fleet. At one point the *Talbot* sighted a four-stacker and ran up a distress signal on the flag hoist; no response. Already listing 20 degrees, the *Ralph Talbot* seemed in bad shape and at one point the order, "Stand by to abandon ship!" was given, misinterpreted by some hands to mean "abandon ship." But Lieutenant Commander Callahan had no such thing in mind—he had decided his vessel could be saved and he meant to do it.

At least twice the communications officer, Lieutenant (j.g.) John F. Adams, a Reserve from Buffalo, New York, asked permission to destroy the confidential publications, and each time Lieutenant Commander Callahan refused. He learned with surprise that someone had given the order to "Secure and abandon No. 2 fireroom"; he countermanded it immediately, and ordered the men back to "get up steam right away."

With Dr. Kveton and his chief pharmacist's mate among the 12 men killed, Pharmacist's Mate Second Class

Leonard A. Peppler took over treatment of the 23 wounded aboard. Overnight he changed from a boy of twenty to a man. He set up emergency sick bay in the crew's washroom, already awash, and worked with his supplies floating in buckets. His skill and courage that night later jumped him from second class to chief pharmacist's mate, certainly one of the Navy's youngest chiefs.

As in all other ships, aboard the *Ralph Talbot* fire was the first problem, and Lieutenant Richard D. Shepard, the gunnery officer, took charge of that. Handy-billys were rigged and bucket brigades formed to fight the main blaze in the topside pyrotechnics locker. The men pitched in and in short order the blazes were out. Before dawn the vessel could raise a little steam and Lieutenant Commander Callahan made plans to put her in shallow water off the west coast of Savo, to see if the underwater hole could be plugged. As the vessel crept in toward shore, the executive officer, Lieutenant Commander Roy A. Newton, moved off ahead in the small boat taking soundings to guide Callahan in.

A few hundred yards from shore (for all they knew a hostile shore), the *Ralph Talbot* came to a stop. Lieutenant Shepard, diving over the side for a survey, found a jagged hole about 4 feet square, which he believed could be patched.

In order to reduce the list and bring the hole nearer the surface, making it easier to work on, Callahan ordered the torpedo tubes on that side jettisoned. Lieutenant Commander Newton took charge of cutting away the 2 starboard quadruple torpedo mounts, and they went over the side with great splashes, reducing the list to 10 degrees.

It was light now, the rain had stopped, and the hole in the hull was easily visible from deck.

Using timbers and mattresses (including one stuffed with a sailor's hard-earned money; he got it back later), a Spanish windlass patch was fashioned on deck. Lieutenant Shepard took charge of fixing it in place, aided by Lieutenant (j.g.) Milton L. Jarrett, Jr., who had had the bridge watch since midnight without relief; Lieutenant (j.g.) Russell E. Walton, a Reserve and damage-control officer, and Carpenter's Mate First Class S. E. Baker, were invaluable in designing and placing the patch.

About 11:00 A.M. the *Selfridge,* with Captain Flynn aboard, nosed around the northern end of Savo Island, looking for the *Ralph Talbot,* the last lost chicken in Destroyer Squadron 4. Captain Flynn sent the *Selfridge's* doctor aboard to help with the wounded, and asked what other assistance he could render. Thank you, said Lieutenant Commander Callahan, but he believed he would soon be under way, and he was. At 12.10 P.M. he rang the engine room and the *Ralph Talbot* set off at 15 knots to rejoin the fleet.

The plight of Admiral Crutchley during this very odd night was moving. He could never find out what was going on.

He had had no luck at all during the battle, and at 3:15 A.M. he had radioed to ask the condition of his sister ship, the *Canberra.*

But the *Patterson* replied, saying, "Disabled on fire in position 7 miles southeast of Savo Island." The Admiral didn't know if this referred to the *Patterson* or the *Canberra.* Twenty-five minutes later he overheard the *Self-*

ridge report that destroyers were concentrated in position 5 miles northwest of Savo Island. This was exactly what he had *not* meant by his order to form a screen on him.

The bad news piled in fast now. At 3:44 A.M. the *Chicago* reported that she was standing in for the transport area, adding, "Believe bulkheads will hold against high speed." At 4:10 the *Patterson* reported "*Canberra* is out of commission," and at 5:15 the *Ralph Talbot,* able to make one radio work, reported "badly damaged near northwest shore of Savo Island."

Ten minutes later Crutchley heard the *Patterson* tell Admiral Turner, "*Canberra* is abandoning ship. Have entire crew aboard. Will destroy her." At 5:30 Admiral Crutchley saw gunfire south of Savo Island, but was spared the knowledge that his own cruiser *Chicago* and destroyer *Patterson* were banging away at each other.

At 5:47 he sent perhaps the most forlorn message of them all. Directed to all his vessels it said: "Situation obscure. Be prepared to give battle at dawn in vicinity of transport groups." Admiral Mikawa and his force were already far up the Slot, making over 30 knots for Rabaul, running from Fletcher's planes, which in turn were moving away from him.

From then on Admiral Crutchley heard nothing to cheer him:

6:22 from the *Chicago:* "Standing by *Canberra.* Have ordered *Blue* alongside to take off remaining 400 men."

6:44 from the *Selfridge:* "American *Astoria* in flames, position 09.07 south, 159.47 east. Four dog dogs [destroyers] picking up many survivors."

6:48 from the *Chicago:* "*Blue, Selfridge, Patterson*

standing by *Canberra*. Am proceeding to concentration area."

8:30 from the *Selfridge: "Canberra* is sunk."

A few minutes before the last message Admiral Crutchley had reported to Admiral Turner that he was "unable to get *Vincennes* or *Quincy* by radio." Both had sunk some six hours before, a few miles away. It was broad daylight now, of a Sunday morning, the water was still dotted with survivors from his smashed cruiser force and the battle to save the *Astoria* was in full swing. Admiral Crutchley reported to Turner that he had "no real information of the night battle." It was a sad Sunday morning.

chapter
22

Admiral Turner's plan to withdraw from the area shortly after dawn was manifestly impossible. At that hour the *Astoria* and the *Canberra* were still afloat and burning, hundreds of men were still struggling in the water, and more supplies simply had to be landed for the Marines.

As the black waters of Savo Sound grew light, the true magnitude of the night's devastation was revealed. The destroyer men could see great patches of oil and islands of debris, shattered timbers and furniture, nets, line, rafts, clothes, ammunition cans, spars, mattresses, wood gratings, potato sacks, and other flotsam spread across the sea where once there had been ships. And twined in all this refuse of violent destruction were men—here one, there a dozen—many living, many suffering, and some dying or dead.

With urgency, yet with great care not to run down their fellow sailors, the destroyers moved about, scooping men from the sea with small boats, lines thrown from deck, or cargo nets strung from the gunwales. Sailors, officers and men, dived into the water to support and guide the shipwrecked to the sides of rescuing vessels, and strong arms reached down to hoist survivors aboard. In every destroyer, crowded ships at best, the wounded, from dozens to hundreds, were received with compassion and offered solace. Crewmen gave their bunks, their bedding, their clothing, cigarettes, coffee, and sympathy to their brothers who at the least had lost their ship and at the most were even now giving their lives. Doctors and dentists, pharmacists mates and hospital corpsmen, boat, swain's mates or anyone who cared to, contributed as he could, from major surgery to rudimentary first aid.

The *Bagley*, herself unscathed, drew alongside the stricken *Astoria* and lifted an incredible 450 men from the cruiser's sloping deck. Lieutenant Commander Charles F. Flower, the *Astoria's* senior medical officer, came along with them, and immediately began work among the 185 wounded, along with the *Bagley's* doctor, Lieutenant (j.g.) Paul P. Pickering. In the wardroom they put Water Tender First Class J. C. Cordle on a mess table. Dr. Flower gave him a local anesthetic and then amputated his leg, using a hacksaw from the engine room to cut through the bone.

The destroyer's other doctor, Lieutenant (j.g.) Donald S. Smith, went aboard the *Astoria* to work there with the more serious cases. Chaplain, Lieutenant M. J. Bouterse II, was still on the fantail, busy with the corpsmen among the living. A special party was collecting bodies and about 30 were there, the sailmaker sewing them up for sea burial. Dog tags were carefully collected and put in a small wooden box. (When the *Astoria* capsized, off they went, bodies, dog tags and all.)

In the *Bagley,* crowded beyond belief, able-bodied *Astoria* men helped injured shipmates or did their best to stay out of the way. Splints and dressings, the regular supply soon exhausted, were improvised from any wood or metal quickly obtainable and from torn clothing and bed linen. The wardroom became an operating theater, with the captain's table as surgical bed, and mattresses, hammocks, and basket stretchers receiving the patients. Even the engineering spaces made way for the refugees, who huddled on the gratings around the boilers and turbines. Strangely, mostly fireman ratings found their way here, as if gravitating to the place they knew best.

Occasionally there was a touch of humor. Gunner's Mate Third Class George A. Cichon, rescued from the *Astoria* by a destroyer, lay in the scupper and vomited blood—except upon macabre re-examination it turned out to be tomato juice, which caused him to enjoy it a second time.

By noon, everything that could be done for these men in the destroyers had been done. Eight *Astoria* men had died in the *Bagley,* and in his tiny cabin the captain, Commander Sinclair, sat down at his desk and wrote, in longhand on a scratch pad, "My dear Captain Greenman." The *Astoria* men, particularly the wounded, had shown wonderful spirit, he said, and Dr. Flower's work had been magnificent, but in spite of their great effort eight *Astoria* men could not be saved.

All bodies had been carefully fingerprinted and official report made, he wrote. Billfolds and other small personal items had been taken from the bodies and would be sent to the captain of the *President Jackson*. The men had been buried at sea, in the area of their travail, with a simple and nonsectarian service, read by Commander Sinclair himself. Then he listed their names: Lloyd Eldred Williams, Bernard Joseph Kam, John Bailes Bear, Samuel R. Gladdin, Norman LeRoy Moon, Francis Gerald Britton, J. A. Knapp, and Warner Raymond.

In early afternoon the *Bagley* went alongside the *President Jackson* and the survivors were transferred, some walking alone, some helped by shipmates, others lifted by cargo booms in basket stretchers. Among them was Ralph Morse, unhurt but minus some 200 negatives he had shot for *Life,* covering the assembly of the forces, the landings, the air raids, and the battle. By 2:00 P.M. the survivors from the sea were in the transport, so lately occupied by young Marines, en route to the new adventure.

The *Wilson,* beginning at 6:40, had picked up 211 men by 10:00 A.M., not stopping to record from which vessels they came. Lieutenants (j.g.) John C. Feick, Jr., and Joseph F. Illick and Ensigns Arnold C. Mealy and Andrew T. Fischer dived repeatedly into the water to rescue struggling men; Lieutenant (j.g.) Leo E. Davison, the medical officer, organized and executed their care, even while the *Wilson* stood alongside the *Astoria* fighting fire. Relieved by the *Buchanan* shortly before noon, the *Wilson* delivered her wounded to the *Hunter Liggett*, completing the task about 3:15 P.M. Next to her, alongside the transport, was the *Helm*, with 175 men she had rescued, mostly *Vincennes* men but a few from the *Astoria* and one from the *Quincy*.

By 7:00 A.M. the *Patterson* and the *Blue* had taken aboard all of the surviving Australians, some 700, of the cruiser *Canberra*. Some of the wounded had received emergency treatment before leaving their ship, but many had not. In the *Blue*, now jammed with nearly 300 survivors, her doctor, Lieutenant Donald L. Martinson, set up shop in the wardroom, assisted by Pharmacist's Mate Second Class Marvin C. Finney, while Chief Pharmacists Mate Randolph R. Payne organized a secondary emergency hospital in the crew's washroom.

Among the *Patterson's* wounded was Captain Getting, whose condition was grave. He died later in the day on the *Barnett* and was buried at sea, a few days after his forty-third birthday.

Some men were beyond help. Able-bodied Seaman Wallace M. Ross, lifted into the *Blue's* charthouse about 6:30 A.M., died before he could be treated. His body was left undisturbed while attention was given to the living, and after all of them had been transferred to the *Fuller* his body was also sent aboard the transport, for burial at sea.

The *Buchanan* came on a Marine sitting in the life ring from the captain's gig of the *Astoria* and lifted him aboard. He was dead.

The *Patterson* lifted about 400 men off the *Canberra's* stern, nearly a quarter of them wounded, and went alongside the *Barnett* about 8:00 A.M. At the same hour, a few miles away the *Canberra* sank.

As the grim task of rescuing battle survivors and disposing of crippled ships progressed, Admiral Turner assessed his situation and found it discouraging in the extreme. He was without air cover (and thus defenseless against sky attack), his surface forces had been badly shattered, and his primary task—landing supplies and equipment for the Marine invaders—had not even begun to be accomplished.

The role of the pioneer is always difficult, and this first amphibious assault of modern times—the first for the United States Navy since the assault on Vera Cruz in 1847 during the Mexican War—had not gone at all according to plan. Unloading of the transports went smoothly during the first few hours of August 7, encouraged by the fact that there was no opposition at the Guadalcanal beachhead and only moderate resistance at Tulagi. The Marines were landed with ease, but when their supplies began to follow a serious administrative flaw was uncovered—there was no clear directive as to who would unload supplies at the beaches and who would move them inland.

The Navy lifted the stuff out of the transports into small boats and dumped it ashore. By late afternoon of August 7 there was no space left on the beach. To the Navy, aboard the transports, it seemed as though hundreds of Marines were standing around on the beach doing nothing. To the Marines, on the beachhead, it seemed that the Navy was not doing its job—the Marines had been landed to fight and they were preparing to move inland to do just that. Finally the Marines pitched in, and Captain Reifsnider ordered 15 sailors from each transport to the beaches to help out. Still it was not enough.

Late that night General Vandegrift was informed by his officers that the situation on the beach was completely chaotic and that further unloading must stop until the beaches could be cleared. At 2:40 A.M. on the eighth, Admiral Turner issued an order to that effect. Later this was modified, but for the rest of the day little unloading took place at Guadalcanal. Each time Japanese planes came over, the transports stopped unloading, put up antiaircraft fire, left their boats, and got under way in an attempt to evade enemy bombs and torpedoes. They churned about Savo Sound, eluding the enemy and avoiding each other, while the dozens of small boats ran for cover or scurried after their mother ship like frightened chicks in a barnyard.

The same scenes took place off Tulagi, except that here virtually nothing had been landed, due to the heavy fighting and unfriendly beaches—coral reefs, high banks and heavy jungle behind the beaches, and no roads or clearings inland. For two days only water and ammunition went in over the beaches. Piers on Tulagi's eastern coast were not captured until the eighth and supplies did not begin moving in over them until nearly midnight. The sea battle that night effectively stopped such activity and some Tulagi units had to go on short rations. A parachute battalion which landed with three days' C and D rations got nothing more. Another unit, landing with three days' food, captured a one-gallon can of tomatoes and some Japanese rice. That rice became their one-meal-a-day from August 11 to August 21.

In view of the supply situation, Admiral Turner knew he could not leave Sunday morning. He had to resume unloading, despite his dangerous situation, and he so ordered. The transports, throughout Sunday, unloaded materials on one hand and received survivors on the other.

The *Barnett* took on 904 officers and men from 8 ships, mostly from the cruisers, including 398 Australians from the *Canberra*. In addition she had 18 Japanese prisoners, 8 of whom were wounded. The *Neville* had 75 *Astoria* men off the *Bagley*, 3 Japanese prisoners from Tulagi, and 5 men rescued from the Japanese planes shot down. The *Alchiba* had 32 *Astoria* men she had rescued in the final moments of that cruiser. The *Hunter Liggett* had hundreds of men, including 190 wounded; all day long the doctors, her own and a half dozen from the sunken ships, labored without stopping to save these men thus far spared. Lieutenant Commander James A. Brown, assistant medical officer of the *Astoria,* worked continuously as a surgeon among his ship's men. The doctors even tried to help a wounded Japanese, but he was uncooperative and he died. Six of the American survivors died in the *Hunter Liggett* the first day.

The *Hunter Liggett,* the only ship present manned entirely by Coast Guardsmen, also retrieved something else that day—an LCVP, one of its small boats which had been lost all night in the Sound, alone in the maelstrom of battle. During the evening of the eighth Coxswain John J. Brady had picked up 3 badly wounded men, a sailor and 2 Marines, from the burning *George F. Elliot.* He had also acquired, by various accidents, 2 coxswains who had lost their boats, a Navy officer, a couple of enlisted men, and a medic who was taking care of the wounded.

En route to the *Hunter Liggett*, flares bright as day had burst overhead, extremely heavy fire opened all around them, and strange ships—possibly their own transports, their own warships, or even enemy vessels—began pounding by on all sides, many at high speed. In the bottom of the LCVP, one of the wounded moaned for water.

The 2 shipwrecked coxswains manned the boat's 30-caliber machine guns, the Navy officer said nothing to anybody, and Brady dodged traffic like a pedestrian in Times Square. Toward dawn he sighted a ship silhouette that looked familiar, took off after it, and came alongside. Over the side a dozen rifles beaded on the little boat and out of the night a roaring voice challenged. It was the Hunter Liggett's executive officer, Lieutenant Commander H. J. Betzmer, whose voice, once experienced, could never be forgotten. For once, Brady welcomed the sound.

With both vessels under way, the transport's deck gang rigged the cargo booms and lifted the stretchers out of the little boat while Brady struggled to hold it steady. This feat of seamanship accomplished, Brady's boat was cast off again, to wander alone until daylight, when it was ordered out to hunt survivors. Hours later a destroyer hailed her: "Get back to your ship, we're pulling out." The battle was over, not only for Brady's boat but for every vessel in the Sound, transports and warships alike.

After her gun battle with the *Patterson*, the *Chicago* stood by the burning *Canberra* until all men had been removed, then attempted to join up with the *San Juan*. But that cruiser was making 15 knots toward Tulagi, and the strain of that speed was too great on the *Chicago's* damaged bow. Captain Bode ordered speed cut to 10 knots and was then summoned by Admiral Crutchley. The *Chicago,* picking her way through haze and rain, found the *Australia* about 9:00 A.M. at the Guadalcanal anchorage, but ten minutes later all ships, including the transports, began maneuvering independently on a report of torpedo wakes in the Sound. The report was false. (Two of Admiral Mikawa's submarines, the *I-121* and the *I-122,* arrived in the Savo area Sunday but made no attack.) About 10:30 A.M. the flurry was over and the *Chicago* put a man over the side to cut away the damaged bow plates impeding her handling. Compartments were pumped and bulkheads shored and by 2:30 P.M. the *Chicago* was ready for sea.

There was no air attack at Guadalcanal on Sunday for good reason. The *Jarvis* was making her fatal sacrifice play. The *Yunagi's* report of the *"Achilles* class cruiser in trouble" got through to Rabaul and Sunday's entire flight destined for Guadalcanal—16 torpedo bombers and 15 fighters—was diverted to look for the crippled "cruiser." She was last sighted by friendly forces just after dawn Sunday, when a *Saratoga* plane spotted her, down at the bow and trailing oil. The Japanese planes found her later and attacked as viciously as if she had been a cruiser. Bombs and torpedoes smashed her and she split and sank, unable to return fire, unable to summon aid. Lieutenant Commander Graham and his 246 men never had a chance; they had jettisoned all boats and rafts before leaving Savo Sound.

One more act remained to be played out. On Sunday

night, Cruiser Division 6—the *Aoba, Kinugasa, Furutaka,* and *Kako,* Rear Admiral Aritomo Goto commanding— broke off from Admiral Mikawa's force, at his order, and headed for Kavieng while Mikawa took the rest of the force toward Rabaul. Monday morning the weather was clear and fine, and CruDiv 6, making 16 knots, was less than 100 miles from Kavieng, without destroyer escort.

This would have been an ideal setup had an American submarine been present. One was. Lieutenant Commander John R. Moore, cruising out of Brisbane in the seventeen-year-old pig boat *S-44,* upped periscope just before 8:00 A.M., sighted the enemy cruiser force 9,000 yards off, headed straight for him. When the last vessel in the formation was 700 yards away "Dinty" Moore fired four torpedoes, and thirty-five seconds later an explosion rattled the bones of the old sub as she plunged to 130 feet. It was the *Kako,* struck fair and full, and for once American torpedoes detonated. The *Kako* sank in five minutes and the *S-44* easily made off in the confusion. The first installment on the Savo debt had been paid—1 cruiser down, with 34 men killed, 48 wounded.

The exodus from Savo Sound began Sunday afternoon. Admiral Turner first ordered out the Guadalcanal transports and screen and they left around 4:00 P.M. by the back door, passing down Lengo Channel, the *Australia* and the *Chicago* in the van. Clear of the island they formed up with the *Hunter Liggett,* Captain Reifsnider as OTC (Officer in Tactical Command), and laid course for Noumea, arriving Friday morning.

Next down the channel went the *Betelgeuse,* half full of supplies; the *Alchiba,* 75 per cent full; the *Fomalhaut,* carrying most of the Marines' earth-moving equipment, only 15 per cent of which had been unloaded. One transport went out with 1,390 Marines, mostly work parties and headquarters' personnel who had never gotten ashore.

The final echelon left about dusk. Led by the *San Juan* it included all remaining vessels, transports and warships alike, Admiral Turner's flag still flying from the *McCawley*. Left behind were the Marines, now without air or sea protection, about 10,000 of them on Guadalcanal and a little over 6,000 on Tulagi. With them were 4 units of fire for their weapons (a unit was a day's supply) and little food. As of that moment the Guadalcanal Marines went on two meals per day.

Also left behind were 4 first-line cruisers, but at the bottom of Savo Sound. Exactly 18 spools of barbed wire had been landed, not 1 power shovel or dump truck, and only 1 bulldozer. This vehicle—by war's end revealed as America's secret weapon—was taken over by a Marine corporal, one Corporal Cates, who literally lived in it, driving it up and down Guadalcanal until it, and he, became famous. (It finally fell apart in October.) Off with the ships went entrenching tools, sand bags, diesel fuel, and indispensable little items like radio batteries.

As night fell the Marines, incredulous on the shore, wheeled up artillery to protect their rear, now exposed as much as the front. Admiral Turner had not said whether he would return, or when, and until he did the Marines would be completely on their own.

General Vandegrift, a hard-bitten realist, had expressed his opinion at the conference with Turner and Crutchley. Now that he saw the Navy actually leaving he wasted no further time on recrimination; he turned with the utmost dedication to the immediate task—fighting off the Japanese single-handed. He had no doubt that his Marines could do it.

Admiral Mikawa had not sunk the transports, to be sure, but his success had been smashing—he had driven transports and warships alike from the scene of battle, and it would be weeks before they returned. In the meantime, the Japanese would be complete masters of Savo Sound. Their submarines and destroyers regularly stood in the Sound, just out of range of the shore guns, and pelted the Marines at will. The First Marine Division, with grim humor, later struck off a little medal for the sailors. The face showed an admiral's arm dropping a hot potato into a Marine's hands, with the motto, *Faciat Georgius* (Let George Do It). The reverse, depicting a cow's rear end facing an electric fan, was inscribed: "In fond remembrance of the happy days spent from August 7, 1942 to January 1943. USMC."

On Sunday morning, the radio watch in Fletcher's ships, far off to the southeast, could hear the beachhead at Guadalcanal calling, "Any friendly planes in the area, come in," "Any friendly planes in the area, come in." There was no answer. Foster Hailey of the New York *Times*, who was with Fletcher's force in the *Minneapolis*, said the sailors were ashamed to look at each other.

In the afternoon Admiral Fletcher cut himself off from the battle with unmistakable finality. He radioed Admiral Ghormley:

"Direct Turner to make reports direct to you, info to me."

chapter
23

Admiral Turner and the routed forces arrived at Noumea, a full thousand miles from the beachheads, on Thursday evening, August 13, four days after leaving Guadalcanal, and Admiral Ghormley was waiting for him. The Commander, South Pacific, theoretically in direct control of events, actually knew little of what had happened.

He had been in a difficult position, anxious to know the progress of the battle, ready to help where possible (although in truth there were no reserves of either men or materials), and hearing only snatches of what went on. What he did hear was foreboding.

Admiral Callahan had brought up the problem of radio silence at the Koro Sea rehearsals in July; Ghormley would be back in Noumea, unaware of what was going on but biting his nails to find out. Admiral Fletcher recognized this, but the only thing he could do would be to send a courier plane from his carrier forces from time to time. He promised to do this, but no planes came. Ghormley did not even have a complete set of Fletcher's and Turner's operations plans; there weren't enough copies to go around at Koro. Fletcher said he would have some copies made, land a set at Suva on July 31, and Admiral McCain would send them back by plane so Ghormley at least would know the whole scheme before the landings. That plane never came either, and Admiral Ghormley never saw a full outline of the Solomons invasion until September, by which time events had rushed far beyond original conceptions.

Ghormley had received some news of the battle—just enough to raise his fears—in the form of radio dispatches from Fletcher as the carriers sped south. There were intercepts, made by Fletcher's communications net, of dispatches among the battle forces at Guadalcanal, and ominous in the extreme.

Ghormley was more than ready to hear the full story from Turner, but first there were the men. Turner's transports were loaded with wounded from the sunken ships, and all local facilities, meager as they were, were put into use. The survivors, thousands of them, who had lost everything when the ships went down, were outfitted in anything that had come their way; they were mostly a tatterdemalion horde in pants and shirts of disparate parentage, Marine, Navy, or merchant, shoeless and hatless, lacking even toothbrush or razor.

Admiral Ghormley had no clothing for them; Navy supplies had not arrived. The Army was little better off, but sent over clothing and shoes to cover the men until they could be reassigned at the front or sent back to Pearl Harbor or the States. Here and there a man found or fashioned a single gold earring, and hung it from the lobe of his left ear, a sign proclaiming to all other men of the sea—survivor.

Turner and Ghormley, in the absence of Fletcher, were faced with a double task: they must report to higher authority what had happened, and at the same time arrange to send reinforcements for the Marines left in the islands. The next days would be critical, for if the Japanese reacted swiftly and in strength they would have the waters of Savo to themselves and could crush the invading force between jungle and sea.

Turner told Ghormley what he knew of the events at Guadalcanal, but the whole story would not be known, even to Turner, for months. This wild battle, one of the strangest in sea history, had been cloaked in mist and darkness, curtained off by sheets of rain, the sea slashed by eerie flashes of heavy guns, the night sky stitched by stuttering lines of tracer bullets, and over it all the roar of cannonading. The fleet had been like a man set upon by thugs in an alley. Stunned and badly hurt, it had dragged itself away and now, in hospital, wondered what had happened.

Admiral Crutchley, who through the long night had never been able to catch up with events, was still thoroughly mystified when he sat down to write his first report to his superior on Monday, August 10, as the force, now in the open sea, moved steadily away from the scene of the debacle. He wrote:

My dear Admiral,

I am sending over this very tentative appreciation of what happened in the cruiser action off Savo as, combined with any other information which you may have, it may help you to make any preliminary report.

But Crutchley really knew nothing, and Turner had no "other information" with which to combine it. The Britisher could not even say when the battle had started.

As you will see from the enclosures, *Chicago's* first report states his first action took place at 0115—I think a phonetic error must have been made and that he means 0150, for the first other record which I have of any alarm is 0146, when the flares illuminated the transport area. I had then just got on board *Australia* as we had great difficulty in finding the minesweeper for the General.

With reserve, and a tinge of sadness, Admiral Crutchley wrote:

There is certainly a great deal to be cleared up, such as:
Why no warning from radar of *Blue* or *Ralph Talbot*?
Why no enemy report from anyone?

These were questions that would be often asked in the months to come, but there was, as yet, no answer to them. In some cases there never would be an answer, at least no clear and satisfying answer.

Admiral Crutchley continued:

The fact must be faced that we had adequate forces, placed with the very purpose of repelling surface attack, and when that surface attack was made it destroyed our force. Why the enemy did not come on and attack the convoy, I do not know.

The only thing that can be said is that the convoy was defended, but the cost was terrific and I feel it should have have been the enemy who should have paid, whereas he appears to have got off free.

I know that at night the odds are heavily in favor of the the attacker, and by the very nature of things our people in this case had to be in the position of defenders; our only chance of reversing that position was warning of the attack by outlying destroyers.

I should be grateful for guidance from you as to what procedure you wish followed to elucidate more facts.

Admiral Turner, faced with a thousand tasks, not the least a report to Washington, would also have liked to know what had happened. In a note to Crutchley, August 12, he said:

I am enclosing a summary of what I can reconstruct from the disastrous battle of Savo Island. It is difficult for me to understand how events could have occurred as they did, but it seems best to face facts.

This was inevitable, for the sinking of 4 cruisers in one night was a very hard fact indeed, and quite aside from what happened or why, Nimitz and King were already facing the fact of how to replace them. They also faced the twin problems of keeping information from the Japanese and from the American public.

The Japanese propaganda forces had leaped into action, somewhat confused and quite inaccurate. Radio Tokyo broadcast on August 9, in world-wide service, that Japanese forces had sunk or damaged 11 transports and 17 "Anglo-American warships" in the first days of the Solomons action, including two *Astoria*-class cruisers and other cruisers of the *Australia* class. Domei, the official news agency, quoted "authoritative quarters" as saying "British and American naval strength has been reduced to that of a third-rate power." In its flight of fancy Domei went on to say that the Japanese had commenced "violent attacks" on Friday and had sunk a battleship of unknown class, 2 cruisers of *Astoria* class, 2 of the *Australia* class, 3 cruisers of unknown class, at least 4 destroyers, and more than 10 transports. In addition, 41 American planes had been destroyed, and heavy damage had been inflicted on 3 cruisers of the *Astoria* class, at least 2 destroyers, and more than 1 transport.

Domei continued: The "damage suffered by the Japanese Navy includes only seven aircraft, which carried out suicide dives against the enemy and destroyed themselves. Two of our cruisers are slightly damaged but are still able to continue fighting and cruising." It added: "Devastating damage was caused among enemy transports." The loss of the *Kako,* even if then known, was not mentioned.

The newspaper *Nichi Nichi* said the Japanese Navy had for weeks been courting battle and finally had succeeded in engaging the Americans. "The Solomon Islands victory is one of the greatest in the history of Japan," the paper said.

On August 10 the German radio said that soon after the landings began the Japanese attacked violently and "one after another [enemy ship] was attacked and sunk by the Japanese planes." The next day Radio Berlin said Allied forces landing in the Solomons were annihilated by the Japanese and their transports sunk. No source was given. The British, with typical understatement, said on August 11 that "it looks as if the action is going not too badly." There will be no official British comment, said "a source," as "it is entirely an American endeavour."

In the face of this, the United States Navy proceeded with great caution:

Communiqué No. 101, of August 8, said attacks had begun in the Solomons, "in force and the attacks are continuing."

Communiqué No. 102, August 9, said the attacks "are continuing. Considerable enemy resistance has been encountered and it is still too early to announce results or to estimate our own or enemy losses. Australian units are participating with our forces."

There was no communiqué the next day, but Admiral King issued a special statement. It outlined the background of the operation and said:

"An initial surprise was effected and planned landings accomplished. The enemy has counterattacked with rapidity and vigor. Heavy fighting is still in progress. Our operating forces are employing all available communications in the conduct of the operations so that our information is incomplete, but it appears that we have had at least one cruiser sunk and two cruisers, two destroyers and one transport damaged."

The final paragraph, ominous in retrospect, said:

"It should be understood that the operation now under way is one of the most complicated and difficult in warfare. Considerable losses, such as are inherent in any offensive operation, must be expected as the price to be paid for the hard-won experience which is essential to the attainment of far-reaching results."

But this paragraph raised no fears at home. The United States Navy had never suffered a defeat in war. (Pearl Harbor was discounted; a treacherous blow when we were *not* at war, and now more than offset by the victories at Coral Sea and Midway.) Actually, the United States Navy, constituted as a unit late in the nineteenth century, had never been in a surface engagement with an enemy fleet, except for the Spanish-American war. The feats of that war glowed in American memory—the smashing of the Spanish fleet at Manila Bay (all seven vessels) and the rout of Cervera at Santiago. How gallant and romantic it all seemed now, but it had been suicide for the Spaniards. They never had a chance.

Rear Admiral Pascual Cervera y Topete, his bottoms foul from the long siege in Santiago, his ships slow and 85 per cent of his ammunition defective, had finally sailed forth—to die. Rear Admiral Winfield Scott Schley, in the *Brooklyn,* accepted battle at 9:30 A.M. and by 1:15 P.M. not a Spanish ship was left. During the chase, American sailors roamed the deck in holiday mood, taking snapshots of the burning Spanish ships.

Dinner was served at noon as usual, and Rear Admiral

William T. Sampson, who had arrived late, clanked about the deck in boots and spurs. He had been riding ashore to confer with General William A. Shafter when the battle began, and before the smoke cleared another battle began, between Schley and Sampson, over who deserved the credit for the victory.

The Americans, busy saving the Spanish sailors from Cubans and sharks, hoisted Captain Don Antonio Eulate aboard the *Iowa* in a chair. As he reached the deck the guard presented arms, the officer of the deck saluted, and Spanish prisoners stood at attention. Eulate, although wounded, straightened with an effort, unbuckled his sword, kissed the hilt, and with a graceful bow presented it to Captain Robley D. Evans of the *Iowa*. Captain Evans declined the sword and took Captain Eulate's arm to help him to the cabin. As they reached the ladder Captain Eulate turned and waved farewell to his ship, "Adios *Vizcaya.*" The last romantic war in history had ended.

In the entire West Indian phase of that war the United States Navy had lost seven men killed in battle. Yeoman George Ellis was decapitated by a shell as he watched the Battle of Santiago from the deck of the *Brooklyn,* the only American lost in the whole battle. The only officer lost in the war was Ensign Worth Bagley, killed as the torpedo boat *Winslow* rashly entered the harbor of Cardenas. Five sailors were cut down with Bagley by the raking Spanish fire.

Now there was a vessel, a destroyer, named in memory of Ensign Bagley, and the destroyer *Bagley* was engaged in battle in a place called the Solomon Islands, and the foe was not a rusting Spanish fleet, manned by romantic officers in sash and sword, who kissed the hilt as they surrendered.

Now it was a ruthless foe, who knew how to fight and who sought death before surrender. His rules were his own: kill or be killed. His weapons were surprise, audacity, and skill; his attacks cunning and deadly. Gone were the days of chivalry and gallantry and "fair play"—as antiquated as the Spanish-American war.

This was the problem, for the Anglo-Saxons were slow in discovering that the rules had been changed. Later, much later, Admiral King called it "lack of battle-mindedness," and what he meant was failure to perceive that this foe was not the foe of yore, and these rules were not the same rules under which the game had been played for centuries in the Western world. When the hand of help was extended to this fallen foe, it was met with a hidden pistol. The Age of Chivalry was dead. Perhaps that is what Admiral King meant when he said that "considerable losses . . . must be expected as the price to be paid for the hard-won experience. . . ."

And so hard-won it was, and so damaging, both materially and psychologically, that the Navy said not a word about it for over three months.

Admiral Nimitz' almost legendary self-control very nearly cracked when news of the Savo debacle first reached him. He was accustomed to take pistol practice daily on a private range just outside his headquarters at Pearl Harbor. It was said that on the day the Savo reports came in he stepped without a word into his range. Long and intense firing was heard and eventually he emerged, tense and stony-faced, silent but under control.

Admiral King's problems were, of course, immense. The grand strategy had been set early in 1942, in conferences and communications between Roosevelt and Churchill and their advisers. The primary objective was the defeat of Germany in Europe, after which Italy and Japan must inevitably fall. The first counterblow would be a second front somewhere in the West, perhaps as early as May, and the United States' role in these undertakings was twofold—first, the fullest support of operations in the West; secondly, the United States must go it alone in the Pacific, doing the best it could in what essentially must be a holding operation. The European operations clearly had precedence and whatever forces Admiral King could obtain for the Pacific would be by scraping and improvising among the forces left over, all within the very clear strictures of the set plan.

Thus the losses at Savo were a severe blow to him. Allied fortunes were extremely low. Rommel was on the loose in Africa, menacing Egypt and the Suez. Hitler's armies were before Stalingrad, and the fall of that great city, possibly all of Russia, was freely predicted. In these harassing days, the loss of ships, any ships, simply could not be supported.

Admiral King had flown to San Francisco early in July to meet Nimitz and discuss Operation Watchtower. He had sketched out the three phases of that campaign:

Task I: Seize and occupy the lower Solomons.

Task II: Seize and occupy the northeast coast of New Guinea.

Task III: Seize and occupy Rabaul.

After that the path would continue up through Truk, Guam, and Saipan toward the Japanese homeland, thousands of miles away. It was an awesome task, and Admiral King emphasized to Nimitz that the forces available for it would be sharply limited. The chance of replacement of losses would be small.

From San Francisco, King flew to London and there, in late July, even as the Solomons invasion force gathered in the Koro Sea, the course of the war in the West was decided. It was to be North Africa and before the end of 1942, and it would require every ship the United States Navy could spare. This settled, King hurried home to Washington; he wanted to be there when the Marines landed on Guadalcanal. This "formidable old crustacean," whose friends said he shaved with a blowtorch and used a torpedo net cutter on his toenails, actually had a heart and it was, as always, in the Pacific.

Unfortunately, his reaction to the news from Savo has not been recorded. It must have been an awesome thing to watch and such was his reputation that his reaction could be awaited with trembling down to the lowest echelons in the Fleet. He loathed inefficiency and it was impossible to explain failure to him. But his control, at least in public, was formidable, and the only thing that issued from his austere office in "Main Navy" on Constitution Avenue was the reserved and reasoned statement of August 10.

After that, the communiqué of the eleventh said the action in the Solomons continues, but "nothing further can be reported at this moment." The next day it was announced that the Navy had been "engaged in bitter fighting, details of which are not yet available." The nation could scarcely have accepted the fact, even had it been allowed to know, that at this moment a mighty American invasion force was creeping away from the Solomons, leaving the Marines to face the enemy alone in land, sea, and air. On that very day, Captain Shoichi Kamada of the Japanese Navy announced that the battle was over, it had been a one-sided American loss, due to poor training of American forces for night fighting. The United States Navy communiqué of the next day was one line, "Operations are continuing in the Solomon Islands area."

In New Caledonia, where he had gone at least partly to escape the Australians, Admiral Ghormley had his own problems. He had purposely concealed the secret of the Solomons invasion from the New Zealand Prime Minister, Peter Fraser. Fraser, perhaps scenting something, had importuned Ghormley for a meeting, and said he would go anywhere for it. Ghormley put him off, and eventually had to flee Auckland for New Caledonia to get away from him. When Fraser learned of the invasion, he was angry that advance knowledge had been withheld from him. But many factors had weighed in Ghormley's decision, not the least of which was the extremely free nature of the Australian press.

In a country with a relatively small, concentrated population, and with so few naval vessels, the loss of the *Canberra* could not long be concealed. Thus on August 20 it was announced simultaneously by General MacArthur's headquarters and by Australian Prime Minister John Curtin. The general's communiqué said the cruiser was "apparently sunk in the first stages of the Allied naval-air-land invasion of the southern Solomons." About 84 men were lost, of a crew of 816, it said, including at least 1 American, Ensign J. W. Vance. "The traditions of

Australia know no greater glory than this dead ship," it concluded.

In his announcement, the Prime Minister said General MacArthur had expressed his "profound regret" at the loss and paid high tribute to the officers and crew. Curtin, in his message to bereaved kin, said "the battle record of this ship, bearing the name of the national capital, will add another illustrious page to the imperishable record of Australian forces in this war."

From Washington there came no word of the loss of the other three cruisers. Nor did any word come from the forward area, where the disaster was the talk of the fleet. Admiral Nimitz wrote to Secretary of the Navy Frank Knox on August 26, saying that Ralph Morse, photographer for *Life* magazine and a survivor of the *Vincennes,* had arrived at Pearl Harbor and had given "a most coherent account of the subject attack to members of the staff at CINCPAC [Commander-in-Chief, Pacific]." The Admiral went on to say that Morse would arrive in New York on August 27 and he, as well as the editors of *Life* and *Time* magazines, should be instructed to divulge nothing of what had happened at Savo. There were no leaks.

But the fleet was seething. The Navy had suffered the worst sea defeat in its history and rumor swept across the Pacific as fast as men could travel, each retelling magnifying the proportions of the disaster. Reports of incompetence and bungling in the American command swelled as each day passed until, bad as they were, the facts were lost in the fiction. The Japanese fleet, which had indeed attacked with intrepidity and smashing force, was built by popular imagination into a dark and dread juggernaut. An aura of near-invincibility began to be built around this force of little yellow men, who could strike such swift and terrible blows in the night, and morale suffered in the American fleet.

Within the command echelon there was a ferment on, by participants to tell their stories and by the higher command to find out what and who had allowed this thing to happen. To those concerned it was a matter of intense moment, for reputations and careers were at stake. For those in the highest command there was a double concern: the causes of the debacle, and the lessons from it, must be discovered and quickly applied to prevent a repetition, for the war was only starting. The very security of the beachheads in the Solomons depended on quick measures to correct deficiencies.

Ghormley wanted to know from Fletcher and Turner what had happened, Nimitz wanted to know from Ghormley, and King wanted to know from Nimitz. So even as the war rushed on—and the Japanese offered little respite—the investigation got under way, not all in one piece, for the participants were widely scattered and many were dead. But by August 23 enough men and reports had reached Pearl Harbor for Admiral Nimitz to prepare his "Preliminary Report to the Commander in Chief." Nimitz had few conclusions, but he had some questions. He said:

The simultaneous departure of all the carrier task forces on the night of Aug. 8–9 was most unfortunate. . . . Was it practicable to fuel one carrier task force at a time, leaving two available for support of operations?

The absence of all the carrier task forces on the morning of the 9th permitted the enemy to make a clean getaway without being subjected to carrier air attack during the early daylight hours of that day. Was it possible and practicable for such attacks to be made by our shore-based planes?

He wanted answers from Ghormley, who bucked them to Fletcher, and on September 9 Fletcher replied. To the question of carriers refueling one at a time "the answer to that is negative," he said. "Due to the fact all task forces were equally short of fuel it would not have been possible to retire one task force at a time."

To the implied criticism of the lack of air pursuit on the morning after the battle, Admiral Fletcher answered:

"This decision [to withdraw] was believed sound in view of the presence of 40 planes equipped with torpedoes on 8 Aug." (Those torpedoes again.) But if Fletcher's powerful force had been in position, and given more fuel, "it is barely possible that with definite information the enemy might have been located after conducting a search the next morning." However, he said, the carriers would have had to be much farther northwest than their supposed position and even then the minimum attack distance would have been 200 miles. In all, " I believe the first sentence [Nimitz' question of morning carrier attack] gives an erroneous impression that the carriers could normally attack the surface forces which attacked Guadalcanal that night, and retired at high speed four or more hours before daylight."

chapter
24

In Washington, Admiral King had little time for Savo, what with Torch in North Africa, the largest amphibious operation in history, then shaping up. But he was by no means through with Savo, and in the meantime his chief of staff, Rear Admiral Richard S. Edwards, was thrown into the breach. It was imperative to discover the causes of Savo and extirpate them without delay, for this was obviously only the beginning of a very long and violent campaign in which not one ship could be spared to incompetence.

Admiral Edwards, a brilliant and tireless worker, quickly put together a critique of the battle of Savo Island and in September it was rushed to commanders in the forward area under the label "Secret." From a long distance away, and from incomplete reports, Edwards concluded:

Admiral Crutchley's instructions (they could not honestly have been called a battle plan) had emphasized (perhaps overemphasized would have been a better word) the fear of attack by Japanese submarines and planes, almost disregarding surface attack. His vessels had been allowed to assume the same disposition each night, which was wrong, for the enemy could easily have learned of this. The cruisers should have been concentrated.

"The fallacy of dividing defending forces is as old as war," wrote Admiral Edwards.

Destroyers should have been sent westward on patrol. Crutchley had 3 groups under his command, really, but left the area without notifying 2 of them (Captain Riefkohl's Northern Force and Admiral Scott's Eastern Force). Of 5 cruiser captains facing the Japanese, only 1 (Captain Getting of the *Canberra*) had been on the bridge when the assault came. No flag officer was present in either force. All OTC's (Captain Bode in the Southern Force and Captain Riefkohl in the Northern Force) were also commanding officers of their own ships. (An officer fighting his own ship has little time to plan and execute tactics for a group of ships.)

The *Canberra*, at a range of under 1 mile, suffered 24 hits in less than a minute.

"The Japanese seemed to illuminate first, shoot first, hit first, after which he needed no more illumination," Admiral Edwards said. The Japanese had a great advantage, he conceded, since they knew that every ship they saw was enemy, but this did not explain everything. When the *Ralph Talbot* first reported a plane entering

Savo Sound, "no one appears to have taken any action on this."

There was far too much ready service ammunition lying around on American ships—50 rounds per 5-inch gun, far more than was used. Admiral Edwards said, "They [the Japs] could not miss a ready service box" on the *Astoria*. He deplored, also, what he called "a subtle change from the offensive to the defensive" after the success of the landings. Similarly he criticized the lack of information given to ship commanders as to Japanese intentions and movements and even as to the plans and actions of friendly ships. All Allied ships present should have known where all other friendly ships were, he said, concluding:

"Sometimes the policy of secrecy is carried too far. Sometimes information is valueless if no use is made of it except to conceal it."

This critique, summing up the most urgent lessons to be learned from Savo, was most valuable in effecting changes down the chain of command, but it still gave little indication of individual performance in the battle. Somehow, that story could not be got at, due mainly to incomplete and conflicting reports and to the sheer press of other events. The question of individual culpability had to be put aside for the moment, while more important tasks were pursued.

By mid-October the time was ripe for changes. The Battle of the Eastern Solomons, August 23-25 (indecisive), and the Battle of Cape Esperance, October 11-12 (an American victory), were behind and it began to be possible to hope that Guadalcanal could be held. Strength had been gathering in the fleet, and the lessons of Savo were beginning to be felt. The defensive phase of the war in the Pacific was coming to a close; it was time to take the offensive, time for action.

Into Ghormley's headquarters came the dispatch from Nimitz, perhaps half expected: "After carefully weighing all factors have decided that talents and previous experience of Halsey can best be applied to the situation by having him take over duties of ComSoPac as soon as practicable. I greatly appreciate your loyal and devoted efforts toward the accomplishment of a most difficult task. I shall order you to report to Halsey for the time being as I believe he will need your thorough knowledge of the situation and your loyal help."

The truth was that Nimitz had decided "the critical situation requires a more aggressive commander," and Halsey, although a year older than Ghormley, was his man. Halsey took over from his friend with feelings of "astonishment, apprehension and regret." After being relieved, Ghormley reported to Nimitz at Pearl Harbor, and went on to Washington to report to Admiral King. He was shocked at the reports that had preceded him.

On October 12, six days before his relief, the Navy had released Communiqué No. 147.

"1. Certain initial phases of the Solomon Islands campaign, not announced previously for military reasons, can now be reported," it began. There followed an outline of the situation in the Pacific and the statement that seizure of the Solomons was necessary to thwart the Japanese advance on Australia and protect its lines of communication to America. The battle was described in a terse and straightforward manner, with no interpretation whatever, and the communiqué concluded:

"Although a majority of the personnel was saved, there were many casualties as a result of the sinking of the four Allied cruisers. The next of kin of those lost and wounded have been notified. The loss of these four cruisers has now been offset by the appropriate reallocation of ships which is made possible by new ship construction."

But censorship was relaxed somewhat now, and Hanson Baldwin, military expert of the New York *Times*, himself a graduate of the Academy (1924), was just back from a tour of the Solomons. He wrote in the *Times* of October 24 that the United States could probably retain its foothold in the Solomons, "barring a repetition of mistakes made in August and September." He said the campaign had started brilliantly, but then came the Battle of Savo Island, when the *Canberra, Vincennes, Quincy*, and *Astoria* were "surprised like sitting ducks." No other phrase stuck like this one, and to this day "sitting duck" is a dirty word to any Savo survivor. To the man of action they are fighting words, to the more introspective, salt in a wound.

Baldwin continued:

They were surprised, first, because they had assumed a defensive station, patrolling back and forth over a fixed course in narrow waters and awaiting the enemy instead of going out to attack him.

They were surprised, second, because their dispositions enabled the enemy to approach almost within gun range without detection; third, because only a small part of their crews were at battle stations when the action started, and fourth, because the admiral in command of the northern [sic] cruiser screen had left the scene in his flagship and, judging from the Navy Department's communiqué, no one had succeeded him in actual tactical command.

This was acceptably accurate, as far as it went, but omitted important lessons, not yet fully known or appreciated. Perhaps the most surprising lapse had been Admiral Turner's, concurred in, however, by every command and staff officer present: he had based his action on what he believed the enemy *would* do, rather than on what he knew the enemy *could* do. This is a fundamental error as old as military science, yet so subtle it seems never fully learned.

A brilliant man (fifth in his class of 201 in 1908), Admiral Turner had progressed through the command structure, qualified as a Naval Aviator at the age of forty-two in 1927 (Admiral King, then forty-one and a captain, had been in the same class at Pensacola), taken the senior course at the Naval War College in 1935–36, and in 1940 become Director of the War Plans Division under Admiral Harold R. ("Betty") Stark. In this post, Admiral Turner's task was to evaluate all intelligence (including that via broken Japanese codes) and predict the actions of the Japanese Navy. His work was distinguished; he was among the few in high places to foresee the Japanese attack on the Philippines, and at the Pearl Harbor investigations he testified he was "not in the least surprised" at the attack there.

Admiral King, on taking over as Commander in Chief, United States Fleet, less than two weeks after Pearl Harbor, thought enough of Turner to ask him to be his Assistant Chief of Staff for Plans. In that post he remained until King sent him to the Pacific for Operation Watchtower, the beginning of his long and brilliant command career in amphibious warfare.

How could a man of this background, a man whose most recent experience had been in the intimate study of the enemy, be misled? It was, after all, exactly the same error made at Pearl Harbor—action was based on what it was thought the Japanese *would* do, rather than on what it was known the enemy *could* do. The Japanese were unorthodox, by American standards, and the thrashing administered at Savo expunged—for all time, it may be hoped—the complacency of a fleet that had never lost a battle.

Perhaps it was Admiral Turner's very background—predicting what the Japanese might do—which led him into the trap. Surely, had he given full weight to his knowledge of what the enemy could do—that is, a night surface attack—he would not have acted as he did. Still, the false estimation of the Japanese was general, and Turner's opinions went unchallenged at the final staff conference in the *McCawley* only hours before the fateful awakening.

Everyone present knew the Japanese *could* arrive that night for a surface attack, yet everyone assumed he *would* arrive the next day, probably for an air attack. The defense strategy was built on this false assumption and the fleet went to bed, with pickets close in to guard the sleepers.

The second most important error was the failure of communications, using the word in its widest sense. The physical system faltered, which is understandable considering the equipment then available in the fleet, but the more serious fault was the human one of failure to communicate to others the knowledge each commander had. The night was replete with tragic breaks in the chain of intelligence. Admiral Crutchley did not tell the Northern or Eastern Forces of cruisers he was leaving the scene, nor did he tell Admiral Turner that he was not resuming his place in the screen. The Southern Force failed to inform the Northern Force that it was under enemy attack, for minutes of warning that were vital. Admirals Turner and Crutchley gave neither group an appreciation of the situation as known to them by midnight, the most damaging omission being the news that the carriers had withdrawn. Had this been known, any planes overhead might instantly have been assumed to be enemy. Each commander lay down on a blanket of assumptions, each his own and a little different from the others', and all of them wrong, and each awoke in a shattering nightmare of death.

The repercussions shook the Navy, and only Turner and Crutchley survived them. Ghormley and Fletcher were gone from the South Pacific by October, the former to duty in Washington, the latter to Seattle. Ghormley, for one, was shocked by what he found in the States. After the war, in a private paper that became known as the "Ghormley Manuscript," he wrote:

Upon my return to the United States in November, 1942, I was very much surprised on reading newspapers carrying late press releases in regard to the August 8 [sic] Battle of Savo Island, and other combats with Japanese land and sea forces in the South Pacific Area, that it all built up, and was so interpreted by some writers, as being an indictment of me. These writers gave this as the reason that Halsey was ordered to relieve me. This I did and do resent very much, as it is not true.

History speaks more kindly of Admiral Ghormley now, and it should. His misfortune lay in being thrust into a critical situation with hopelessly inadequate forces to meet it. It is questionable whether any commander, even Halsey, could have done better at the time and under the circumstances.

As to Fletcher, the powerful carrier task forces then building for the South and Central Pacific offensives passed to other commanders.

There were rough seas ahead for Captains Bode and Riefkohl. The former retained command of the *Chicago* until the end of the year, returned to the States, and in January, 1943, went to Balboa, Canal Zone, as commander of the Naval Station there. His travail lay ahead. Captain Riefkohl was back in Washington by September, 1942, and the next month went to Mexico City, with duty there and at Vera Cruz as liaison officer for the Gulf Sea Frontier. He knew now that he would not make rear admiral, as had been promised him at the end of the *Vincennes'* cruise. Captain Greenman remained in the Pacific, shifted now to the Service Forces.

The blow to American morale, Navy and civilian, had been harsh. Americans were not accustomed to defeat, either by history or by temperament. Other shocks awaited, to be sure, but one could hardly perceive as yet that the era of romantic war was dead. This was the first defeat, therefore felt the keenest. France had suffered German occupation, Britain had known its Dunkerque, now America knew its Savo. What had happened?

The Navy had been severely shaken by Savo, and individual reputations were being demolished at the bar of every officers' club. As soon as conditions allowed—and it was December by then—the Navy set about finding out. Secretary of the Navy Frank Knox ordered Admiral Arthur J. Hepburn, former Commander in Chief of the United States Fleet, to investigate and determine the "primary and contributing causes of the losses and whether or not culpability attaches to any individual engaged in the operation." Admiral Hepburn, then sixty-four and near retirement, was at this time Chairman of the Navy General Board, senior advisory group to the Secretary of the Navy. He was the Navy's most senior officer, Signal No. 1, a man highly regarded as tactician and strategist.

Hepburn reported to King in Washington two days before Christmas, and on Christmas Eve began work in a talk with Admiral Ghormley, who confided later in his memoirs his surprise and resentment at the blame heaped on him at home for the Savo debacle. The day after Christmas, Admiral Hepburn left for Pearl Harbor, beginning a quest that took him all the way to Australia. He became ill on January 2, the day he arrived in Pearl

Harbor, and remained in the hospital until January 25.

During this period, *American Mercury* published in its January, 1943, issue, an article by Representative Melvin J. Maas, Minnesota Republican, entitled "Mistakes I Saw in the Pacific—A Plea for Unified Command." Representative Maas, ranking minority member of the House Naval Affairs Committee, an airman and a colonel in the Marine Corps Reserve, was just back from the Pacific.

As to the Solomons [he wrote] I have already indicated the confusion and lack of co-ordination in the initial stages. The later engagement in which we lost four heavy cruisers can be charged to negligence and to divided responsibility. Our force was warned during the afternoon that three Jap cruisers were approaching at a speed of 15 knots. Our commander did not believe the three enemy warships would dare attack our much larger force, and even if they dared, they would not come within range until the following morning. But the Japs increased their speed, executed a daring maneuver, and within eight minutes [sic] our four cruisers had been hit mortally and the attackers were gone.

Now why do I insist that this tragic mistake be recognized, since it cannot be undone? Because an effort has been made to "alibi" this disaster. We have been told that it was necessary to sacrifice these ships in order to protect our transports; that by resisting the Japs these ships saved our landing party from attack. None of this is true. Because the Japs were so heavily outnumbered, they obviously had no intention of pressing the attack and reaching our transports. They planned a hit-and-run engagement and they pulled it off. I believe it is safer for us to admit this and be on guard against recurrence than to pretend that we were not asleep.

Admiral Hepburn's illness did not delay the investigation; his aide, Commander Donald J. Ramsey, was already at work. Ramsey, a destroyer commander just back from action in the forward area, reached Pearl Harbor in late December and was immediately told of his new assignment. He had previously served in the Navy Judge Advocate General's office in Washington, including a year in charge of the section on Courts of Inquiry and Investigations.

During January, Ramsey began examination of records and reports on the Savo action, conferring daily with Admiral Hepburn in the hospital. As soon as the admiral left the hospital, he and his aide interviewed Lieutenant Commander Elijah W. Irish, navigator of the *Chicago*, and Lieutenant Commander Heneberger, senior survivor of the *Quincy*, who were then at Pearl Harbor. On February 15, Admiral Hepburn and Commander Ramsey left by plane for Brisbane, via Noumea. At Brisbane, Admiral Hepburn talked alone with General MacArthur and on February 18 Admiral Crutchley arrived. He said he welcomed the opportunity to make a written statement and this was entered in the record. On February 22, Hepburn and Ramsey conferred again with Crutchley at Melbourne aboard the *Australia*, and on March 3 arrived in Noumea, where Ramsey examined the records and Admiral Hepburn talked with Admiral Turner. By March 8 they were back at Pearl Harbor, where Captain Greenman of the *Astoria* was interrogated.

No officer of the Eastern Force was interrogated. Admiral Scott could not be; he had been killed in the terrible night Battle of Guadalcanal, November 12–15,

1942. His powerful force, containing the newest cruiser and destroyers, was never brought into the action at Savo, though Admiral Mikawa's force passed within a few miles of it. The Eastern Force watched the battle with confused interest, but received no orders nor asked for any.

Late in March, Admiral Hepburn and Commander Ramsey returned to the West Coast, and on April 2–3 at Corpus Christi, Texas, they talked with Captains Bode and Riefkohl. Captain Riefkohl was his usual self, affable and voluble, secure in his belief that he had done no wrong. Captain Bode was quiet, a bit tense, and puzzled. He seemed to be learning, for the first time and with surprise, that his actions during the battle were under question. The next day he flew as far as New Orleans with the interrogators, and it was obvious from his conversation that his puzzlement was growing. From New Orleans he flew back to Panama, and in the days following appeared depressed to those who knew him. On April 19, he sat down in his quarters and wrote a personal letter to Admiral Hepburn. Upon his return from mailing it, he entered the bathroom of his quarters, taking a .45 Colt with him. There was a shot. Captain Bode died the next day in the Naval Hospital at Balboa, just past his fifty-fourth birthday, his goal of flag rank unachieved. His Navy biography appends the parenthetical note: "(Not a war casualty.)"

chapter
25

Admiral Hepburn returned to Washington on April 7, and submitted his report under date of May 13, 1943.

The Hepburn Report has never been made public. It was a curiously parochial paper, containing severe criticism of two relatively junior officers. Summaries of it have, however, been allowed (minus the personalities) and of these presumably the most authoritative is that of Rear Admiral Samuel Eliot Morison in his multi-volume *History of United States Naval Operations in World War II.*

Admiral Hepburn concluded that the principal cause of the defeat was "the complete surprise achieved by the enemy," and he said the surprise was due to:

Unreadiness in the ships to meet sudden night attack, failure to guess the meaning of enemy planes overhead just before the attack, too much confidence in radar, delay in contact reports, and lack of knowledge that there had been no effective air search on August 8.

"As a contributory cause," Morison quotes Hepburn, "must be placed the withdrawal of the carrier groups on the evening before the battle. This was responsible for Admiral Turner's conference . . . [and] for the fact that there was no force available to inflict damage on the withdrawing enemy."

This order of primacy of causes has been substantially changed by subsequent studies. Admiral Nimitz made a somewhat different listing. He spoke of communications weaknesses and poor air search, but he listed third the "erroneous estimate of enemy intentions" and went on to note ineffective radar, disregard of unidentified planes, and "want of a flag officer in the Southern Force," concluding with "the probability that our force was not . . . sufficiently battle-minded."

These statements, particularly those concerning the mistaken estimate of what the Japanese planned to do and the lack of that ineffable thing called battle-mindedness, were striking closer to the heart of the matter, but were not the whole of it. It was not yet possible, in the din of daily crises around the world, to bring full attention to bear on this debacle and its causes. That would remain a postwar task.

In the meantime, it was necessary to focus on one of the main purposes of the Hepburn investigation—"whether or not culpability attaches to any individual engaged in the operation." Little can be known of the inner searchings that went on within the Navy Department, but the final and official answer of the Navy is known. It is contained in a letter, stamped "secret," from Admiral King to Secretary of the Navy Knox, under date of September 14, 1943. The letter, suppressed until long after the war was over, at Admiral King's recommendation, follows in full:

1. As you are aware, Admiral A. J. Hepburn, USN (Ret), was directed to report to the Commander in Chief, U.S. Pacific Fleet, for the purpose of conducting an investigation of the circumstances attending the loss of the USS *Vincennes*, USS *Quincy*, USS *Astoria*, and HMAS *Canberra*, sustained during the action off Savo Island early in August, 1942. Admiral Hepburn was chosen for this assignment because of his distinguished career in the Navy, during which he was Commander in Chief, U.S. Fleet, and because of high professional attainments which made him particularly well qualified for the duty. In order to facilitate his work and at the same time interfere as little as possible with current operations, his inquiry was conducted informally. His report, together with the endorsement of the Commander in Chief, U.S. Pacific Fleet, is forwarded herewith as Enclosure (A), with the request that it be returned when it has served its purpose.

2. The objects of the inquiry were first, to find out exactly what caused the defeat, and second, to determine whether or not any responsible officers involved in the planning and execution of the operation were culpably inefficient. Admiral Hepburn's report has been valuable to me in both respects, and I consider it an excellent presentation and analysis of the operation. I note that both he and the Commander in Chief, U.S. Pacific Fleet, are of the opinion that surprise was the immediate cause of the defeat, but that they differ somewhat as to the circumstances responsible

for the surprise. So far as that particular question is concerned, I incline to the view that the Commander in Chief, U.S. Pacific Fleet has listed them more accurately.

3. Granting that the immediate cause of our losses was the surprise attack, the question is whether or not any officer should be held accountable for failing to anticipate it. Considering that this was the first battle experience for most of the flag officers involved, and that consequently it was the first time that most of them had been in the position of "kill or be killed," the answer to that specific question, in my judgment, must be in the negative. They simply had not learned how and when to stay on the alert.

4. The strategic situation preceding the operation was such as to require execution of the operation on a date which made the planning and mounting matters of the greatest urgency. The planning, and to a lesser degree the exercise of command, reflect the urgency with which the operation was undertaken, and in that respect, fell short of the usual standards. The fact that the operation was not well executed may have been due in part to lack of experience.

5. The deficiencies which manifested themselves in this action, with particular reference to communications and the condition of readiness, together with erroneous conceptions of how to conduct this type of operation, have long since been corrected. Furthermore, adequate administrative action has been taken with respect to those individuals whose performance of duty did not measure up to expectations.

6. For the foregoing reasons, and because I see nothing to be gained thereby, I contemplate no further action, but I deem it appropriate and necessary to record my approval of the decisions and conduct of Rear Admiral R. K. Turner,

U.S. Navy, and Rear Admiral V. Crutchley, Royal Navy. In my judgment, these two officers were in no way inefficient, much less at fault, in executing their parts of the operation. Both found themselves in awkward positions and both did their best with the means at their disposal.

7. I am furnishing copies of this report and accompanying endorsements to the Admiralty and to the Australian Naval Board.

8. I recommend that no part of this report be made public before the end of the war.

Numbered copies of this letter went to Admiral Hepburn, Admiral Nimitz, Admiral Turner, The First Sea Lord, Admiral of the Fleet Sir Dudley Pound, G.C.B., O.M., G.C.V.O., the Australian Naval Board, the Commander 3rd Fleet (Admiral Halsey), and the Commander 7th Fleet (Vice Admiral A. S. Carpender). For the rest of the war, nothing more was heard of Savo.

chapter
26

Historians agree that the Battle of Savo Island was not decisive, and of course it was not, but no one could say that at the time, or for weeks afterward. In the first step of its war of reconquest, with thousands of miles of hostile sea and land before it, the United States Navy had faltered. The record of confusion, timidity, and unpreparedness had been shocking. If the Imperial Japanese Navy had followed up with the vigor and dash exhibited by Admiral Mikawa, the consequences could have been exceedingly grave. That it did not was a boon the Allies had no right to expect, but the time granted was used to repair the neglect of decades, revealing the secret of American success—the ability immediately and honestly to assess mistakes and correct them.

That, perhaps, is the meaning of Admiral King's valedictory: A severe defeat had been absorbed, lessons had been learned and applied, eventual victory was in sight, it was pointless to punish individuals. For by September, 1943, the situation was sharply different than it had been a year earlier. The tide had turned. The Russians had crushed the German armies before Stalingrad, the Allies had driven Rommel from Africa, were firmly based in Sicily and were even then landing at Salerno. In the Pacific, Allied forces had the offensive in the Solomons and New Guinea, were soon to strike in the Marshalls. American power, in men and ships, was beginning to accelerate in tremendous ratio, while Japanese power had passed its peak. The eventual outcome was inevitable.

Admiral Turner had become Commander, Amphibious Force, Pacific Fleet, a post he held until the end of the war. Admiral Crutchley commanded a Task Force in the Seventh Fleet (MacArthur) until June, 1944, and then returned to the British Fleet. He was the last Britisher ever to command His Majesty's Royal Australian Squadron, was knighted in the Birthday Honors of 1946, and retired the following year as Vice Admiral. Admiral Ghormley was Commander Hawaiian Sea Frontier when Admiral King's letter was written, subsequently served as Commander U.S. Naval Forces in Germany, where he ended the war, and served on the General Board until he retired in 1946. Admiral Fletcher spent the last two years of the war as Commander North Pacific Force and North Pacific Ocean Area, led the occupation of the northern Japanese islands at the end of the war, served as chairman of the Navy General Board in 1946, and retired the following year.

Savo left scars at this echelon, without question, but Admiral King's "all's well that ends well" letter undoubtedly reflected the feeling of the highest command—recrimination would serve no purpose. Among the cruiser captains there was none left to feel aggrieved but Captain Riefkohl, who, although he spoke wistfully of returning to a sea command, served out the war in shore commands. But he felt the burden of Savo, and tried to have it placed where he felt it belonged, on an echelon higher than his.

He had help in this, as Savo flared into the news for a brief period in mid-1946. On April 11, Senator C. Wayland Brooks, Illinois Republican and member of the Senate Naval Affairs Committee, had written to Secretary of the Navy James Forrestal, asking whether any disciplinary action had been taken after the Battle of Savo Island and "if not, why not." He said failure to act seemed "to stand out in bold contrast" to the prompt action taken against Captain Charles B. McVay, III. (He referred to the loss of the USS *Indianapolis* shortly before the end of the war, and the court-martial of Captain McVay.) Was it true, the Senator asked, that Admiral Crutchley had been absent from the battle and had designated no commanding officer?

The reply came in the form of a story in the Chicago *Tribune* on June 6, headlined: "Navy Refuses to Act Against British Admiral," with the subhead, "Shuns Discipline Despite Loss of 3 U.S. Ships." The Washington dispatch by Chesly Manly started out: "The British Admiral who commanded at Savo was completely absolved of negligence and inefficiency by the Navy Department, it was disclosed today in correspondence between Navy Secretary Forrestal and Senator Brooks, R., Ill."

The Senator's letter and Forrestal's reply, dated May 13, were given in part, and the story said: "Forrestal quoted a hitherto secret letter from Adm. King, former CinC of the fleet, to the late Navy Sec. Knox, which acknowledged that 'the operation was not well executed' but blamed the shortcomings of the commanders on their lack of experience." This was Admiral King's letter of September 14, 1943, summing up the whole affair. Forrestal outlined the battle and the aftermath, and as to Admiral Crutchley admitted that he had been absent but said this "did not preclude his maintaining over-all command of his screening groups." The Action Reports showed however, that Admiral Crutchley had not succeeded in establishing command during the battle.

A week later the Chicago *Tribune*, in those days well known for its anti-British views, published a lead editorial headlined: "The Savo Whitewash." It declared:

Secretary of the Navy Forrestal has now joined the British Admiralty in stating that there will be no disciplinary action against the naval commanders at the battle of Savo Island, which was second only to Pearl Harbor as the greatest disaster in the history of the American navy. . . .

The American navy concealed the battle losses for more than two months and did not acknowledge for more than a year and a half that a Briton had been in command of the American vessels which were lost. . . .

Adm. King dismisses the defeat with the casual statement that Crutchley and Turner "found themselves in awkward positions." That position is a good deal less awkward than that of the 952 Americans who were sacrificed to ineptitude, for Crutchley and Turner not only survived but were complimented by King for "doing their best." Other American commanders who were to a more considerable degree the victims of circumstance than either of them have not been so fortunate.

The tender treatment of Crutchley may be compared with the vindictive manner in which Adm. Kimmel and Gen. Short . . . were branded with sole responsibility for that disaster (Pearl Harbor) and driven in disgrace from the services. . . .

Crutchley did not order precautions of any sort, tho he was in the midst of active operations against the enemy, but the navy has no blame for his omissions. The authorities seem to be covering up for some purpose. Somebody seems to have too much pull. It appears that the way to get along in the American navy is to be a British admiral in command of American ships. The Savo Island episode does not present our navy in a favorable light, but it may still serve some purpose if it demonstrates the advisibility of keeping Americans in command of American forces.

Things were hotting up now, and on August 19 *Time* magazine jumped in with a piece on Savo, "the worst blue-water defeat in U.S. history." *Time*, noting that some documents had been declassified on the fourth anniversary of Savo, said they added little to the picture: "The new detail that did come out was an explanation of how the command failed. Its mistake: Given ample warning of the approach of a powerful Japanese force, it failed to read the warning right." The magazine then recounted the battle, noted that the cruiser captains had been ruined while Admirals Turner and Crutchley went on to honors, and summarized:

But the stubborn fact remained: four great ships had been lost with 952 U.S. officers and men and 84 Australians. The Japs (it was disclosed later) had a slight edge in ships and guns, but not enough to foreclose the decision. The crux of the matter was the misjudgment of what the Japs were up to. If the enemy's actions had been properly appraised, all the physical factors of human fatigue, poor visibility, unreliable radar and stuttering communications might have been overcome.

[Casualty figures quoted above are those first announced. The final figures given by the Navy were 1,024 men killed, 709 wounded.]

Riefkohl was not finished. The interrogations of Japanese naval officers, including three who had taken part in the Battle of Savo Island, had just been made public by the U.S. Strategic Bombing Survey. Commander Ohmae, operations aide to Admiral Mikawa; Captain Kato, executive officer of the *Chokai*, and Rear Admiral Matsuyama, who had ridden the *Tenryu* through the battle, all agreed that the Japanese objective had been an attack on the American transports at the beachhead.

That was all Riefkohl needed. Under date of August 9 he was writing to Admiral Nimitz, who had succeeded Admiral King as Chief of Naval Operations. Captain Riefkohl said the interrogations gave positive proof that the

Japanese objective was the transports, that the defense by the Northern Force (his) had driven them off, and that therefore, far from a defeat, Savo was an American victory. He concluded:

> Inasmuch as I had command of the *Vincennes* group and was senior U.S. naval officer of our ships actively engaged in the battle, I feel it incumbent on me to bring the above observations to the attention of the Navy Department. As the veil of wartime secrecy is being lifted, it is believed that the true story of the First Savo Island Battle should be published in order to correct any false impressions that may linger in the minds of the American people, regarding the role played by ships of our Navy in that battle. Such action by the Navy Department is recommended in behalf of the parents and relatives of the personnel lost in this action, as well as for the survivors, and the prestige of our Navy.

There was no reply, and on August 30 Riefkohl wrote to his friend "Chips" Carpender. Vice Admiral Arthur S. Carpender, who at the time of the battle had been MacArthur's naval chief, was now the Navy's Director of Public Relations. Riefkohl told him:

> I felt quite certain that our aircraft would attack the Japs that afternoon [August 8, after the sighting reports], and if for any reason they were not attacked we would be alerted by our Force Commander. As we received no such alert, I naturally assumed that the enemy had been attacked.

Nevertheless, he said, he warned his ships to be alert, particularly after the late afternoon report of their approach. He went on:

As I was not aware of Admiral Crutchley's absence from the Southern Screening Group, I could not even order the Southern Group to illuminate the enemy or turn on searchlights, thus clarifying the situation and silhouetting the enemy for our group, which was then in column on course 315 True. [He did not say it here, but actually Captain Riefkohl's force was very nearly in the classic position of crossing the enemy's T, that is, being in position to fire all guns in enfilade while only part of the enemy's guns could bear.]

The action at Savo Island was really fought by our Northern Group of three heavy cruisers and two destroyers, against an enemy force of five heavy cruisers, two light cruisers and one destroyer.

Why, then, when our small Northern Cruiser group single-handed and under most unfavorable conditions, prevented a far superior Japanese force from accomplishing their mission, is this action of ours called a defeat?

We have permitted the first Savo Island Battle to be called a defeat as we lost several ships, and did not know, or could not let on that we knew, the size of the enemy force that attacked our small Northern group. Also, we did not know for sure that the mission of this enemy force was to destroy our transports at Guadalcanal and Tulagi. Nor did we then know that but for certain valuable hits made by our cruisers on the Japanese flagship, Admiral Mikawa would have returned to destroy those transports and smash our initial Guadalcanal campaign.

The above information now having been ascertained from Japanese interrogations, it seems that we could well afford to change the story, and tell the public the truth about this so-called defeat of Savo Island.

It was a good try, but not good enough. Back came "Chips'" reply: He had given the matter "a great deal of thought," but "frankly I do not feel that I should take any action towards reopening this issue." This was a hard letter to write, he said, "but I definitely do not feel that anything beneficial would be accomplished. And I question very seriously, as I said above, the advisability of any further action."

After that there was little more to be said. Riefkohl did get a letter in December, 1946, from Representative George J. Bates of Massachusetts, a member of the House Naval Affairs Committee.

"It certainly is a confused situation the more thought one gives to it," said Bates, "but I cannot get it out of my mind how Turner or Crutchley or the commanding officer of the *Blue* [H. Nordmark Williams] can avoid direct responsibility for this disaster."

Bates' interest in the battle was more than legislative. His son-in-law, Lieutenant Ginty, had been lost with the *Vincennes*. Bates' inquiries in 1943 led him to conclude that a large share of the blame for Savo lay with Turner. So much so that in mid-1943 when Turner's name came before the Senate Naval Affairs Committee for promotion to vice admiral and appointment as Commander, Amphibious Forces, Pacific, Representative Bates made formal objection. Only after Admiral King sent Commander

Ramsey to call on Bates was the objection withdrawn, and then reluctantly. Now that the war was over, Bates would still have liked to see action on the matter. No action followed.

In human suffering the cost of the Battle of Savo Island was high; in terms of experience gained it was cheap. In one night the United States Navy had been blasted from a distant and romantic past to a harsh and violent present. The Solomon Islands campaign, now beginning, was unique in ferocity, duration, losses, and lessons. During the seventeen months between the landings at Guadalcanal and the landings on New Britain, the United States Navy lost in the Solomons 2 aircraft carriers, 9 cruisers, 18 destroyers, and dozens of lesser vessels, including an oiler, a PT tender, 2 attack cargo ships, 7 transports (including Admiral Turner's own *McCawley*, shot from under him), 3 LST's, 15 PT boats, a gunboat, and a seagoing tug.

This mere recital of losses cannot begin to indicate the intensity of the fighting, at sea by the Navy and ashore by the Marines and Army, such vicious and unremitting warfare as has never been seen before. Nor can it tell the prodigies of courage, ingenuity, labor, and sheer heroism expended here by thousands of nameless Americans.

The Japanese losses in the Solomons included 2 battleships, 2 aircraft carriers, 8 cruisers, at least 37 destroyers, 11 submarines, and numberless transports, torpedo craft, and auxiliaries. There were two important considerations: the Japanese could not begin to replace their losses while the United States not only replaced theirs but greatly expanded its fleet; and the Japanese losses were light early in the campaign while American losses were heavy, but the situation slowly reversed itself. The tide of American fortunes could almost be told in the monthly ship losses. By December 1, 1942, the American losses were nearly over while the Japanese had just begun to suffer, and as the tide turned the Americans began to lay it on. There was retribution and they began to harvest it. The lessons learned at the Battle of Savo Island, and the five other major naval engagements which followed it within three months, were bitter indeed, but from this holocaust emerged a fleet—men and ships—without equal in the world.

appendices

A   *Casualties*
B   *Admiral Fletcher's Force*
C   *Destroyers, Transports for "Operation Watchtower"*
D   *Japanese Forces*
E   *Allied Screen Forces*

A   Casualties
Battle of Savo Island, August 9, 1942

American and Australian

Vessel	COMPLEMENT Officers	Men	Killed	Wounded
Quincy	76	944	370	166
Vincennes	85	1,059	332	258
Astoria	83	989	216	186
Canberra	Total 816		85*	55
Ralph Talbot	17	234	11	11
Patterson	16	235	8	11
Chicago	68	956	2	21
Total	345	4,417	1,024	709

* Includes one U.S. Navy officer

257

COMPLEMENT

Vessel	Officers	Men	Killed	Wounded
Chokai	77	847	34	48
Aoba	54	626	None	None
Kinugasa	50	607	1	1
Furutaka	50	589	None	None
Kako	50	589	None	None
Tenryu	30	292	None	2
Yubari	30	310	None	None
Yunagi	12	142	None	None
	353	4,002	35	51

NOTE: *Kako* sunk next day by *S–44* approaching Kavieng, with loss of 34 killed, 48 wounded.

Jarvis sunk next day by Japanese planes west of Guadalcanal, with loss of 247 men, all hands.

B   Admiral Fletcher's Force at the Battle of Savo Island

Battleship: *North Carolina*, Capt. George H. Fort

Aircraft Carriers:

> *Saratoga*, Capt. DeWitt C. Ramsey
> *Enterprise*, Capt. Arthur C. Davis
> *Wasp*, Capt. Forrest P. Sherman

Heavy Cruisers:

> *Atlanta*, Capt. Samuel P. Jenkins
> *Minneapolis*, Capt. Frank J. Lowry
> *New Orleans*, Capt. Walter S. DeLany
> *Portland*, Capt. Laurance T. DuBose
> *Salt Lake City*, Capt. Ernest G. Small
> *San Francisco*, Capt. Charles H. McMorris

Destroyers:

Aaron Ward	Lt. Cmdr. Orville F. Gregor
Balch	Lt. Cmdr. Harold H. Tiemroth

Benham	Lt. Cmdr. Joseph M. Worthington
Dale	Lt. Cmdr. Anthony L. Rorschach
Farenholt	Lt. Cmdr. Eugene T. Seaward
Farragut	Lt. Cmdr. Henry D. Rosendal
Grayson	Lt. Cmdr. Frederick J. Bell
Gwin	Cmdr. John M. Higgins
Laffey	Lt. Cmdr. William E. Hank
Lang	Lt. Cmdr. John L. Wilfong
MacDonough	Lt. Cmdr. Erle V. Dennett
Maury	Lt. Cmdr. Gelzer L. Sims
Phelps	Lt. Cmdr. Edward L. Beck
Stack	Lt. Cmdr. Alvord J. Greenacre
Sterett	Cmdr. Jesse G. Coward
Worden	Lt. Cmdr. William G. Pogue

C   Transports for Operation Watchtower
Capt. Lawrence F. Reifsnider, Convoy Commander, in *Hunter Ligget*

Group X-Ray, for Guadalcanal
(Capt. Reifsnider)

Ship	Formerly	Tonnage *
-o-	-o-	-o-
Commanding	Built	Type
Alchiba (AK 23)	Mormacdove	8,656 D
Cmdr. James S. Freeman	1939	C-2
Alhena (AK 26)	Robin Kettering	10,000 D
Cmdr. Charles B. Hunt	1941	C-2
American Legion (AP 35)	Army transport	13,763 G
Capt. Thomas D. Warner	1926	
Barnett (AP 11)	Santa Maria	7,857 G
Capt. Henry E. Thornhill	1928	
Bellatrix (AK 20)	Raven	9,274 D
Cmdr. William F. Dietrich	1941	
Betelgeuse (AK 28)	Mormaclark	8,656 D
Cmdr. Harry D. Power	1939	C-2

Crescent City (AP 40) Capt. Ingolf N. Kiland	Delorleans 1940	9,021 D
Fomalhaut (AK 22) Cmdr. Henry C. Flanagan	Cape Lookout 1941	7,400 D
Fuller (AP 14) Capt. Paul S. Theiss	City of Newport News 1919	11,773 D
George F. Elliot (AP 13) Capt. Watson O. Bailey	City of Los Angeles 1918	11,773 D
Hunter Liggett (AP 27) Cmdr. Louis W. Perkins, USCG	Pan America 1922	13,712 G
Libra (AK 12) Cmdr. William B. Fletcher, Jr.	Jean Lykes 1941	7,400 G C-2
McCawley (AP 10) Capt. Charlie P. McFeaters	Santa Barbara 1928	7,856 G
President Adams (AP 38) Cmdr. Frank H. Dean	ex-American President Lines 1941	9,937 D C-3
President Hayes (AP 39) Cmdr. Francis W. Benson	ex-American President Lines 1941	9,937 D C-3

* G—gross,   D—deadweight

Group Yoke, for Tulagi
Capt. George B. Ashe, commanding

Colhoun (APD 2) Lt. George B. Madden	Commissioned 1918—1919 as	Displaced 1,060 tons
Gregory (APD 3) Lt. Cmdr. Harry F. Bauer	4-stack DD's of 1916—1917	when built. Converted
Little (APD 4) Lt. Cmdr. Gus B. Lofberg, Jr.	Class, refitted for WW II use	1938—40, two boilers re-
McKean (APD 5) Lt. Cmdr. John D. Sweeney	as fast troop transports	moved, ca- pable 25 knots

Heywood (AP 12) Capt. Herbert B. Knowles	City of Baltimore 1919	11,773 D
Neville (AP 16) Capt. Carlos A. Bailey	City of Norfolk 1918	11,773 D
President Jackson (AP 37) Cmdr. Charles W. Weitzel	ex-American President Lines 1940	9,937 D C-3
Zeilin (AP 9) Capt. Pat Buchanan	President Jackson 1921	14,000 G

AK—Cargo   AP—Personnel   APD—Destroyer Transport

Destroyer Screen for Transports

Selfridge	Lt. Cmdr. Carrol D. Reynolds
Mugford	Lt. Cmdr. Edward W. Young
Henley	Cmdr. Robert H. Smith
Hull	Lt. Cmdr. Richard F. Stout
Dewey	Lt. Cmdr. Charles F. Chillingworth, Jr.
Ellet	Lt. Cmdr. Francis H. Gardner
Southard	Lt. Cmdr. Joe B. Cochran
Hopkins	Lt. Cmdr. Benjamin Coe
Trever	Lt. Cmdr. Dwight M. Agnew
Zane	Lt. Cmdr. Peyton L. Wirtz
Hovey	Lt. Cmdr. Wilton S. Heald

D Japanese Forces at Battle of Savo Island
Eighth Fleet—Rear Admiral Gunichi Mikawa, Commanding

Ship -o- Commanding	Class -o- Completed	Tonnage -o- Speed	Main Guns	Torpedo Tubes	Rounds Fired	Depth Charges Fired
Chokai (CA) (FF) Capt. Mikio Hayakawa	*Atago* 1932	9,850 35.5	10 8-in. 6 4.7-in.	8 24-in. 24 torpedoes	308 8-in. 120 4.7-in. 8 torpedoes	
Cruiser Division 6 R. Adm. Aritomo Goto						
Aoba (CA) (F) Capt. Yonejiro Hisamune	*Kako* 1926	7,100 34.5	6 8-in. 4 4.7-in.	8 24-in. 16 torpedoes	182 8-in. 86 4.7-in. 13 torpedoes	6
Kinugasa (CA) Capt. Masao Sawa	*Kako* 1926	7,100 34.5	6 8-in. 4 4.7-in.	8 24-in. 16 torpedoes	185 8-in. 224 4.7-in. 8 torpedoes	6
Furutaka (CA) Capt. Tsutoo Araki	*Kako* 1926	7,100 34.5	6 8-in. 4 4.7-in.	8 24-in. 16 torpedoes	153 8-in. 8 torpedoes	6
Kako (CA) Capt. Yuuji Takahashi	*Kako* 1925	7,100 34.5	6 8-in. 4 4.7-in.	8 24-in. 16 torpedoes	192 8-in. 130 4.7-in. 8 torpedoes	

Cruiser Division 18
R. Adm. Mitsuharu Matsuyama

Tenryu (CL) (F) Capt. Shinpei Asano	Tenryu 1918	3,230 33	4 5.5-in. 1 3-in.	6 21-in. 12 torpedoes	80 5.5-in. 23 3-in. 6 torpedoes	20
Yubari (CL) Capt. Masami Ban	1923	2,890 35.5	6 5.5-in. 1 3-in.	4 24-in. 8 torpedoes	96 5.5-in. 4 torpedoes	
Destroyer Division 29 Capt. Takemi Shimazui						
Yunagi (DD) Lt. (sg) Shizuichi Okada	Kamikaze 1925	1,270 34.5	4 4.7-in.	6 21-in. 12 torpedoes	32 4.7-in. 6 torpedoes	1

Total Rounds Fired - 1,020 8-in. 176 5.5-in. 592 4.7-in. 23 3-in. 61 torpedoes 39 depth charges

E Allied Screen Forces
Rear Admiral Victor A. C. Crutchley, RN, Commanding

Ship -o- Commanding	Class -o- Completed	Tonnage -o- Speed	Main Guns	Torpedo Tubes	Rounds Fired	Hits Sustained
Australia (CA) (FF) Capt. Harold B. Farncomb, RAN	Kent 1928	10,000 31.5	8 8-in. 8 4-in.	None	None	None
Southern Force						
Chicago (CA) Capt. Howard D. Bode	Northampton 1931	9,300 32.7	9 8-in. 4 5-in.	None	No 8-in. 44 5-in. star	1 5.5-in. 1 torpedo
Canberra (CA) Capt. Frank E. Getting, RAN	Kent 1928	9,850 31.5	8 8-in. 4 4-in.	None	No 8-in. 3 4-in.	28 8-in. and 4-7-in.
Bagley (DD) Cmdr. George A. Sinclair	Craven 1937	1,500 35	4 5-in.	16 21-in.	No 5-in. 4 torpedoes	None
Patterson (DD) Cmdr. Frank R. Walker	Craven 1937	1,500 35	4 5-in.	16 21-in.	33 5-in. No torpedoes	1 shell
Blue (DD) Cmdr. H. Nordmark Williams	Craven 1937	1,500 35	4 5-in.	16 21-in.	No 5-in. No torpedoes	None
Northern Force						
Vincennes (CA) Capt. Frederick L. Riefkohl	Astoria 1937	9,400 32	9 8-in. 8 5-in.	None	33 8-in. 20 5-in.	57 8, 5.5 and 4-7-in. plus perhaps 17 more. 2 torpedoes

Ship / Commander	Class / Year	Displacement / Speed	Guns	Torpedoes	Rounds Fired	Ammunition Remaining
Quincy (CA) Capt. Samuel N. Moore	Astoria 1936	9,375 / 32	9 8-in. / 8 5-in.	None	21 8-in. / No 5-in.	36 8, 5;5 and 4.7-in., plus perhaps 18 more. 3 torpedoes
Astoria (CA) Capt. William G. Greenman	Astoria 1934	9,950 / 32.7	9 8-in. / 8 5-in.	None	53 8-in. / 59 5-in.	34 8, 5;5 and 4.7-in. plus perhaps 29 more.
Helm (DD) Lt. Cmdr. Chester E. Carroll	Craven 1937	1,500 / 35	4 5-in.	16 21-in.	4 5-in. / No torpedoes	None
Wilson (DD) Lt. Cmdr. Walter H. Price	McCall 1939	1,500 / 36.5	4 5-in.	16 21-in.	212 5-in. / No torpedoes	None
Ralph Talbot (DD) Lt. Cmdr. Joseph W. Callahan	Craven 1937	1,500 / 35	4 5-in.	16 21-in.	12 5-in. / 4 torpedoes	5 5.5-in.
Eastern Force Rear Adm. Norman Scott						
San Juan (CL) (F) Capt. James E. Maher	Atlanta 1942	6,000 / 40	12 5-in.	8 21-in.	None	None
Hobart (CL) Capt. Henry A. Showers, RAN	1936	7,105 / 32.5	6 6-in. / 8 4-in.	8 21-in.	None	None
Monssen (DD) Cmdr. Roland N. Smoot	Benson 1940	1,630 / 37	4 5-in.	5 21-in.	None	None
Buchanan (DD) Cmdr. Ralph E. Wilson	Bristol 1942	1,700 / 37	4 5-in.	10 21-in.	None	None

Total Rounds Fired - 107 8-in.. 385 5-in.. 3 4-in. 8 torpedoes
CA—Heavy Cruiser   CL—Light Cruiser   DD—Destroyer   FF—Fleet Flagship   F—Division Flagship

bibliography

Action Reports by vessels concerned, including statements by surviving officers and enlisted men, U.S. Navy, Naval History Division.

Admiral Halsey's Story, by Fleet Admiral William F. Halsey, USN, and Lieutenant Commander J. Bryan III, USNR, Whittlesey House, 1947.

The Army Air Forces in World War II, edited by Wesley Frank Craven and James Lea Cate, University of Chicago Press, 1953.

The Battle of Savo Island, by Captain Toshikazu Ohmae, IJN, United States Naval Institute *Proceedings*, December, 1957.

Campaigns of the Pacific War, Naval Analysis Division, by the United States Strategic Bombing Survey, U.S. Government Printing Office, 1946.

The Coastwatchers, by Commander Eric A. Feldt, RAN, Oxford University Press, 1946.

The Discovery of the Solomon Islands by Alvaro de Mendaña in 1568, edited by Lord Amherst and Basil Thomson, Hakluyt Society Publication, 1901.

Fleet Admiral King, A Naval Record, by Fleet Admiral Ernest J. King, USN, and Walter Muir Whitehill, W. W. Norton & Co., Inc., 1952.

Fundamentals of Naval Warfare, by Lee J. Levert, The Macmillan Co., 1947.

Ghormley Manuscript, by Vice Admiral Robert L. Ghormley, USN, unpublished.

The Great Sea War, edited by E. B. Potter and Fleet Admiral Chester W. Nimitz, USN, Prentice-Hall Inc., 1960.

The Guadalcanal Campaign, by Major John L. Zimmerman, USMCR, U.S. Marine Corps, Historical Division, 1949.

Guadalcanal Diary, by Richard Tregaskis, Random House, 1943.

A Guide to Naval Strategy, by Bernard Brodie, Naval War College Edition, Princeton University Press, 1958.

Hepburn Report, by Admiral Arthur J. Hepburn, USN.

A History of the United States Navy, by Commodore Dudley W. Knox, USN, G. P. Putnam's Sons, 1936.

History of United States Naval Operations in World War II, Vols. IV and V, by Rear Admiral Samuel Eliot Morison, USNR, Atlantic-Little, Brown and Company, 1949 and 1951.

HMAS Mark II, published by the Australian War Memorial, Canberra, 1944.

Interrogations of Japanese Officials, by the United States Strategic Bombing Survey, 2 vols., U.S. Government Printing Office, 1946.

The Landings in the Solomons, Office of Naval Intelligence Combat Narrative, 1943.

Logs by vessels concerned, National Archives.

A Log of the Vincennes, by Johnathan Truman Dorris, The Standard Printing Company, Louisville, Ky., 1947.

Midway, by Captain Mitsui Fuchida, IJN, and Commander Masatake Okumiya, IJN, United States Naval Institute, 1955.

Naval War College Analysis, by Commodore Richard W. Bates and Commander Walter D. Innis, 2 vols., also the Navy film, 5 reels, made from the *Analysis,* U.S. Navy.

Pacific Battle Line, by Foster Hailey, The MacMillan Co., 1944.

Preliminary Report Solomon Islands Operation, by Fleet Admiral Chester W. Nimitz, USN, Aug. 23, 1942.

Royal Australian Navy 1939–1942, by G. Hermon Gill, published by the Australian War Memorial, Canberra, 1957.

Samurai! by Saburo Sakai with Martin Caidin and Fred Saito, E. P. Dutton, 1957.

The Splendid Little War, by Frank Freidel, Little, Brown, 1958.

They Call It Pacific, by Clark G. Lee, Viking Press, 1943.

Through the Perilous Night, by Joe James Custer, The MacMillan Co., 1944.

United States Naval Chronology, World War II, by the Naval History Division, U.S. Government Printing Office, 1955.

The War Against Japan, Vol. II, British official war history, Her Majesty's Stationery Office, 1958.

index

269

271

Guam Is.: 13
Gunthorp, CY G. J.: 106
Gwin: 62

Hager, S 1/c Lynn F.: 160
Hailey, Foster: 211
Hall, Lt. Walter A., Jr.: 152
Halsey, Adm. William F., Jr.: relieves Ghormley, 231; 235
Hamilton, Gen. Sir Ian: 69
Hansen, Cmdr. Raymond A.: 182, 184
Hartt, Cmdr. William H., Jr.: 171
Hatch, S 1/c Howard M.: 111
Hayes, Lt. Cmdr. John D.: 94, 121, 130, 137, 139, 162, 186–7
Healey, Lt. (j.g.) Vincent P.: 160
Helm: 68, 88, 166; misses battle, 170–71; rescues survivors, 182–3, 203
Henderson Field: 70
Heneberger, Lt. Cmdr. Harry B.: 134–5, 153–4; interrogated, 239
Henley: 68
Hepburn, Adm. Arthur J.: ordered to investigate, 237; investigation, 237–45
Hepburn Report: 241–2
Herzberger, Ens. Raymond G., Jr.: 128
Hill, Ens. H.I., Jr.: 180
Hitchcock, Cmdr. Norman R.: 74
Hobart: 47, 69–70
Hole, Lt. Cmdr. D. M.: 105–6
Hopkins: attempts to tow *Astoria,* 188–9
Hopkins, Lt. (j.g) Everett S.: 181
Hornet: 48, 85
Hudsons: *See* Lockheed Hudsons
Hull: 71, 118
Hunter Liggett: 189, 203, 206–7, 209
Hyakutake, Lt. Gen. H.: 17

I-121: 33, 208
I-123: 33, 208

Illick, Lt. (j.g.) Joseph F.: 202
Inca Seer: *See* Yupanqui, Tupac Inca
Indianapolis: 248
Inoue, V. Adm. Shigeyoshi: 14, 18
intelligence, failures of: *See* under sightings
International News Service: 57
Irish, Lt. Cmdr. Elijah W.: 239
Ironbottom Sound: 7, 38, 44, 58, 62, 71, 118
Isquith, Lt. Cmdr. Samuel A.: 158

Jacobs, Lt. (j.g.) Robert M.: 149, 178
Japanese approach: reports of, 82–3, 86–7, 118, 152, 160–61
Japanese Navy: night battle doctrine, 27–8, 32, 39, 41, 174, 176; losses in Solomons, 255–6
Japanese planes: *See under* Type number
Jarrett, Lt. (j.g.) Milton L., Jr.: 196
Jarvis: 68; hit, 71; 88, 103–4, 115, 117; sunk, 208
Johns, FC 1/c W. W.: 159
Joint Chiefs of Staff: 53
Joslin, SM 3/c Leonard A.: 181

Kako: 21, 33; described, 35; 36, 42, 124; sunk, 209; 217
Kalish, Ens. Ralph W.: 92
Kam, Bernard Joseph: 202
Kamada, Capt. Shoichi: 224
Kami, Capt. Shigenori: 14
Kamikaze class: 36
Kato, Capt. Kenkichi: 173, 251
Kavieng: 20, 21, 30, 72, 209
Kempf, Lt. (j.g.) E. L.: 147–8
Kendrick, CTC C. L.: 149
Kenney, Lt. Gen.: 80
Kieta: 76
King, Adm. Ernest J.: 15; Pacific strategy, 16; 46; instructs Ghormley, 50, 216–7; Pacific plans, 221–3; 226; letter summarizing debacle, 242–5

Patrick, Cpl. James L.: 182–4
Patterson: 68, 87, 93, 99; gives warning, 104–5; in battle, 108–110, 122; 132, 170, 173; aids *Canberra,* 191, 193; battle with *Chicago,* 191, 193; 196–7; rescues survivors, 203–4, 207
Payne, CPhM Randolph R.: 203
PBY: 73–4
Peck, Brig. Gen. DeWitt: 51, 53
Peppler, PhM2/c Leonard A.: 194–5
Phelps: 62
Philip II: 4
Pickering, Lt. (j.g.) Paul P.: 200
Portland: 62
Port Moresby: 11, 14–15, 17, 19–20, 25, 80–81
Pound, Sir Dudley: 245
President Adams: 46
President Hayes: 46
President Jackson: 46, 57, 187, 202
Price, Lt. Cmdr. Walter H.: 170
Provost, CWT Sidney: 139

Quincy: 46, 57–8, 63–4, 68, 70, 85, 88, 95, 103, 120–22, 125; in battle, 128–136, 140–143, 146–154; sinks, 154; 167, 173, 177, 179; officers killed, 185, 198, 203, 232

Rabaul: 13–15, 17–18, 20, 22, 24; B-17 raid, 25; 29, 33, 36–7, 41, 72–4
radar: 67, 69, 95, 105, 114, 118, 120, 127–8
Radke, QM 2/c R. A.: 130
Ralph Talbot: 60, 67–9, 92; warns of planes over Savo, 93–4, 103, 118–121, 166–7; in battle, 175–6; fight to save, 194–6; 197, 215
Ramsey, Cmdr. Donald J.: 239–40, 255
Ray, CMM H. F.: 139
Raymond, Warner: 202
Read, Jack: 71
Reagan, Lt. (j.g.) L. H.: 147
Reifsnider, Capt. Lawrence F.: 66, 205, 209

Rekata Bay: 91–2
Rendova Is.: 3
Riefkohl, Capt. Frederick L.: 69; biographical, 83-4; 89, 93–4, 97, 102–3, 117–8, 120, 124, 135–6, 155–8; abandons ship, 182–3; 229; reassigned, 236; interrogated, 240; seeks exoneration, 248, 251–4
Rieve, Lt. (j.g.) Roland: 153, 179
RO-33: 33
RO-54: 33
Ross, AB Wallace M.: 203
Royal Australian Air Force: 75

S-38: 25, 32–3, 73
S-44: 209
St. George's Channel: 25, 31, 72
Saito, Hirosi: 56
Salt Lake City: 47, 62
San Cristobal Is.: 171
Sanderson: 106
San Francisco: 62
San Juan: 64, 69–70, 94, 167, 207; leaves Savo, 209
Santa Barbara: 57
Santa Cruz Isls.: 9, 73
Santa Isabel (Ysabel) Is.: 5–6, 33, 65
Saratoga: 46, 48–9, 55, 62, 64, 66, 73; fuel 79–80; 111, 208
Sarmiento de Gamboa, Pedro: 4, 6
Savo Is.: 3; discovered, 7; 39, 42–3, 46, 60, 62; flares over, 96–7, 121
Savo Sound: *See* Ironbottom Sound
Schuessler, 2nd Lt. Carl I.: 184
Schwitters, PhM 3/c Merlin J.: 151
Scott, R. Adm. Norman: 68, 70, 167, 229, 239–40
Scott, PhM 2/c Paul W.: 152
SC radar: *See* radar
Seabees: 51
Seal, Lt. (j.g.) John D.: 120
Sealark Channel: 60, 68, 167, 209
searchlights: 35, 124–5, 136, 156, 160
Selfridge: 64, 68, 93, 166; sinks *Canberra,* 194, 196–8

Sells, MM 1/c O.S.: 162–3
Sersain, Mach. Simon L.: 184
Seventeenth Army: 17, 24
SG radar: *See* radar
Shannon, Ens. E. F., Jr.: 120
sharks: 178
Shepard, Lt. Richard D.: 195–6
Sherman, Capt. Forrest: denied permission to help Turner, 172
Shinohara, Cmdr. Tamao: 30
Shoho: 13
Shortland Is.: *See* Faisi
Shoup, Cmdr. Frank E., Jr.: 162, 186, 190
sightings: 30–33, 36–7, 72–6 80–81
Silver Sound: 21
Simko, AMM 2/c Andrew J.: 148
Simpson Harbor: *See* Rabaul
Sinclair, Cmdr. George A.: 109, 164, 169–70, 201–2
Singer, Jack: 57
Skaife, Lt. (j.g.) Douglas C.: 134
Slot: 32, 38; plane search, 74–5; 197
Smith, Lt. (j.g.) Donald S.: 200
Smith, Lt. (j.g.) H. W.: 147–8, 180
Smith, Lt. James C., Jr.: 178
Smith, WT 1/c L. M.: 142
Smith, CWT M. K.: 138
Snark: 9
SOC-3: 146–7
Society Isls.: 16
Solomon Isls.: discovered 3–9; 14–16; Japanese infiltrate, 17–18; 46, 73; U.S. losses, 255
Southard: 96
Southern Force: 68, 87–9, 100, 102, 104, 117–8, 124–5, 136, 156, 166, 170, 235
Soya: 25
Spalding, CWT Earl O.: 180
Spanish-American War: 28, 47, 219–221
Stack: 62
star shells: failure of, 111, 114
Sterett: 62
Stolz, F 2/c William H.: 180

Storey, CMM Harvey, A.: 142
Strobel, CBM G. J.: 179
Stucker, CY Leonard E.: 182–3
Sullenberger, WT 1/c Lynn: 141
Sutherland, Gen. Richard: 53
Suva Is.: 51
Swinson, CPC B. Q.: 161
Sykes, Morgan C.: 183
Szoka, CSM F. C.: 133, 179–80

Tangier: 52
Task Force 62.6: 47
Task Group X-ray: 63
TBS: 88, 93, 117–19, 121–2, 126, 175
Tenryu: 13 22, 30; described, 35; 38–9; 76, 124; hit, 172; 175, 251
Thompson, Lt. (j.g.) G. W.: 138
Time: 225, 250–51
Tinian Is.: 15
Tokyo Express: 42
Tonga Is.: 16
Tongatabu: 50
Topper, Lt. Cmdr. James R.: 94, 121, 125–131, 162, 187, 189–90
torpedoes, American: 28; tubes removed from cruisers, 84; 118; faulty, 194
torpedoes, Japanese: 27, 104, 110–11, 156–7
Touve, WT 2/c Norman R.: 163
Townsville: 25, 80–81
transports: unloading problems, 72, 204–06; withdrawal, 209–211
Tregaskis, Richard: 57
Truesdell, Lt. Cmdr. William H.: 127–8, 161–2
Truk: 14–15, 17–18, 74, 126
Tsugaru: 25
Tulagi: 3; Japanese occupy, 17; Allies invade, 21–22; last message, 23; 24, 26, 36–7, 39, 42, 46; approach, 62; landings, 63–66; 70
Turner, R. Adm. Richmond Kelly: 48–9, 51; opposes withdrawal of carriers, 55–6, 58; 60–61; plane

277

About the Author

RICHARD NEWCOMB, one of the pioneers of narrative nonfiction, is the author of the bestselling *Abandon Ship!* and *Iwo Jima*. He lives in Florida.